Nightside *of the*
RUNES

"Here Thomas Karlsson takes us on an inner journey to the secrets of the North. His insight brings new light to the topics of Johannes Bureus, the runic mage of the Renaissance North, and to the enigmatic Uthark, first explored by the Swedish runologist Sigurd Agrell. Karlsson's access to obscure sources makes this work a true gem."

STEPHEN FLOWERS, PH.D., AUTHOR OF *ICELANDIC MAGIC: PRACTICAL SECRETS OF THE NORTHERN GRIMOIRES* AND *LORDS OF THE LEFT-HAND PATH: FORBIDDEN PRACTICES AND SPIRITUAL HERESIES*

"Thomas Karlsson's *Nightside of the Runes* is a curious and fascinating compendium, not just for the largely forgotten theories of the Swedish luminaries from earlier centuries that he resurrects and works with (the Uthark rune-row of the mystical scholar Sigurd Agrell and the *Adulruna* of the scholarly mystic Johannes Bureus) but also for what it shows of the author's own personal journey. The first part of the book reveals a youthful and at times naive magician drawing great power from forsaken research, while the second part shows Karlsson himself having blossomed into a fine researcher and seasoned scholar, yet one who is still very much a magician at heart. A careful reader will find numerous insights at both ends of this runic spectrum."

MICHAEL MOYNIHAN, COAUTHOR OF *LORDS OF CHAOS* AND COEDITOR OF THE JOURNAL *TYR: MYTH—CULTURE—TRADITION*

"The runes, symbolic letters deriving from the primal word refer-ring to 'secret' or 'whispering,' are the primal mysteries and forces latent in nature, to which the actual rune-stavs are mere mark-ers. The runes take many forms, as does man's understanding and conceptualization of them, and the rune-rows themselves have his-torically both expanded and contracted with time. Yet, they keep speaking to those that look for them. In *Nightside of the Runes,* Thomas Karlsson explores the work of two pioneering Swedish runologists, Johannes Bureus and Sigurd Agrell, and sheds light on this heretofore relatively obscure area of runic knowledge, which is of interest to students of runosophy and all Odinic seekers in their ever-unfolding quest for wisdom."

AKI CEDERBERG, AUTHOR OF *JOURNEYS IN THE KALI YUGA:*
A PILGRIMAGE FROM ESOTERIC INDIA TO PAGAN EUROPE

Nightside *of the* RUNES

Uthark, Adulruna, and the Gothic Cabbala

THOMAS KARLSSON, Ph.D.

Inner Traditions
Rochester, Vermont

Inner Traditions
One Park Street
Rochester, Vermont 05767
www.InnerTraditions.com

Part 1 of this book was originally published in Sweden in 2002 by Ouroboros Produktion
    under the title *Uthark, Nightside of the Runes*
Part 1 of this book was also published in German in 2004 by Arun Verlag under the title
    Uthark, Im Schattenreich der Runen

Part 2 of this book was originally published in Swedish in 2005 under the title *Adulrunan
    och den götiska kabbalan* by Ouroboros
Part 2 was also published in German in 2007 under the title *Adulruna und die Gotische
    Kabbala* by Edition Roter Drache
Part 2 was also published in Italian in 2007 under the title *Le rune e la kabbala* by Atanòr

First U.S. edition published in 2019 by Inner Traditions

Cataloging-in-Publication Data for this title is available from the Library of Congress

ISBN 978-1-62055-774-7 (print)
ISBN 978-1-62055-775-4 (ebook)

Printed and bound in the United States

10 9 8 7 6 5 4 3

Text design and layout by Debbie Glogover
This book was typeset in Garamond Premier Pro with Appareo and Gill Sans MT Pro
    used as display typefaces
Illustrations and rune images in part 1 are by T. Ketola except where noted
Illustrations and rune images in part 2 are by T. Ketola where noted; all other images in
    part 2 are by Johannes Bureus

To send correspondence to the author of this book, mail a first-class letter to the author
c/o Inner Traditions • Bear & Company, One Park Street, Rochester, VT 05767, and we
will forward the communication, or contact the author directly at
thomas@thomaskarlsson.net.

This book is dedicated to my family.

✳

*I wish to thank Stephen Flowers, Ph.D., for all his work
in the field of true magic and runic esotericism.
Sincere thanks to Timo Ketola for the artwork,
and to the National Library of Sweden, Stockholm;
Carolina Rediviva library, Uppsala;
and the University Library of Linköping
for letting me work and study the original manuscripts of
Johannes Bureus from the early seventeenth century.*

On the mountains of truth you can never climb in vain: either you will reach a point higher up today, or you will be training your powers so that you will be able to climb higher tomorrow.

FRIEDRICH NIETZSCHE

CONTENTS

THE NORTHERN LIGHT OF ORIGINAL GENIUS

By Stephen E. Flowers

Sweden has a relatively small population, yet over the centuries it has produced more than its share of innovative thinkers with ground-breaking ideas, from Carl Linnaeus to Alfred Nobel. This innovative spirit is especially evident in the field of runology. *Nightside of the Runes* brings together two works of original genius concerning the runes. Both are written by Thomas Karlsson, an ingenious master of the mysterious ways of the North. Each of the two is in turn rooted in the ideas of two Swedish geniuses in the field of runology: Sigurd Agrell and Johannes Bureus.

Part 1, "Uthark: Nightside of the Runes," follows the pioneering work of Sigurd Agrell (1885–1937) on runes, magic, and mysticism; it highlights the Uthark's symbolic connections with Norse spirituality and provides an experiential guide allowing readers to apply these hidden aspects of rune wisdom in their lives. Part 2, "The Adulruna and the Gothic Cabbala," investigates in detail the world of Johannes Bureus (1568–1652) and his profound insights regarding the spiritual dimensions of the fifteen "noble" runes, the adulrunes, and their connections to the Cabbala.

Sigurd Agrell came of age in a world in which the scientific study of the runes was in full swing. Scholars from Scandinavia, Germany, and Britain were all contributing to a lively debate on the origin of the runes and the use of these mysterious characters in the culture of the North. Agrell's interest in runes was multidimensional. He took note of the subculture in which he saw this writing system being used as well as the crosscurrents with other cultures, such as the Greeks and even the Lapps. His controversial Uthark theory is the contribution for which he remains best known, and in "Uthark: Nightside of the Runes" Karlsson describes how this theory can be applied today.

Johannes Bureus is not only considered the father of modern, scientific runology but also an early leader of the international Rosicrucian movement of the sixteenth century. He was innovative on two fronts: first, he scientifically learned to read and record many of the runic inscriptions that he found in his native country, and second, he brought the spiritual insights of the Paracelsian revolution to the lore of the runes in an unexpected way. Bureus was both a scholar and mystic. In "The Adulruna and the Gothic Cabbala," Karlsson offers the first book-length study of Bureus to be published in English. (It should be noted that Karlsson also wrote his doctoral dissertation on the subject of Bureus.)

To both of these innovators Karlsson brings his own pioneering spirit to provide readers with new intellectual and magical experiences as they follow his journey though the mysteries of the northern lights.

STEPHEN E. FLOWERS, Ph.D., studied Germanic and Celtic philology and religious history at the University of Texas at Austin and at the University of Göttingen, West Germany. He received his Ph.D. in 1984 in Germanic Languages and Medieval Studies with a dissertation titled *Runes and Magic*. He is the author of numerous books, including *Original Magic, Icelandic Magic, The Fraternitas Saturni,* and *Rune Might* (under his magical name, Edred Thorsson).

PART I

Uthark:
Nightside of
the Runes

Sigurd Agrell (December 1921).
Lund University Library Collections

SIGURD AGRELL
AND THE UTHARK

By Stephen E. Flowers

Thomas Karlsson's intriguing text *Uthark* explores the mysteries of the runic tradition that was discovered and brought to the light of day by the Swedish philologist Sigurd Agrell (1885–1937). Agrell's theories gained widespread authority in esoteric circles in Sweden during the late twentieth century because his ideas opened the doorway between runic and Germanic magic and the more familiar magical ideas rooted in the Mediterranean. This was an important insight on his part, that these worlds of the North and the South were not as separate or distant from one another as people might think. I offer the reader this short survey about Agrell and his contributions.

During Agrell's relatively brief lifetime he contributed intellectually and artistically in diverse ways. He was obviously a talented linguist who translated poetry into Esperanto at the age of sixteen. As a young university student, he belonged to a circle of symbolist poets at Uppsala who called themselves *Les quatre diables* (The four devils). His early academic career was spent in Slavic philology, in which he earned his doctorate in 1908 from Lund University. He taught and wrote scholarly articles in that field and also undertook the translation of works of Russian literature—for example, Tolstoy's *Anna Karenina* (1925)—as well as various folktales and short stories by the Nobel Prize laureate Ivan Bunin.

In the late 1920s Agrell began to publish scholarly works on the subject of runes and runology. His interest was especially within the context of Late Antiquity European culture as regards magic and mysticism. Works by him on these topics appeared in both Swedish and German. Agrell's major works in the field of runology included *Runornas talmystik och dess antika förebild* (Number mysticism of the runes and its ancient model) (1927); *Rökstenens chiffergåtor och andra runologiska problem* (The cypher puzzles of the Rök-stone and other runological problems) (1930); *Senantik mysteriereligion och nordisk runmagi: En inledning i den nutida runologiens grundproblem* (Late Antiquity mystery religion and Nordic rune magic: An introduction into the basic problem of current runology) (1931); *Die spätantike Alphabet-Mystik und die Runenreihe* (Late Antiquity alphabetic mysticism and the rune row) (1932); *Lapptrummor och runmagi: Tvenne kapitel ur trolldomsväsendets historia* (Lappish drums and rune magic: Two chapters from the history of the essentials of sorcery) (1934); *Die pergamenische Zauberscheibe und das Tarockspiel* (The magic disk of Pergamon and the game of Tarock) (1936); and *Die Herkunft der Runenschrift* (The origin of runic writing) (1938).

In addition to his philological studies, Agrell continued his interest in poetry, and he published several volumes of verse.

THE UTHARK

Runes are a well-known subject to the average Swede of any time period, since the Swedish landscape is covered with thousands of runestones, which give the land a mysterious pedigree. The runes were used by the ancient Germanic peoples to write their language before they adopted the Roman script after the various tribes were Christianized. But even after Christianization, runes continued to be used for several centuries, especially for inscriptions on memorial stones.

This form of writing was first used in the last century or so BCE. But the oldest actual surviving inscription comes from about 45 CE. Runes were used for relatively short inscriptions, most of which could have some kind of magical meaning or function. Over the first several centuries of runic history, the runes and rune carvings underwent several historical phases.

Much to Agrell's credit, he did not just look at the runes and runic inscriptions as lines on paper in books and as something separate from the actual culture and lives of the people from the times when the inscriptions were made. Agrell had a lively interest in the actual culture and psychologies of the people who made these monuments.

As the rune carvers came into ever-increasing contact with the peoples of southern Europe—the Italic and Hellenic peoples especially—they also came into contact with the theories and ideas about writing that would have been of great interest to their craft. Many Germanic men joined the Roman army. In this context many of them were initiated into the Mithraic mysteries. Mithrasim was an initiatory cult for men of all social and economic classes in the Roman Empire. It had its origins among the ancient Iranians, but in the exact form as practiced by the Romans the cult was highly Latinized with mythic elements from the Iranian and Hellenic cultures of the ancient Near East.

Closely related in some respects to the Mithraic system were the practices reflected in the Greek magical papyri, mostly originating from Egypt. These documents show a use of language for magical purposes that often mirrors the practices that seem to be in use by the rune magicians of the same time period (between 200 and 500 CE). In both styles we see inscriptions or written formulas that begin in natural language but at some point break off into what historians of magic call *ephesia grammata,* or *voces magicae*—strings of letters/sounds that make no linguistic sense but rather are thought to be the voices of the gods or some secret encoding of sound in a "divine language" understood by the gods or directly by the universe itself. Additionally, such strings of runes or letters could, in Agrell's theory, be numerological codes believed to have the power to alter reality.

The Uthark theory is rooted in the study of the numerical values of the runes. Since the early twentieth century runologists had been speculating about the role of number symbolism in runic inscriptions. Agrell was among the first to apply the theory of gematria (that is, the idea that a letter has a numerical value and that words and texts can be analyzed on an esoteric level according to the sums of these values). He did so with the following twist: he shifted the numerical values by one place so that the first rune was taken to the end of the row, and the second rune (*uruz*) in the row received the numerical value of 1. This created a new order of the runes called the Uthark. One of the main things that made this theory plausible to Agrell was the fact that when he made this numerical alteration the resulting sums of runic inscriptions seemed to be more in line with the numerical symbolism found in the Mediterranean world.

The controversy about the role of the Uthark in the *origin* and history of the runic tradition is, I think, solved when we look at it as an alternate number code used to help synthesize the systems of the runes and the Greco-Roman magic of Late Antiquity. If we view the rune row as a ring of runes and numbers, and all we do is shift the runes one numerical place, we have a new set of numerical values such that the whole system can be seen as a decoder ring. With this decoding, or re-encoding, a new set of correspondences is produced that links runic, Roman, Hellenic, and Hebraic signs. With this encoding too, the runes can be brought into the so-called mainstream of Western esotericism.

INTRODUCTION TO PART 1

For nine days, the Nordic god Odin hangs in the world tree, Yggdrasil. He hangs there sacrificed by himself, to himself. Without food or water, deeply wounded by his own spear, he endures the long nights in the tree. Odin's sacrifice in the tree is not an attempt to save humankind from its sins. He is not sacrificing himself to redeem a sinful world. Odin hangs in the tree by his own free will. The Nordic world picture does not include belief in an original sin from which humanity and its world must be saved. The Nordic tradition does not emphasize any messiah. There are other reasons behind Odin's sacrifice. He hangs there for his own sake. He hangs there to gain wisdom and power. Odin hangs in the world tree in his quest for the utmost secrets of the universe, the secrets that he picks up from the depths in a scream of ecstasy.

Odin is not a messiah. He is in many ways a dark and demonic god, feared by most. But he is a role model. Through his uncompromising search for knowledge and power we can learn the secrets known only by him. Odin can become our teacher and initiator. He will not save us from any sins. But the path of Odin will reveal a magical initiation of knowledge and power. He can teach us to save ourselves from weakness and uncertainty. Odin can teach us the secrets of the runes.

This book is an introduction to *runosophy,* the wisdom of the runes, and to practical rune magic. The runes are dynamical symbols that characterize hidden forces. The outer shapes of the runes have changed through history, but the principles that they symbolize are as similar today as during the ancient Norse times. This book does not claim to include a historical description of runes or rune magic. It is an introduction to a rune magic that is constructed around practical work with the runes in modern time. The ambition, however, has been that the runosophy in this book shall be deeply rooted in historical Nordic magic. Even if some of the *runosophical* knowledge in this book cannot be recognized from archaeological findings, the aim has been to describe keys to the same hidden reality that unites modern humans with our ancestors in the past. Time has passed, but we are the same now as then; just as with the hidden reality.

To many people the spiritual quest is associated with heavenly spheres and a striving up toward the light. This reflects the great influence from religions like Christianity, Judaism, and Islam. In these religions the divine world exists somewhere in a distant heaven, and God is a masculine sky god of light. In the older pagan traditions the divine could also be found on earth and inside it, in the underworld. There were not only a male god but also equally powerful goddesses. Humans sought not only the light: the wise also entered the dark in their spiritual quest. The night sky with all its stars was as important as the daylight sky. The underworld was as important to visit as the heavenly spheres. This is reflected in the ancient Norse tradition. In the Nordic tradition the darkness is a prerequisite for illumination. When Odin hangs in the world tree he gazes into the depth to find the runes. The secrets of existence are hidden in the underworld.

The runes consist of a light outer form and a dark inner dimension. Rune magicians during all times have sought the inner secrets of the runes, striving with an iron will like Odin to discover the hidden meanings of the runes. The runosophy of this book is based on a disputed thought that the rune row is written in a cipher to hide its secret meaning from the uninitiated. The hidden and dark side of the rune row has been called the Uthark. This has been viewed as the inner esoteric rune row that is hidden behind the more common rune row, called the Futhark. When discussing this type of occult thought there is no actual right or wrong, true or false. Many have doubted the historical anchorage of the Uthark, and many deep and advanced magical books based on the Futhark have been written. But the Uthark has revealed itself as a very powerful tool for entering the secrets of the runes and for exploring their nightside.

THE SECRET WISDOM
OF THE NORTH

The word *rune* in itself might give us a hint of what the runes really are. In Old Norse and the Germanic languages, the word *rune* signifies "secret," "mystery," or "secret whisper." The runes were not used in normal writing at first but were magical symbols or signs to describe different forces and principles in the universe and human existence. These signs are not only the runes that we can recognize from the rune rows. In a deeper sense the runes are hidden forces that are illustrated with certain writing signs, as well as with galders, songs, and other magical practices. The runes and songs that Odin received after his initiation in the world tree are magical expressions of the hidden forces of the universe. Thus the runes can have many different meanings. In an outer aspect the word *rune* denotes the Old Norse writing sign; on a deeper level it denotes the forces of the universe and the whole of occult spirituality.

The runes and Norse spirituality are codified after a classification that indicates a sophisticated intellectual ability and a profound understanding of existence. Today we can only acquire a fraction of the knowledge possessed by the wise ones of ancient times, but through wholehearted studies we can hopefully discover what is essential regarding the secrets of the runes.

Many modern scientists and scholars tend to underestimate the old cultures and reduce their thoughts and religious beliefs to the level of the plain or trivial. One can easily get the impression that the old spirituality was mainly concerned with harvest cults and burial ceremonies. The myths are interpreted as if they are naive and puerile descriptions of life. The majority of all archaeological findings are alleged to be grave artifacts. It is almost as if the interpretations reveal more about the worldview of scientists than about ancient religion. This positivistic worldview that has deeply influenced modern science claims that man has progressed from simple and primitive levels to more and more advanced and sophisticated ways of thinking. This is a conception that logically arises through the meeting of the old monotheistic worldview and the materialism of industrialism. It is an unconscious analogy to how one experiences the self as developing from the state of childhood to the more complex world of the adult.

There is no reason to believe that we are now on a higher intellectual or spiritual level than during ancient times. If an analogy is drawn to humankind, perhaps we are now as children and the peoples of ancient times were adults, but from the generation of a different cycle. Or else we are now senile and confused elders! The reason why archaeological sites are described as graves can be the fact that they are connected to the feeling of the past being dead and buried. The absence of corpses in many of the so-called graves is interesting. In any case, we must be prepared to accept that the ancients were more advanced than us, intellectually and spiritually. In fact, industrial society and our postindustrial information society are the type of societies where people have been forced to focus most of their time on material work and have thus had less time to develop the spiritual and intellectual side. One can draw the conclusion that the materially most advanced societies might be in danger of producing the intellectually and spiritually weakest persons. In the societies of the past, life was often very hard, but there were also long periods where the inner work could take place, with sophisticated religious practice, advanced philosophical views on existence, and rich traditions of myths and stories. Thanks to Snorri Sturluson and others, parts of this knowledge have been kept alive to the present day.

Our knowledge about the runes and old Norse spirituality is derived from the *Eddas* and the sagas, from archaeological findings, from cave paintings, picture- and runestones, and village names. Besides the *Eddas,* a book by the Danish historian Saxo Grammaticus from the thirteenth century also presented views on the old Norse worldview. We can also derive information from the Roman Tacitus's (55–120) *Germania* and from Adam of Bremen's descriptions. For those who wish to explore the secrets of the runes it is of great importance to investigate these sources. But one should not get stuck in the archaeological information. One must keep in mind that the runes and the old Norse tradition have gone through constant change. Runic knowledge has progressed and changed through the ages and with its practitioners. The runes and the myths are exoteric pictures of an esoteric reality that exists outside time.

There is profane time and there is mythical time. We normally exist in profane time, and here history occurs through death and return. Here we can attain knowledge through historical and archaeological research. Mythical time is archetypal and lies beyond profane time and space. This is the time described by the myths. A shaman or magician can reach mythical time through extraordinary states of consciousness. Mythical time is, however, more easily accessed through knowledge on the profane level. Theory will enable practice, but one should not be too overly focused on archaeological or historical details. The power that the runes denote is the same today as it was during the age of the Vikings.

There are many theories regarding the origin of the runes. The four main theories are called the Latin theory, the Greek theory, the Etruscan theory, and the Nordic theory. The Latin theory is most common today in academic circles. It is based on facts derived from archaeological findings and the similarities between certain runes and Latin letters. The Greek theory points out similarities between Greek letters and runes, like Omega (Ω) and Odal ($\rtimes$). The Etruscan theory is based on the fact that certain artifacts of Etruscan origin were written with Etruscan letters but in the Old Norse language. The Nordic theory claims that the letters originated in the North and influenced the other alphabets. There are also theories describing the runes as the letters that were used in Atlantis.

THE RENAISSANCE OF THE RUNES

Rune magic, as we know it today, is derived from two main sources. One is from those who are researching old material and revitalizing the old tradition. We can call them the revivalists. The other source is from those who have kept patterns of ancient knowledge alive. We can call them the preservers. The first category is often based in academic circles. The other is more commonly found in the countryside. Among the revivalists, the theories are often centered on the intellectual and philosophical patterns in the runes. The magic of the preservers, on the other hand, is more down-to-earth and mixed with concepts—such as certain aspects of Christianity—that have arisen through the years. This approach can be found in the so-called black-arts books that were written in the Nordic countries, such as the Icelandic *En Isländsk Svartkonstbok från 1500-talet* (An Icelandic black-arts book from the sixteenth century). The revivalist theories can be divided into three epochs or generations: the Swedish, the German, and the Anglo-Saxon.

The rebirth of Nordic spirituality began during the decades preceding the "great power" epoch of Sweden (1611–1718). During these times many grandiose books were written; for example, the *Atlantica* by Olof Rudbeck that describes Sweden's connections to Atlantis. The interest in the occult and the old Norse tradition was growing. Interest in *storgoticism* (or *megleogothicism*) was a current that connected Sweden with the Goths and explored hidden and occult aspects in a nationalist, romantic way. Johannes Bureus (1568–1652), an underestimated writer, was part of this current and was the first great runic revivalist. He collected a vast amount of material about runes and runestones. He held that the runes had an occult side that was similar to the letter mysticism and numerology of the Cabbala.* He called this system of hidden runes *adulrunes* (noble runes).

The next generation of revivalists can be found in Germany between the Romantic period and the Second World War. During the Romantic period and the following epochs the interest in ancient Nordic and Germanic religion was great. The Grimm brothers collected folktales, and the Nordic mythological operas of Richard Wagner were popular all over the world. In nationalistic circles, people explored the connection between the runes and Germanic spirituality. The rune-master of these circles was Guido von List (1848–1919). After a period of blindness caused by a surgical operation, he claimed to have been initiated into the mysteries of the runes. He wrote the very influential book *Das Geheimnis der Runen* (*The Secret of the Runes*). List claimed, like Bureus, that there are hidden meanings in the runes. He described the three levels, called *kalas,* of the runes. The first level was the outer exoteric level; the second was the inner esoteric level; and the third was the most secret "Armanen" level. The Armanen was, according to List, the secret of initiated runic priests, those who had been initiated by Odin. Guido von List created his own runic row called the "Armanen-Futhark," and it consisted of eighteen runes that represent the eighteen runes or songs that Odin is described as receiving in the *Hávamál*. List wanted to reestablish the old Germanic spirituality and the cult of Odin in an Odinistic (Wotanistic) movement.

List had many followers, which led to the creation of a Guido von List society and an Armanen society. The Edda Society led by Rudolf Gorsleben and the Germanen Order founded by Hermann Pohl were inspired by List. Many of these societies became increasingly political and were partly involved in the creation of the Nazi Party, the NSDAP. The swastika and the use of the two *sieg* runes in the SS symbol are derived from List. Another follower of List, Siegfried Adolf Kummer,

---

*In this book the term Cabbala is used to describe the entire cabbalistic tradition from the original Hebrew texts through the later Christian and occult forms.

included rune yoga, rune yodeling, rune mudras, and magical circles connected to the zodiac. He was forced to flee Germany when the Nazis reached power. Friedrich Marby (1882–1966) was a rune magician who was more independent in his relation to List. He developed a runic gymnastics that might have inspired the rune yoga of Kummer. Marby connected the runes to cosmic energies that could be channeled through the body. He was of Swedish origin and traveled to Sweden in 1928 to find the roots of the runes. In Germany he was imprisoned by the Nazis and sent to a concentration camp during the war.

The third generation of revivalists is found in the Anglo-Saxon and North American parts of the world. From the 1970s until today these revivalists have been active in publishing books and starting societies. Some of these Odinistic societies focus on racial-mystical neo-paganism, while others are purely occult groups.

THE NORDIC WORLDVIEW

If the magical language of the runes is to be understood one must have a basic knowledge of Nordic myths. We will not enter into these particular myths now, but one should study the *Eddas,* the *Hávamál,* and the *Völuspá.* H. R. Davidsson's *Gods and Myths of Northern Europe* is a basic introduction to Nordic mythology.

There are numerous important principles in the Nordic worldview. One may get the impression that many characters and events in Nordic mythology are similar to the Bible. This is of course due to the later influence of Christianity—Balder as Jesus, Loki as Satan, Ragnarök as Armageddon, and so forth, are all later interpretations. Although parallels might exist in many of the stories, there are obvious differences in the basic structure of the two religions. The Bible is based on a monotheistic and linear worldview: The belief is that there is a god who created the world at the beginning of time. Then time marches on until it is all destroyed in Armageddon, after which the righteous will reach paradise. This thought is a unique abnormality shared by the monotheistic religions: Judaism, Christianity, and Islam. In the pagan religions, on the other hand, time moves in cycles. The Nordic world picture is built on cyclic time. Worlds are created and destroyed in a way that resembles the cycles of nature.

Also, the world was not created by a god but rather came into existence through a meeting of polar energies. In the oldest pagan religions there is not only a god but a god and a goddess as well. There are also numerous polar powers from which the world arises. The Nordic myth describes creation as coming about through the interaction of two primordial principles, Niflheim and Muspelheim, the realms of heat and cold, respectively. This is the primordial polarity of the universe. We can see the continuity of polar thinking into the nineteenth century and how important it was to the Romantics; Goethe, for instance, relied on ideas about polarity in his works of alternative natural science. The basic terms in the creation myth are these:

Muspelheim: the principle of fire, heat, expansion; takes a convex form;

Niflheim: the principle of ice, cold, astringency; takes a concave form; and

Ginnungagap: the great nothingness from which the world existence arises through a balance between these two primal opposites.

The first being formed is Ymer, the primeval giant, whose name means "twin." He has a twin nature and is described as two-headed and/or a hermaphrodite. The two-sexed or two-headed primeval being can be found in many occult traditions.

There are two main races or kinds of higher beings in Norse mythology. The giants, or *thurses,* are the oldest beings and belong to an ancient race of giants. The gods are younger and created the world by slaying Ymer. The younger gods fighting against the older gods or giants of chaos is a common mythological theme. In Norse mythology there is a struggle between the giants and the gods, but it is not obvious who are in fact the good ones. Unlike the monotheistic religions, the Nordic tradition did not use terms like *good* or *evil*. The universe was viewed as a struggle as well as a cooperation between different powers. The giants are in possession of the greatest wisdom. Odin gains wisdom through the giant Mímir, and he is taught the secrets of the runes by the giant Böltorn. The giants are dark powers or chaotic forces in possession of ancient hidden wisdom and power.

Time is connected to destiny, and it is woven by the three dark Nordic goddesses called the Norns: Urd, Verdandi, and Skuld. They represent the past (Urd), the present (Verdandi), and the future (Skuld). Urd means "fate" or "primeval" (as in the prefix *ur*); Verdandi, "being"; and Skuld, "result." Skuld is connected to the idea of karmic energy that can be used or gained. The web of the Norns connects the universe together. The runes are the different powers or aspects of the web. Through the runes the magician can influence the web of destiny. Odin's dark blood brother, Loki, is also called "Locke," the spider weaving a web. He invented the net. Loki is the "trickster" or "culture hero" who attaches the newly created universe and forms the web on which existence is built. From Loki, both humans and gods learn how to use nets. These nets are the ability to control one's destiny. Loki can be compared to Prometheus, a figure who reveals secret and forbidden knowledge.

In the Nordic worldview, space is created when the three gods Voden, Vile, and Ve slay Ymer and create the world from his body. From chaos, order is created through the triad of gods. Space is held up by the four cardinal dwarves, Nordre, Södre, Östre, and Västre.

Time is created through the female triad of Urd, Verdandi, and Skuld as they weave the thread of destiny.

There is also a dark triad of demonic beings who have important roles in the end of the world in the great transformation of Ragnarök. This triad represents the disintegrating and destructive forces that enable rebirth and change. They are Loki's three children with the giantess Angerboda: Hel, Jörmundgandr (the serpent of Midgård), and the wolf Fenrir.

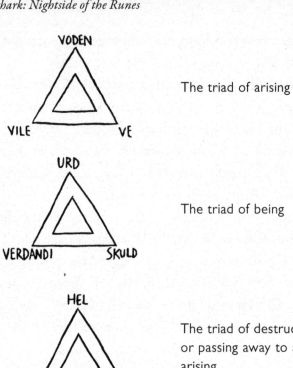

The triad of arising

The triad of being

The triad of destruction, or passing away to a new arising

The three triads intertwined as a whole

Thus there are three triads:

Voden (according to Snorri Sturluson, Voden is the oldest name for Odin; the alliteration creates VVV), Vile, and Ve: the creating triad that creates space.

Urd, Verdandi, and Skuld: the triad of being and time.

Hel, Jörmundgandr, and Fenrir (or the Fenris wolf): the triad of destruction and departure.

The four dwarves represent the four cardinal directions on a surface. In Nordic spirituality two more directions are used, which make six in all. The directions up and down are represented by the eagle (Veðrfölnir) and the reptile (Nidhögg), the two foremost archetypes for the sky and the underworld. The eagle and the reptile are the two poles of the vertical line, and they interact through the communication carried by the squirrel Ratatosk. In all ancient religions and worldviews the world pillar is of great importance. The world pillar is the vertical line that exists in the center of the world and links what is above with what is below. The bird and the reptile are archetypal symbols of the two poles of the pillar, and the dragon symbol represents the unity of the poles and the above with the below. In the Nordic tradition the world tree Yggdrasil is the world pillar. Shamans, magicians, and witches could travel between the worlds on the world pillar. They could climb up to the worlds of the sky or travel down to the underworld. The world pillar became like a steed for the magicians. Thus the world pillar in the Nordic traditions was called "Odin's steed." The term *ygg* or *yggr* is an epithet of Odin, and *drasil* denotes his steed.

NORDIC NUMEROLOGY

Numbers have always been of great importance in religion, myth, and magic. Numbers seem to be part of the basic structure of the mind. Nature as well can be constructed from mathematical principles. Some philosophical (Pythagorean and Platonist) and mystical (Cabbala) systems describe everything being constructed according to mathematical principles, and numbers represent aspects of existence. In the Nordic tradition numbers are also of great importance. The essential numbers in the Nordic tradition are built upon the triad. Triads of gods and goddesses create the basic structure of the world. There are 3×3 worlds. Odin hangs in Yggdrasil 9 nights and is taught 18 (2×9) power songs. The triad is a pivotal idea in the whole of the Nordic spirituality. From two opposites the third is born.

This idea lived on in Hegel's philosophy of thesis-antithesis-synthesis.

One. The number 1, important in monotheistic theology and Platonic-Hermetic philosophy, is not as significant in Nordic spirituality. Yggdrasil as the world pillar corresponds to this number.

Two. The number 2 is more significant. The world is created through two poles, Niflheim and Muspelheim. Not even the primal being Ymer can be connected to the number 1; his twin aspect and connection to Tuisto (from *tvistra,* "to separate") assigns him to the number 2. The eagle and the dragon Nidhögg are two polar principals. Hugin and Munin (the ravens of Odin) can be connected to the number 2, and also Gere and Freke (Odin's wolfs). Odin and Loki are a magically complementary couple.

Three. The number 3 is the cardinal number representing the eternal movement in the universe (thesis-antithesis-synthesis). A triad of gods—Voden (Odin), Vile, and Ve—structures the universe. Odin, Hönur, and Lodur (probably the same triad but with altered names) give humans the qualities of the soul. Urd, Verdandi, and Skuld are rulers of time. The number 3 is the foundation of the runes and the power songs.

Four. The number 4 represents order. The symbol of this number is the sun wheel (swastika), which is the symbol of Thor. He fights the forces of chaos and maintains order. The world is supported by the four cardinal dwarfs, Nordre, Södre, Östre, and Västre. Four stags are chewing on the buds of the world tree and can be viewed as four necessary destructive cardinal forces making the world order and the number 4 move in a cycle.

Five. The number 5 is connected to time. A week in the old Germanic society consisted of five days and was called a *fimmt.* The pentagram was used in later old Norse magic.

Six. The number 6 is connected to space. There are six directions (north, south, east, west, up, and down).

Seven. The number 7 is associated with "the other side." The rainbow bridge, Bifröst, is sometimes described as having three colors, and other times as having seven.

Eight. The number 8 represents the order of the runes. The Elder Futhark is divided into three groups of eight, called *ættir*. The Scandinavian Futhark can also be divided into two groups of eight (three groups of five and six are more common, however). The thirty-three-stave Northumbrian rune row is divided into four ættir of eight and one separate rune. There is also a very uncommon rune row of forty runes that can be divided into five ættir of eight. The magical practice of the runes can be divided into eight kinds.

Nine. The number 9 is the most important number in Nordic spirituality. In the Cabbala the number 10 represents the total; in the Nordic tradition the number 9 fills the same function. There are nine worlds, and in the underworld there are nine more. Odin hangs nine nights in Yggdrasil and gains nine power songs. In the Ynglinga tale, Snorri Sturluson presents Odin as having nine magical abilities. The three triangles joined in the *valknut* is the symbol of completion, the number 9, and Odin.

SACRED PLACES

Knowledge about the Nordic tradition cannot be found simply by researching written material on this subject. Many secrets are only revealed when one visits the old Nordic sacred places. These areas are often ridiculed by common archaeology; they are described simply as being graveyards or playgrounds. An initiate in magical or religious thought will realize that the sacred places are powerful areas and important centers that are surrounded by advanced cults. The stone labyrinths, the so-called *trojeborgar*, have been described as being playgrounds. They are in fact created through an advanced knowledge of the power of the ground and the area in general. The paths of the labyrinth will deeply influence the mind. It is claimed that these labyrinths are pictures of the mind and the brain. To enter these ancient stone labyrinths is a form of initiation. It stages an entry into the center of the underworld where the core of the soul and secret of existence, the diamond, can be found.

Ship tumuli were not only places where the dead were burned but were also used in astral travels to the worlds beyond our own. They were constructed with the most intricate knowledge about the directions and the magnetic area of the tumulus. The construction itself reveals a certain logic in its form and place. The fact that they also resemble wombs is no mere coincidence. They represent wombs from which the living can be born into new worlds. These tumuli are the proof of the thought that the grave and the womb are the two gates to the other side and that they are, mystically, the same. When we die we are born, and when we are born we die. The old sacred places are placed in relation to each other. They are part of a gigantic net. One way to explore these places is using a divining rod or a pendulum. Earth energy and magnetism have much information to give. The stones are not placed randomly but where the power is strongest, or where it naturally creates vacuums in time and space, which enables journeys between the worlds.

2

THE UTHARK AND
THE RUNES

THE RUNE ROWS

The rune row or runic alphabet is not an alphabet comparable to the Greek or Roman alphabets. The rune row begins with another set of letters—*f, u, th, a, r, k*—and thus the rune row is called the Futhark. The order of the runes in this rune row was found on Gotland, on the Kylver stone, and on other items like the Vadstenabracteate and the Grumpanbracteate. The most common theory regarding the origin of the runes is that they are derived from the Greek or Roman alphabet. But the fact that the runes are placed in the Futhark order makes this rather unlikely, since it is no ABC alphabet. The position of the runes indicates a strong connection to the old Nordic spirituality and world-view. This might indicate that the runes appeared independently in the old Norse tradition. The runes were not originally letters used for writing but were instead magical symbols. This is made clear through the oldest discoveries of the runes, which reveal a magical character. Only after the cultural decline in the Viking Age were the runes degraded to trivial use, something that can be observed on the numerous rune-stones. Even after the arrival of Christianity the runes were used for protection, even in churches. In the church of Hemse on Gotland, the priest's pulpit is protected with a couple of Futharks. If the Christian powers could not protect the church, they must have thought it best also to let the old runes of Odin be of assistance.

The elder rune row consists of twenty-four runes, and this is the most common row in magical use. The rune row is divided into three *aetts*, each aett having eight runes. The three aetts are named after Frej, Hagal, and Tyr. The younger rune row has sixteen runes. This row exists in two versions, the Norwegian-Swedish and the Danish (also called the "common") rune row. It was not used as frequently in magical practice. There is also an Anglo-Saxon rune row of thirty-three runes where the Elder Futhark is extended with nine additional runes. Even if the Scandinavian sixteen-stave rune row was not commonly used in magical practice, it has had great influence on magical traditions through the Armanen Futhark of Guido von List. It is thought to represent the power songs and runes that Odin obtained during his initiation. Although the Armanen Futhark is lacking in historical evidence it is used in many modern runic magical circles.

A disputed version of the Elder Futhark is the "Uthark." According to Professor Sigurd Agrell, who published books on the subject during the 1930s, the first rune should be placed last. Thus a rune row with a new meaning, in accordance with numerological theories, will arise. In his book *Lapptrummor och Runmagi,* Agrell writes: "At the positioning of the runes in a Futhark (one beginning with the runes *f, u, th, a,* etc.) a cryptographic trick has been used: the last rune is placed before the others. Thus it has been made impossible for the uninitiated to know the real order of the runes."

In *Runornas Talmystik och dess antika förebild* and *Senantik Mysteriereligion och Nordisk Runmagi,* Agrell reveals similarities between the numerology of certain antique mystical cults and the runic tradition. The problem of the Uthark theory is the lack of archaeological evidence to support it. There are some occasional artifacts found that could be Utharks, but the first rune might be missing. The fact that the Uthark theory makes sense from a numerological perspective of the Nordic tradition supports its probability.

It could be that Agrell is right that the rune row was enciphered, so as only to be recognized by initiates. We know that the Nordic magicians created numerous secrets and hidden runes and that the runic tradition consists of many levels. The Futhark could be the outer, exoteric rune row, while the Uthark is the inner, esoteric one.

The twenty-four-stave Elder Futhark is commonly used in runic magical circles. It exists in two main versions used by different practitioners. Some place the *d*, Dagaz, last, while others place the *o*, Odal, last. The latter version is derived from the Kylver stone, but the first is more common. In German runic magical circles and among those inspired by national Romanticism and Guido von List, the Armanen Futhark is used. Some are also leaning toward the racial-mystical theories of List while others are excluding this dimension. In Sweden, the Uthark has been used by some runic magical groups. The twenty-four-stave Elder Futhark is presented by Edred Thorsson in his books *Runelore* and *Futhark: A Handbook of Rune Magic* and by Freya Aswynn in her *Leaves of Yggdrasil.* Thorsson describes the sixteen-stave Scandinavian Futhark in *Northern Magic* and the Armanen row in his book *Rune Might.*

The Uthark is a magically potent version of the rune row. Even if its historical roots are in dispute, it corresponds to the language and mythology of the old Norse culture. The wealth rune Feh, representing the goal and reward, is placed last, which also seems logical. Also, Ur denotes the wild primeval ox, while Feh represents the tame cow, which creates two opposites in polarity in the Uthark. Let us now explore the Uthark.

THE UTHARK

Ur (*u*): The Ur rune denotes the primeval state and the origin. The Ur rune is the Ur- ("original") ox or the Ur-cow that in many myths represents the state before creation. In Nordic mythology it is the cow Audhumbla. If we were to turn the Ur rune so that it would look like a normal *u* we can see how it illustrates the horns of the animal.

From the udder of Audhumbla flow four rivers of milk, feeding the other primeval being, Ymer. The rivers of milk are the inherent nourishing force of the original state that spreads out in the cardinal directions of space. From a salt stone covered with white frost Audhumbla licks out the god triad of Voden, Vile, and Ve. The salt stone is the crystal-shaped form in which gods and runes can be found. This is the potentiality of the original state that is actualized and manifested through the following runes of the Uthark. The crystal returns in the Hagal rune. The Ur rune also illustrates Ginnungagap, the wide-open crack of primeval chaos and the original emptiness. The Ur rune is the womb from which everything is born and created.

Thurs (*th*): This is the rune of the giants and the *thurses*. It represents the two primal forces of chaos: the giant realm Muspelheim, the world of fire, and Niflheim, the world of ice. These worlds are inhabited by fire thurses and rime thurses, respectively. Thurs represents the extremes—the forces and worlds that are outside the order of the cosmos. These are the forces of darkness that are both frightening but also contain the wisdom and power of creation. The two primal forces of chaos are driving the world forward and are preventing it from becoming stagnant.

The forces of chaos are in the end destroying the gods and their world to enable the creation of a new world. Thurs is "the other," the antithesis and the opposite. Thurs is the world of giants, trolls, and all dark beings. The giants are often fighting with the gods. But the gods are receiving their wisdom from the giants who are in possession of the utmost wisdom. The giants are a race of gods who appeared before the Æsirs. The twin being Ymer belongs to the Thurs rune and the number 2. Thurs is the rune of witchcraft and dark magic.

As (*a*): The rune of the Æsirs. This rune belongs to Odin and the gods. It represents the wind and the breath. Odin is the god of storms and winds. He gives life and spirit to the first human couple: Ask and Embla. The As rune is connected to *önd*, which is breath and spirit—the spiritual core humans are given by Odin. In the Uthark it is the third rune, 3 being the divine number. As noted above, the original gods appear in triads: Voden, Vile, and Ve; and Odin, Höner, and Lodur. The As rune is the synthesis of Ur and Thurs. As is the rune of the power of creation—the rune that shapes cosmos from chaos. The first Æsirs kill the giant Ymer and create the world from his body.

Reid (*r*): The rune of order. This is the rune of the god Thor and is called the wagon rune. Thor is *reidatyr,* the wagon god who rides in his wagon with his hammer, Mjölnir, to fight the forces of chaos. This rune is connected to the number 4 (the wheel, the cross, etc.) and is also the fourth rune in the Uthark. The wagon rune also represents the swastika and the sun cross (an equal-armed cross in a circle), which illustrates the wheel of the wagon and the journey of the sun in the sky that banishes the forces of darkness. The Reid rune symbolizes the four seasons, and Thor is the god of agriculture and the protector of farmers. The name of the rune is also connected to riding and illustrates the four legs of the animal. Reid also denotes "right" and the Sanskrit *ṛta*—cosmic order. Thor is the upholder of order. If the Tyr rune illustrates the power of laws, the Reid rune makes sure that the laws are followed.

Reid is connected to agriculture, the wheel of the year, and the cycles of nature. Life is a journey through different levels of change, loss, and return. Reid as the wagon rune denotes this journey. The four dwarves of the cardinal directions belong to this rune. The Reid rune is the rune of rhythm, and Thor marks the time, the pulse and rhythm of existence with his hammer. Reid corresponds to the blood and the heartbeat.

⟨ **Ken (k):** The rune of fire. This rune is called the torch rune. The name of the rune has numerous meanings. *Ken* means "torch" but can also signify "to know" or "to feel," as in in the Swedish word *känna,* but even more clearly in the German and Dutch *kennen.* The word is connected to art (SW: *konst*). The torch rune is the inner fire that gives light in the form of intellectual illumination as well as feelings. This inner fire is ruled by the Nordic Prometheus figure Loki, whose name is connected to Loge, the deity of the flame. The torch rune belongs to the realm of Muspelheim and beings of fire like Surt and the sons of Muspel. The torch rune can be dangerous, similar to illumination. The rune brings both heat and light as well as destruction. One of the names of the rune is *kaun,* which can be interpreted as "a boil." The heat can bring illness, but the fire can also destroy illness.

⟨ **Gifu (g):** The name of this rune means "giving" and "sacrificing." In Nordic spirituality, gifts and giving are essential. In the *Hávamál* it is written of gifts: "So hospitable and generous no one I found, that he was not glad when given gifts, and no one so rich that a reward to him was weary," and "With his friend, man should be friendly and reward gift with gift." The Nordic tradition views life in a karmic pattern, that equal demands equal. Thus the advice is given not to give or ask for too much: "Better is not to ask or pray, than to offer (Old Norse: *blota*) too much, gift seeks gift in return; better not sacrificed than too much wasted." The relation to the divine powers in Nordic spirituality is not obsequious as in monotheistic religions. In the North it is a question about gifts and gifts in return. A religious foundation for this is the fact that the gods did not create mankind. The first humans were made of wood: Ask and Embla. These were given spirit, understanding, and feelings by the gods Odin, Höner, and Lodur. The gods gave humans the soul qualities of happiness, force, and success and thus receive gifts from humans in return. The Gifu rune reveals an exchange of gifts, knowledge, and force. It reveals how the above communicates with the below and how they are united in the middle.

This rune also has erotic aspects that are connected with the sexual interchange between persons. The rune also represents the six directions: the four elemental directions and up and down. The Gifu rune is often found on round sacrificial breads, marked with the *X* sign. The most important sacrifice or gift is self-sacrifice. No magical power or wisdom can be reached without this process. The shape of the rune denotes a man standing with outstretched legs and arms. Odin, the archetype of magicians, received the runes by sacrificing himself to himself: "given to Odin, myself to myself."

Wynja (*w*): The rune of happiness. The name of this rune means "happiness," "joy," or "pleasure." The gothic form of Wynja also denotes pastureland, "a place where the cattle can be at ease." The joy of the rune denotes a place and a state of mind.

Wynja is an old Germanic term meaning "perfection." Words like *wish* in English and *Wunsch* in German are related to this term. The rune represents the fulfillment of wishes and the joy that follows. The rune of happiness gives power and ability to *win,* which is also a related word. The rune is the seventh in the Uthark. Seven is traditionally associated with perfection, which suits the name of the rune. It corresponds to the spectrum of seven colors. The rainbow is the bridge to worlds of joy. The seventh heaven is a place of bliss and happiness, and Wynja denotes both a place and a state of mind. The number 7 has also been frequently used in Germanic magic denoting luck. Wynja corresponds to the god Frey, who according to Snorri not only rules the grains of the earth but also sunshine and peace among men. "He brings the mortals peace and pleasure," according to Adam of Bremen.

Hagal (*h*): The hail rune Hagal is one of the most important runes in rune magic. It contains the other runes. The Hagal rune is the esoteric counterpart of the Promethean fire. But instead of fire it is ice that falls from the sky, the world of the gods, down to the earth, the world of humans. This is a force that can cause great destruction but also contains great knowledge. The Nordic word *hagel* originally meant "stone," "crystal," or "crystal stone." The word *crystal* is borrowed from Greek in which its counterpart means "that which froze." Crystals, diamonds, and gems were believed to be pieces that had fallen from the "crystal sky"—the eighth heavenly and divine sphere that can be found beyond the seven planetary spheres. In the Scandinavian Futhark the shape of the rune illustrates the connection to hail. This form can easily be used as a sigil for a hailstone. The arms are then linked by a line that is surrounded by a circle ⊗. This symbol reveals the crystal shape of the rune, and in this shape all other runes can be found. In an extended form (✳) this rune has eight arms, which reveals its position in the Uthark. The number 8 is connected to the word *aett*. Hagal is the "mother rune" that contains all the other runes in potential. As the eighth rune in the Uthark it gives birth to the aetts of eight runes each. Hagal is related to Hel and the realm of cold, Niflheim/Niflhel. The English word *hail* (both meaning ice and the greeting) and *hel* are connected. Hagal can also be viewed as a piece of the original salt stone from which the primeval cow Audhumbla licked out the ancestors of the gods.

Naud (*n*): The ninth rune is the need rune. *Naud* denotes "need," and above all, "necessity." It is the rune of fate and is connected to the three Norns who weave the web of destiny. Naud is also the rune of magic and initiation. Magic is the ability to influence destiny, knowledge of which sometimes not even the gods possess. Not even the gods can influence the decisions of the Norns. Destiny is the thread of life that humans have been given. Skuld, the youngest of the Norns, is veiled since she represents the future. She cuts the thread when the time comes for a person to die. Destiny is connected to time and death. The magical initiation is the path to control destiny and to enter the deepest levels of the realm of death. Odin hangs nine nights in Yggdrasil, deeply wounded by spears so he can be initiated in the mysteries of the runes. The realm of death consists of nine worlds. The distance is nine days by horse, as we know from Hermod's journey to bring back Balder and thus change destiny. Naud is the ninth rune in the Uthark. The fact that the number 9 is connected to the Naud rune is revealed on the Sigtuna amulet where the phrase "have nine necessities, wolf" is written. The connection between the Norns and the number 9 is reflected in the *Late Edda* poem "The Sun Song" in which it says: "On the chair of the Norns, for nine days I sat." In Nordic magic the number nine is recurrent. The Icelandic books of black arts teach us to carve nine Naud runes, thus revealing the connection between the number 9 and this rune. Nine is 3 × 3 and is thus a higher aspect of the magical power of the trinity. The three witches in *Macbeth* (who might have been inspired by the Norns) chant: "Thrice to thine and thrice to mine, and thrice again to make up nine." Nine is not just destiny and necessity but also the possibility of influencing fate. Naud is time, destiny, necessity, and death, and thus also rebirth. The Naud rune is connected to the nine months of gestation and childbirth, and the pains involved are an initiation into a new reality. In Nordic spirituality death and life are intimately connected. Certain aspects of the initiatic meanings of the Naud rune continue in the eighteenth rune (9 × 2).

Is (*i*): The meaning of the ice rune is, as the name reveals, connected to ice, winter, and cold. It is the rune of Niflheim, and it represents the primal forces of the ice realm: astringent and materializing. Fire and heat make water into steam that rises upward, while cold makes water fall back to earth. For this reason the forces of ice are associated with the materializing principle. Cold makes the souls return to earth from heaven. Thus the ice rune has been used to "cool down" minds that are disturbed or in psychotic states. The ice rune is the rune of the self and represents concentration and focus. It is focusing, absorbing, and egocentric. The torch rune corresponds to feelings and the ice rune to thoughts. Its forces are like clear ice. In ice things from the past are kept. Ice belongs to the realm of death and its lowest regions, Niflhelm. In the old North, the expression "to make cold" meant to kill someone. Ice belongs to the period of rest in the winter and in death: the bears' hibernation and the state just before rebirth. In the Nordic tradition the ice represents the fifth element. The ice rune resembles a spike, and it corresponds to its qualities. The ice rune nails things down.

Jara (*j*): The year rune. Jara represents the year and especially a good year. The rune represents a good harvest and fertility. In the traditional Futhark it is the twelfth rune, which fact connects it to the twelve months of the year. In the Uthark it is the eleventh. The number 11 is connected to harvest and fertility magic, as Sigurd Agrell reveals in his books. In *Runornas Talmystik och Dess Antika Förebild,* Agrell writes that an ancient mystical numerological observation may have connected the number 11 with fertility and yearly harvest. A solar year (365 days) excedes a lunar year (354 days = 12 × 29½) by 11 days. These 11 days were believed to have a mystical influence on the growth of the year. This does not seem unlikely when viewed in the light of the fact that the sun and the moon were used to measure time in ancient days. The rune consists of two stylized half-moons circulating around each other. The moons are connected with Frey and Freya, who rule over fertility that in turn contributes to a good year. In the *Edda,* Frey gives the female giant Gerd eleven golden apples. They correspond to the fertile power of Frey.

Pertra (*p*): Pertra is often called the rock rune. The word *pertra* is generally viewed as related to the Greek and Roman word for "rock" or "stone," which is *petra.* The rune is also called *peorth* and is connected to the English word *birth.*

Mythologically the god is born out of the world mountain (as was Mithras and others). The rock is Mother Earth, from whose womb life is born, but it can also represent the night sky (as the ancient Egyptian Nut, for example), the womb from which the gods are born. This would explain the placing of the rune as the twelfth one in the Uthark. The night sky and the twelve signs of the zodiac are the womb from which life is born. But the place of the rune is far from obvious.

On certain artifacts the order of the Pertra rune and the following Eihwaz rune are reversed. On the Kylver stone the Pertra rune is before Eihwaz, but on the bracteate medals the Eihwaz rune precedes the Pertra rune. Runes twelve and thirteen are the center of the rune row. The exchange of places here could denote the central dynamics of the rune row. There are numerological reasons for both placements. But the fact is that both runes are quite mystical. *Pertra* can also mean "secret." Pertra is not only the womb but also the grave, and that would correspond to its place as the thirteenth rune, since this number is traditionally associated with death. Pertra is sometimes interpreted as the bowl used in the casting of dice or of runes. In the Anglo-Saxon rune song it is said, *"Peorth byth symble plega and hleter wlancum Thor wigan sittah on beorsele blithe aetsomne,"* or "Peorth is both game and joke for the proud . . . where warriors sit in the beer hall happy together."

Pertra can be understood as a game where chance decides the throw of the dice or which rune turns up. This game illustrates the wheel of destiny, and Pertra is the rune of destiny from which all other runes are born. Pertra is the power of fate and Lady Fortuna. It can also be so that the runic poem cited above originally revealed another meaning where the word for "warriors," *wigan,* was *wifan,* "wives," and the word for "beer hall," *beorseele,* was *beorthseele,* the "hall of birth." The runic song would then say that Peorth is "game and joke for the proud, where wives are sitting in the hall of birth happy together." This other reading would suggest the birth aspect of the rune and its connection to fertility.

Perchta is a deity of death and fertility who rides together with Odin during the wild hunt. She lives in the rocks or in the underworld.

Eihwaz (*ei*): Eihwaz, also called "Eoh," corresponds to the yew tree. On numerous artifacts this rune precedes Pertra. But the thirteenth place suits this rune, since it is connected to death. In northern countries the yew tree has been a typical graveyard tree. It is also a symbol of death and eternal life, since it can grow to be more than two thousand years old. The Anglo-Saxon rune song says: "Eoh is on the outer side not a happy tree, hard, earthbound, the guardian of fire, supported by roots, a joy on inherited land." The yew is a holy tree in the Nordic tradition, and the sacrificial tree in Uppsala was probably a yew tree. The yew represents the world tree, Yggdrasil. Yggdrasil has often been thought to be an ash tree, but it is called "eternally green," which fits the yew. The yew tree was also called the "needle ash." Eihwas represents the world pillar that unites the worlds above with the worlds below. Eihwaz is the means of communication and way to journey between the worlds.

Through his initiation, Odin has the knowledge to make such journeys, and Yggdrasil is the steed of Odin. The yew is a very poisonous tree. Properly prepared, the poison can be a powerful hallucinogen. Hallucinogens have been used in all old cultures as a method of "riding" between the worlds. The yew was also used to make magical amulets and wands but above all to make bows. The god of the yew tree is Ull, the god of hunting and archery. The *Grimnismal* relates that he lives in Ydalir, the valley of the yew trees: "The Ydalir is the home of Ull; there he founded his house." Eihwaz is the arrow and the pillar and represents the phallus. Pertra is the womb. Together they form the middle of the rune row.

Algiz (*z* or -*r*): This rune is commonly called the elk rune since its name can be interpreted as "elk." The horned look of the rune also points to this reading. Algiz represents the animal kingdom and the horned god (these aspects also correspond to the sun goddess Sol). Algiz is not only the elk but also other horned animals such as deer. Four deer are eating the leaves of the world tree and can be connected to this rune. The names of the rune have many meanings. *Algiz* means "protection," and this rune is known as the classical protection rune, especially when four Algiz runes are placed in an *aegishjalmur* (✳), the "helm of dread," a symbol from the dragon Fafnir. Algiz is also connected to the word *ahl,* which means "sacred place." According to Agrell the rune is connected to Alcis, the divine twins worshipped by the Germanic tribes according to Tacitus. This might be Frey and Freya. Algiz can be carved in two directions, denoting in each direction the male and the female sex. These two variations have also been used to denote birth and death. In the rune row from Charnay, the Algiz rune is in the same form as the Scandinavian form of Hagal (✳).

In this version the two forms of the Algiz rune are connected—masculine and feminine in one. In Holland this symbol has traditionally denoted marriage. The connection to the word *ahl*—"sacred place"—could have a sexual meaning. In the Scandinavian rune row this is the rune of man—Mannaz—and it is easy to see it as a man with outstretched arms. The rune is then interpreted as a man who is channeling forces from the world of the gods.

Sol (*s*): The rune of the sun. This rune symbolizes the sun in the sky as well as the divine force behind it. In *Alvíssmál* we read: "'Sol' it is called among men, 'Sunna' among the gods." Sunna is the goddess of the sun. In the Nordic tradition the sun was not a masculine force as in many other cultures. At least in its inner form the sun is a goddess whose nurturing power brings fertility and life on earth. The god Balder also belongs to this rune. He is a sun god, and his death represents the entering of the sun into the realm of the dead. The sun cult is very old in the North, and the motion of the sun, its disappearance and return, was a central theme in the cult. The sun represents protection and victory. The sun is a fertile force connected to virility and to the power of will, which can survive even death. The sun is also the eye of the sky. The sun is one of Odin's eyes. The eye that he sacrificed in the well of Mímir (dreams and memories; the unconscious) is symbolized by the moon. The sun rune corresponds to the destructive sun giant Surt, who lives in Muspelheim. He represents the most powerful but also most destructive aspects of the sun.

↑ **Tyr (*t*):** Tyr is the ancient war and sky god, and the rune that bears his name symbolizes his power. The Tyr rune is above all the rune of struggle and victory. In the *Edda* poem *Sigrdrífumál* we can read: "Victory runes you shall know if victory you desire, and carve them on the handle of the sword, some on the hilt and on the pin and two times mention Tyr." Tyr represents courage and justice. Tyr is the law-giving force and represents balance and order (something that is kept by the Reid rune). The shape of the rune is both the scales and the spear. The rune also illustrates the pillar that supports the roof of the sky. The Tyr rune symbolizes the part of Yggdrasil that is above earth, like the Irminsul of the Saxons. Tyr is the rune of bravery and self-sacrifice. Tyr places his hand in the mouth of the Fenris Wolf as a security when the gods are placing it in chains. The wolf bites his hand off when the chains are placed on him. The Tyr rune brings victory but victory that includes self-sacrifice. The rune is masculine and phallic. It is often viewed as the male rune while the one following is the female rune.

ᛒ **Bjarka (*b*):** The birch rune. The name of this rune means "birch" or "birch branch." The shape of this rune has been interpreted as two female breasts or as a pregnant woman in profile. The rune represents fertility and childbirth. In old fertility rites young men chased the young women and whipped them with birch branches.

This ceremony took place in the spring. The female soul was believed to be connected to the birch, and it was commonly believed that the female soul inhabited the birch after death. The birch represents the flow of life from both birth and death. The birch is also connected to witchcraft and the *sejd* trance. The bristle on the witch's broom was traditionally made from birch. The birch is a typically Nordic tree. It was the first tree to return after the latest ice age and symbolizes rebirth and new creation. The goddesses Frigg and Freya are connected to the birch.

Eh (*e*): This rune is called the horse rune. The word *eh* means "horse," and the most common interpretation of this rune is partnership, friendship, and cooperation. The rune has been used in marriages and partnership ceremonies. The rune also has a more occult significance. It is rune number 18 in the Uthark, and 18 is the number of Odin (2 × 9, Odin knows 18 power songs, and magic connected to Odin is constructed on the numbers 9 and 18). The rune is thus connected to Odin. The horse is also connected to Odin. Odin's eight-legged horse, Sleipnir, carries him between the worlds. As noted above, the word *Yggdrasil* means "Odin's steed," and Yggdrasil is the axis between the worlds used by the magicians when traveling between them. The horse rune is connected to journeys between the worlds. It is also connected to the Reid rune. The horse is viewed as the most magical animal in the Nordic tradition. A horse head would frighten the *landvættirs* (nature spirits) and was believed to cause bad luck. But at the same time a horse's head was placed over a well to protect it. The horse is intimately connected to death. At the winter solstice Odin rides with the legions of the dead in the feared "wild hunt." The horse also belongs to Hel. The underworld consists of another nine worlds, apart from the nine worlds of Yggdrasil. These worlds are called "Heldrasil," which can be translated as "Hels horse," the dark female and underworld counterpart of Yggdrasil. Among certain farmers, "Hels horse" is a mystical conception related to death and its kingdoms.

The Eh rune is also connected to karma and justice. In many myths a person's good and bad deeds are placed on a scale in the underworld. This rune can illustrate a scale. The shape of the rune has also been interpreted as illustrating a horse, but sometimes as two people shaking hands. The meaning of partnership is then revealed. The Eh rune is connected to a person's totem, the *fylgja*. This totem animal helps us to travel between the worlds and is perhaps our greatest guide through life and death. It is said that *"Marr er manns fylgja,"* "The horse is man's fylgja."

ᛗ **Mannaz (m):** The rune of man follows the horse rune; Mannaz represents man in balance. The shape of this rune is sometimes interpreted as a man and a woman holding each other. The X shape can also be found in the rune, illustrating the communication between the worlds above and below, and the four directions. This rune belongs to the world of humans. The rune is the nineteenth in the Uthark. The number 19 unites the seven planets and the twelve signs of the zodiac. It is a very old conception that humans are created by forces from the planets and stars. The rune Manna in the Gothic Futhark has the double meaning of tree and man. In Nordic spirituality man was connected to the trees. This is also evident from the Scandinavian rune row, where the rune of man has a shape similar to a tree (identical to the elk rune).

ᛚ **Lagu (l):** This is the rune of water. The name of the rune can be found in many words: the Swedish *lag* and *lagun,* the English *lake, lagoon,* and so forth. Lagu does not only denote water but also the word for "fluid" (SW: *vätska*). Lagu is the basic law (SW: *lag*) of life. The rune represents the original waters of Niflheim that are the prerequisite of all life. Lagu, like water, is closely connected to the moon. The tides ebb and flow with the phases of the moon. The cycle of the moon also reflects menstruation, and Lagu is the rune of blood and bodily fluids. Lagu corresponds to witchcraft and magic, and in the names *logr* or *laukar,* it signifies "witchcraft." The rune is connected to dreams, which are influenced by the moon and the balance of the bodily fluids. Lagu is also connected to the goddess Nerthus and the god Njord as well as the god Ägir and his wife, Ran, and their nine daughters. The rune is twentieth in the Uthark. Twenty is often connected to water and the moon. Sigurd Agrell has a theory about how the number 20 is found in the Nordic tradition by pointing this out about Ägir, Ran, and their nine daughters: "If we would dare to suppose that they also had as many sons—such a symmetry is common in mythology—the water in Nordic folk belief would have been represented by 20 water demons (2 + 9 + 9)."

In the Nordic tradition a ceremonial pouring of water on people—*vatni ausa*—was common; one poured water as a sort of baptizing.

◇ **Ing (*ng*):** The Ing rune represents the masculine power of reproduction. The rune illustrates a sperm or a phallus. The word *ing* means "sperm" or "seed" (SW: *frö*). Ing is a god corresponding to Frö or Frey. This god is the husband of Freya and a god of fertility. Ing might also have been the male counterpart to Nerthus, the goddess of earth. The mythical Swedish royal dynasty, the Ynglingarna, could supposedly trace its family lines back to the god Yng or Ing. The Swedish word *yngling* means a young, virile man. The rune is connected to the spring. From a magical perspective the rune contains the potential. The rune is the seed of what is to come.

ᛟ **Odal (*o*):** Odal denotes "real property/estate" or "inheritance." The *odalman* is an independent landowning man. Odal also denotes "noble" (SW: *ädel*), which alludes to the *odalman* who, according to tradition, has the power to claim life, power, and land. The word *nobility* can also be traced to Odal (SW: *adel*). The Odal rune is also connected to the family and one's historical right. The Odal rune is the rune of the clan, the relatives, and the nation. It represents limit and protection. The rune illustrates a wall with a large opening. It is also the Ing rune standing firmly with two legs on the ground. The magical aspect of the rune is to find one's roots and one's anchorage in history. The oldest forms of spirituality were ancestor cults in which people lived in direct relation with their ancestors and the places they inhabited. The ancestors often lived on in magical objects, especially trees, that were connected with their souls. The tree cult and the ancestor cult have always been intimately connected. The Odal rune represents a person's roots and historical foundation. As a rune of protection, it can be found on old houses. The place of the rune in the row is not obvious. Sometimes it is placed after Dagaz, as in the Kylver stone. But in many places it comes before Dagaz.

ᛗ **Dagaz (*d*):** This is the day rune. It denotes daylight itself rather than the day as a period of time, although it does represent the time between dawn and dusk. Dagaz represents illumination, clarity, and awakening. It is used as protection against witchcraft and was carved on doors and windows. Dagaz is the rune of culmination. It represents the zenith and the climax. The Jara rune represents the year cycle when it turns at the winter solstice, and Dagaz represents the summer solstice. Dagaz is the highest point of a cycle and the beginning of a new. It is similar to the butterfly and represents the step out of the chrysalis and into a new reality.

ᚠ **Feh (*f*):** The name of this rune denotes "cattle" or "livestock." Cattle were equivalent to wealth, and the rune is often called the wealth rune. In the Elder Futhark this is the first rune, which is the best argument for the Uthark theory. It seems reasonable that the primeval animal Ur comes first and the tame cattle, Feh, would be last. The name "wealth rune" also denotes that this rune is connected to rewards and riches that one has gathered. Logically, this would be the last step in a process.

According to the Uthark this rune represents the completion of a process and the reward that comes from that completion. The enormous primordial and chaotic powers of the Ur rune with which the rune row begins have been tamed and are under the magician's control at the Feh rune. The relationship between the first and the last rune reveals how they are like two sides of a coin. They represent the extremes that easily will pass over into each other. Since Nordic spirituality is not created around the perspective of linear time, but rather cyclic time, a new cycle begins after Feh, starting with a new Ur rune.

THE UTHARK VERSUS THE FUTHARK

The Uthark theory is controversial. Many runologists doubt that it has any real significance. But there are also a number of serious runologists who believe that it might be possible. It all depends on how we look upon the runes. The Uthark theory is not mainly dependent on archaeological findings but on its correspondence to Nordic mythology, numerology, and magical tradition. The most important evidence that to a certain extent supports the Uthark theory is the Kylver stone from Gotland, which is the oldest artifact that reveals a complete rune row. It begins with a vertical line before the Ur rune (some scholars believe the line is a broken or incomplete Feh rune). The last rune is a classical cryptic rune, or a sign that could be a version of the rune Feh. This oldest evidence of a complete rune row, which was found in a tomb, could very well reveal the original rune row.

It is also known from other artifacts that this very code that turns the Uthark to a Futhark was common among rune magicians. Often the runes were moved one place to conceal the meaning of what was written. If we were to move the runes one place back in the rune row, the name *Hel* would become WBM. The complete rune row could be arranged in this manner to avoid the uninitiated grasping its true secrets. In the story of Egil Skallagrímsson it is told how the rune magician Egil arrives at a farm where the daughter in the family is seriously ill. Egil finds a piece of whalebone carved with runes under her bed. It was made by a young man in the area who has tried to carve love runes to win her love. But he has carved the wrong runes and instead made her ill. Egil removes the young man's runes and carves new runes to heal the girl. Afterward Egil states that "a farm boy shall not carve runes, if he places them not right: many men may be misled by marks upon dark staves." Thus we are taught there is a great risk that those uninitiated in the secrets of the runes will arrange them erroneously.

It is interesting from a rune-magical perspective that the oldest finding of a rune row is from Gotland and that it could be depicting an Uthark. The runes might have their origin in the tradition of the Goths, whose tribal name comes from the god Gaut (Gotos, Got, Gut). *Gaut* means "god" and is one of Odin's names. Odin is the one who is initiated in the runic mysteries, and it is from him that humans can get the knowledge about the runes. The Goths are Odin's people, and it is often claimed that Gotland is the native country of the Goths.

The Futhark is sometimes viewed as an outer, exoteric form of the rune row. It begins, as noted above, with the tamed—Feh—which is followed by the wild in the form of Ur. The Uthark is a darker form of the rune row that, in accordance with Nordic myth, begins in the beginning with the forces of chaos.

From a magical perspective the rune row is not only a linear row but should be arranged in a circle. In this circle of twenty-four runes, the runes also represent the twenty-four hours of the day and the twelve signs of the zodiac. Placed in a circle we can see how the rune row can be read both as a Futhark and an Uthark.

Not only the separate runes, but the whole rune row was used in magical operations. The rune row itself contains magical power, and it summarizes all the magical qualities of the separate runes. Thus it is not unlikely that the widespread magical formula ALU can confirm the Uthark theory. If the runes in the formula are added numerologically (A = 3, L = 20, U = 1), it makes 24—the number of runes in the complete rune row. The ALU formula includes the complete rune row and is a synthesis of the powers of the twenty-four runes. The ALU formula is interesting also from the perspective of the Futhark, where its number becomes 27, which is 3 × 9. To repeat a magical number like 9 three times is believed to increase its power. The term *alu* means "holy" and is related to the English word *ale* (SW: *öl*) and denoted divine inspiration and magical power.

The Elder Futhark and the Uthark are divided into three ættir. In the Futhark the first rune in each ætt signifies the ætt: Frey (Feh), Hagal, and Tyr. In the Uthark these runes come last in each ætt. There are three ways to divide the ættir in the Uthark: (1) One can begin from the end, with Frey (Feh), Tyr, and Hagal, but this will complicate the logic of the Uthark disposition. (2) The last rune of every ætt can signify the ætt; thus we have Hagal's, Tyr's, and Frey's ætt. Or (3) one names the ættir after other runes and powers, like in the Futhark using the first runes of each ætt. We will then have the ættir of Ur, Naud, and Bjarka. This indicates three female ættir: Ur/Audhumbla, Naud/the Norns, and Bjarka/Frigg or Berchta. These ættir would represent creation, time or death, and finally, resurrection.

3

RUNOSOPHY

Knowledge about the nine worlds described in the old Norse tradition is as important as the knowledge of the runes. The nine worlds are not only the abode of mythological characters but also represent aspects of existence and human consciousness. The nine worlds are linked by the world tree, Yggdrasil, which is the axis in the middle of the universe. The worlds can be divided into three triads: the first three represent the shamanic "upper world," or human superconsciousness; the three following represent the "middle world" and the conscious mind; while the three lowest represent the "underworld," the unconscious and unknown. Starting with the first triad, these are the nine worlds.

Muspelheim: The realm of heat and fire. One of the two extreme poles of cosmic forces. The word *muspilli* means "world fire," and this is the abode of the powers that initiate Ragnarök. Muspelheim is in the south. It is ruled by the fire giant Surt who commands his legions, the sons of Muspel. Surt carries a flaming sword.

Muspelheim represents the expanding and convex force in the universe. Muspelheim is plasma and pure energy.

Asgård: The world of the gods. Asgård is the home of the Æsir and also the Vanir. Around Asgård there is a wall that was built by a giant. The Æsir are gods of war and the builders of the universe. They are keepers of order in the cosmos. They are at war with the giants, but there is also some cooperation between the two. Asgård is the center of önd, the spirit and breath that brings life.

Vanaheim: The world of the Vanir. The Vanir is the other group of gods, and it is often thought that they might belong to an older and more powerful race than the Æsir. Odin was taught the secrets of magic by the Vanir goddess Freya. The Vanir are connected to fertility and water. They are also the gods of witchcraft. Vanaheim is the realm of sexuality. The Vanir god Frey is depicted with a huge, erect phallus. Frey and Freya are united in a *hierosgamos,* a sacral sexual intercourse and wedding. The fylgja belongs to Vanaheim. The fylgja is the totem animal and female guardian spirit guiding man. The fylgja is connected to the Dises, and the main Dis is Vanadis, an epithet of Freya.

Ljusalfheim: The *ljusalfar,* or light elves, are the heavenly elves. They are related to the Vanir, who are called elves in the *Lokasenna*. The god Frey lives in Alfheim. Frey was given Alfheim by the Æsir. The elves had a greater cult around them than what is revealed through the myths. The elves are spirits of nature, and the light elves are related to the fairies. The sun is called *alvglans*. Ljusalfheim is, like Vanaheim, connected to sexuality and fertility as well as to intellect and clearness of mind. Ljusalfheim is the seat of the *hugr,* thought.

Midgård: The world of humans; the material world and physical nature. In the human, Midgård represents the physical body, called *lik*. It was not created by the gods. The first two humans were created from two pieces of wood. Through Voden, Vile, and Ve the physical body/pieces of wood were given life and spirit, understanding, and sensory perception as well as emotions and other senses.

Svartalfheim: The *svartalfar,* or black elves, are the elves of the underworld. They are craftsmen and goldsmiths and create the finest treasures and weapons. They are related to the dwarves. The black elves, like the light elves, are spirits of nature. They live under rocks, in mountains, and underground. They represent the shaping force, or that which brings forth the shape, the *hamr*. If the light elves are the intellect, the black elves represent the feelings.

Jotunheim: The realm of the giants, the *jötnar*. Compared to the gods, the giants belong to an ancient race. They represent chaos, the forces that lie outside the cosmos of order, created by the gods. The castle of Utgård is in Jotunheim. The giants are extremely wise, and all memories from ancient times are kept among them. The well of Mímir is in Jotunheim, and Odin sacrifices his eye in it to gain access to the secrets of Mímir, the *minni*. Jotunheim represents *minni,* the magical memory. The well of Mímir corresponds to what in occultism is sometimes called the "akashic records," the place or level where all things from all times are kept.

Helheim: Helheim or Hel is the world of the dead. It is the most misunderstood and misinterpreted of the Nordic worlds. The true meaning of Hel has been shrouded in ignorance. This is hardly surprising since the name *Hel* itself means, among other things, "the hidden one" or "the shrouded one." Helheim is the world of nothingness and includes the nine worlds that are dark counterparts to the nine worlds of Yggdrasil. Hel has been interpreted as the Nordic hell where all who have died in bed (by disease) will end up. Hel is the world of hidden mysteries. It is not just death but also that which foreshadows life. Hel is like the earth, giving life through decay and death. Hel is a dark goddess, a double nature of life and death. This is reflected in her face, which is half blue and half flesh colored, or in other interpretations, white and black. The road to Hel leads deep down into the underworld through dark valleys and over the river Gjöll. Helheim is guarded by the young maiden Modgunn, who will only let one pass after one has revealed one's name and ancestors. Helheim is also guarded by the terrible hellhound Garm. The road to Hel takes nine days and leads through innumerable difficulties. This corresponds to Odin's nine days on Yggdrasil. Hel is the realm of death where the secrets of existence—the runes—are hidden. Hel is completion. Hel is not a place for suffering but a place where complete knowledge can be found, the hidden or shrouded knowledge. Hel is the seat of the soul double called *vård*.

Niflheim: The realm of winter and ice. This is the deepest of all worlds and lies under Hel. Niflheim is the other extreme of the universe and is opposite to Muspelheim. This is the astringent and concave principle. Niflheim is the utmost heaviness and is connected to black holes. Hel, the goddess of death, was thrown down into the realm of ice and built her world above it. Niflheim is sometimes called Niflhel and is thought to be a darker and more frightening place than the realm of death. This is where criminals will arrive after death. From the center of Niflheim the spring Vergelmer flows into eleven rivers. At Vergelmer the dragon Nidhögg lives.

Nidhögg represents the anti-force of the universe, the destructive principle embodied. But one must not forget that it was from the waters of Niflheim that all life came.

NINE WORLDS AND TWENTY-FOUR PATHS

The most important symbol in Western occultism that illustrates the structure of the universe is the Tree of Life in the Cabbala. It consists of ten worlds representing ten levels of manifestation and creation, from the first idea to completion or manifestation. The ten worlds are linked by twenty-two paths corresponding to the twenty-two trumps of the tarot and the twenty-two letters of the Hebrew alphabet. Nordic spirituality also has a symbol for the universe, but it is constructed according to another system.

Instead of viewing creation as flowing from one single source, the Nordic myth of creation begins with a meeting of two polar forces. In the created worlds there are both life and death, while the Cabbala focuses on a dualism between good and evil, where death and "evil" are not included in the structures of creation. Instead a gigantic shadow of the Tree of Life is created, called the Tree of Death. This is to a certain extent represented by Heldrasil and the nine underworlds of Hel in Nordic spirituality. But at the same time there is no such extreme dualism in the Nordic system. Death and life are interwoven in a unity. The gods and their enemies, the giants, often cooperate.

The Nordic world tree Yggdrasil could be compared to the Tree of Life. Yggdrasil can be drawn in a manner that is slightly reminiscent of the cabbalistic Tree of Life but which contains twenty-four paths representing the runes. The runes are aspects of the web called "the web of Urd" (or Wyrd), which connects the universe and the different worlds. The paths of the world tree are like the rune row constructed according to three ættir of eight runes each.

THE UTHARK AND THE TWENTY-FOUR PATHS

There are, of course, variations in the arrangement, the meaning of the ættir, and their names, as well as the position of the worlds and the paths. We are here using a method that is based on the Uthark focusing on the idea that everything was created through the meeting between two primordial polar forces. There are three ættir: The Ur ætt, which represents the flow of the forces from the realms of fire and ice and how this is the foundation of the other worlds. The Naud ætt represents time and the wheel of destiny. These are the cosmic forces that by necessity move outside the control of man. Through the initiation in the secrets of the runes, a person will gain control over the wheel of destiny and the worlds outside Midgård. The Bjarka ætt belongs to the human world, to human life and soul qualities. This is also connected to initiation and rebirth. The two primal realms of thurs are here isolated from the human being, who creates a complete soul (the lik, vård, önd, hamr, fylgja, hugr, and minni are here connected) that exists between the two extremes, without being torn in either direction.

The Ur Ætt

1. UR. Nifl–Hel: Vergelmer and the primordial river that gave rise to the universe.

2. THURS. Nifl–Jotun: The *rimthurses* are created through Niflheim and inhabit Jotunheim.

3. AS. Muspel–As: The gods are created from the heat. Divine dynamic energy.

4. REID. Nifl–Svartalf: From the primordial giant the dwarves are created. The four cardinal dwarves support the world.

5. KEN. Muspel–Ljusalf: A fire spark from Muspel becomes the light in Ljusalvheim and gives rise to the sun, Alvglans.

6. GIFU. As–Mid: The gods give man the qualities of life and soul as a gift. Man responds through sacrificial gifts in return.

7. WYNJA. Muspel–Vana: Light and energy. Joy and fertility. The rune of the Vanir.

8. HAGAL. Mid–Hel: Death and the hidden. Man's initiation in the secrets of the runes.

The Naud Ætt

9. NAUD. Hel–Jotun: Urd and Mímir. Destiny and memory. Contains the secrets of the runes.

10. IS. Jotun–Svartalf: Layers of ice in the underworld that cross man's path into Hel.

11. JERA. As–Vana: A meeting between the Æsir and the Vanir. Odin and Freya.

12. PERTRA. Jotun–Ljusalf: The well of Mímir (or Urd), which unites memory and thought.

13. EIHWAZ. Svartalf–Vana: A phallic principle that unites the center of basic instincts with the center of fertility.

14. ALGIZ. Ljusalf–As: Nature as a divine sanctuary. The fairies' home in the trees.

15. SOL. Ljusalf–Vana: Alvglans: the sun, as the solar nature of the god Frey, as ruler of both Vanaheim and Ljusalfheim.

16. TYR. Hel–Svartalf: The wolf of hell is fettered by the chain Gleipner, made by the dwarves.

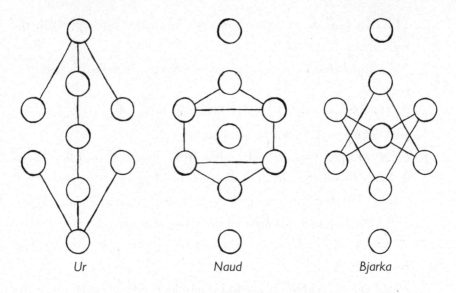

Ur   Naud   Bjarka

The Bjarka Ætt

17. BJARKA. Mid–Vana: Rebirth. The fertile power of the Vanir.

18. EH. As–Jotun: Cooperation between the giants and the Æsir. The birth of Sleipnir. Rides to Utgård.

19. MANNAZ. Mid–Svartalf: The shape of man is created.

20. LAGU. Hel–Ljusalf: The water of the underworld arises in the spring.

21. ING. Vana–Hel: The seed fertilizing the underworld.

22. ODAL. Mid–Jotun: The world of man is demarcated and protected from the forces of chaos.

23. DAGAZ. Mid–Ljusalf: The intellect of man. Illumination. Clarity.

24. FEH. As–Svartalf: The gods' treasures, obtained from the dwarves of the underworld.

THE MULTIDIMENSIONAL UTHARK

The runes are not meant to be understood only from a linear perspective where Ur is the first and Feh the last. The runes also symbolize multidimensional principles. By looking at different arrangements of the runes one can discover hidden meanings.

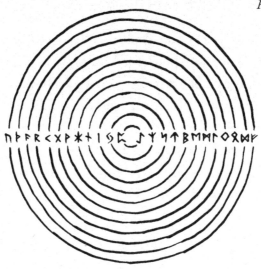

One can place the 24 runes in 12 circles inside each other as in the figure above. The first and last runes are on each side of the outer circle. The runes from the two ends of the Uthark will then appear in pairs on each side of the circle. The inner circle consists of the middle rune pair Pertra and Eihwaz. Thus we have 12 rune pairs. The numbers 12 and 24 are important in many ways: they represent the zodiac, the day, the months, and so forth. The rune pairs create complementary and polar forces. Some are obvious.

> Ur–Feh (1–24): the primordial ox/the tame ox, nature/culture
> Thurs–Dagaz (2–23): night/day
> As–Odal (3–22): Asgård/Midgård, heaven/earth
> Reid–Ing (4–21): Thor/Frey, structure/nature
> Ken–Lagu (5–20): fire/water
> Gifu–Mannaz (6–19): giver/receiver
> Wynja–Eh (7–18): harmony/cooperation
> Hagal–Bjarka (8–17): Hel/Frigg, death/life
> Naud–Tyr (9–16): Odin/Tyr, descent/preservation
> Is–Sol (10–15): winter/summer, Nifl/Muspel
> Jara–Algiz (11–14): field/forest
> Pertra–Eihwaz (12–13): the womb/the phallus

It is also possible to create triple rune arrangements, or groups of 4, 6, and 8. This will create powerful sigils but also new groups of runes that can reveal even more inherent meanings. The most common runic sigil in Northern magic is constructed around the Scandinavian Hagal rune (✳). The six spokes are filled with runes or flowerlike patterns. A very powerful sigil is the aegishjelmur (see below). On its twelve arms the 24 runes can be placed in two rounds. This will create even more rune pairs with interesting meanings.

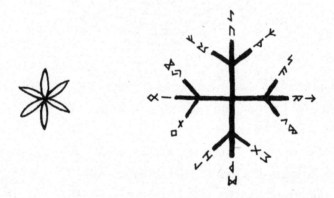

There are three main methods for exploring the significance of the runes. These are through their (1) name, (2) shape, and (3) position. All three of these aspects contribute to the probable likelihood of the Uthark theory. The Ur rune can be used as an example. The word *ur* indicates a connection to the "origin" (SW: *ursprung*), "the first," and so on. If one bears this in mind, the placement of the Ur rune as number 1 in the row seems logical. The shape of the Ur rune will be even more striking if we turn it upside down, as then it bears a resemblance to our modern letter *u*. The rune will thus symbolize the chalice or the womb from which everything is born. In mythology this "container" is the Ginnungagap. The shape of the rune also represents the two horns of the primordial cow or ox, and it is known that the first being besides Ymer was Audhumbla, the primordial cow. Thus it is almost obvious that a rune called Ur, corresponding to mythological descriptions of the primordial state, is the first rune in the row.

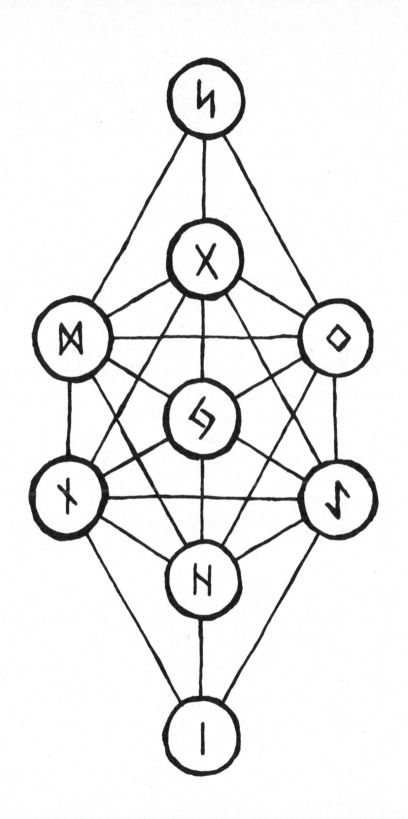

The name of the rune is what principally denotes its significance. What the shape reveals is more or less evident in the different runes. A good exercise to learn the meanings of the runes is to draw or carve them many times and meditate on what they seem to represent. The significance of many runes will appear rather distinctly. The ice rune resembles an icicle, the Ing rune a seed. It is not too far-fetched to see the Bjarka rune, which is the feminine rune, also illustrating a female body. The Tyr rune has a phallic shape but also illustrates the function of Tyr as the god of order. Tyr is the pillar holding up the roof of heaven. The Algiz rune signifies elk, tree, and human, simultaneously illustrating all three of these meanings (the horns of the elk, a tree with stem and branches, and a man with outstretched arms). The positions of the runes are connected to their numerology. The Ur rune is the first rune and denotes number 1. The Thurs rune is number 2. The number 2 is associated with the powers of darkness. It is possible to read many connections between the position of the rune and its meaning through the rune row. Sigurd Agrell uses mainly numerological arguments to support his theory.

There is another way to see significance in certain runes, which is evident when the runes are used for divination. Some runes will then appear upside down, or they will be reversed. The runes will then behave in four different ways.

Some runes are symmetrical and can appear upside down; when they do, the meaning will be inverted. The significance also becomes inverted.

Odal	Mannaz	Eh	Tyr	Algiz	Ur
ᛟ	ᛗ	ᛖ	ᛏ	ᛉ	ᚢ

Some runes are not symmetrical and do not change when inverted but are reversed. The meaning is thus reversed but not inverted.

Thurs	Ken	Pertra	Bjarka
ᚦ	ᚲ	ᛈ	ᛒ

The third group can be both reversed and inverted. Their meaning will then become both inverted and reversed.

Feh Lagu Wynja Reid As

The fourth group is of greatest importance. They can neither be reversed nor inverted. Their meaning is never changed. Significantly, they are also nine in number.

Gifu Hagal Naud Is Jara Eihwaz Sol Ing Dagaz

In chapter 7 we will take an in-depth look at how the runes are used in divination. The difference between the runes appearing inverted and those reversed can at first be difficult to understand. Only through experimentation can one reach a true understanding. We will now limit ourselves to a deeper study of the nine unchangeable runes. They also denote the nine worlds.

Muspelheim: The rune that represents the world of fire is Sol. It is shaped like a flash of lightning and indicates the power and dynamics of Muspelheim. In its primal and destructive form, the rune corresponds to the giant Surt. The rune is also a picture of the flaming sword of Surt.

Asgård: Generally the As rune is associated with Asgård, but Gifu also belongs here. The gift rune represents the meeting between gods and men, the gifts we are given from the gods and the fact that Asgård is often described as the center of the universe.

Vanaheim: The obvious rune here is Ing. This rune is related to fertility, and the main god of the Vanir is Frey, who is also named Ing.

Ljusalfheim: This is the world of light and clarity, and the rune that belongs here is Dagaz. This is the world of the fairies, which is indicated by the butterfly or fairylike form of the rune.

Midgård: The world of humans is characterized by cycles and the return of the seasons. The rune that belongs to Midgård is Jara, the rune of the seasons.

Svartalfheim: The elves from the underworld are harsh beings, but very important in magic. They are living in the tunnels under the roots of Yggdrasil, and the rune that belongs here is Eihwaz.

Jotunheim: The world of the giants is a world of ancient extreme forces that resist the cosmos that the gods have created. They are forces of chaos and necessity as well as wisdom. In their world the well of Mímir can be found. The well of Mímir is related to the well of Urd. The ninth rune, Naud, corresponds to Jotunheim.

Helheim: Hel is the goddess of death, and her realm contains the secrets of the runes that are inherent in the hail crystal. The rune Hagal belongs to the world of Hel.

Niflheim: The ice rune belongs to Niflheim.

Nordic spirituality is not dualistic in the sense that good and evil stand opposed in an unsolvable conflict. The old wise ones of the Nordic tradition were more nuanced in their views and realized that there was no absolute good or absolute evil. Often the gods are more treacherous and immoral than the giants. Darkness and light are not connected to good and evil. Both darkness and light exist in a balance like night and day. Every rune has a dark and a light side. But one could create a group of dark runes, a group of light runes, and a group of neutral runes from the rune row. One would then have three groups of eight runes.

The dark runes are called *rökkr* runes or *myrk* runes:
Ur, Thurs, Hagal, Naud, Is, Pertra, Eihwaz, Lagu.

The so-called light or *heid* runes are
As, Ken, Gifu, Wynja, Sol, Tyr, Dagaz, Feh.

The remaining runes are neutral:
Reid, Jara, Algiz, Bjarka, Eh, Mannaz, Ing, Odal.

But every rune has a dark and a light side. This must, however, not be interpreted in an ethical way. The dark runes do not have to be equivalent to evil. The dark runes are connected to functions related to death and the underworld but also to the hidden wisdom of the runes. Some aspects of the dark runes are connected to the womb and the primordial force from which the world is born. The light runes can cause stagnation and exhaustion. In Nordic spirituality, the world is a balance between two extremes.

THE NORDIC COLOR SCALE

Colors have been experienced and categorized in different ways in different epochs and traditions. In the *Edda* of Snorri the rainbow is described as having three colors, while other sources describe it as having seven. The Nordic color scale can be divided into nine colors that correspond to the nine worlds. The nine colors are the four primary colors (red, yellow, green, and blue), black and white, gold and silver, and the color of the earth— brown. They are connected to the nine worlds in the following way:

Brown: Midgård. The color of earth and soil, of Mother Earth, the one who gives life and takes it back through decay. Nourishment and stability.

Green: Vanaheim. The color of fertile and flowering nature.

Yellow: Ljusalfheim. The color of the intellect. Lightness, clarity, and communication.

Red: Svartalfheim. Power, emotions, and instincts. Magical force. Potency. Iron and smithery.

Blue: Jotunheim. The realm of the giants at the edge of the sea. Water and the well of Mímir. Memories and dreams of the past.

Gold: Asgård. Divine power, önd. Glory and power. The sun and its beams.

Silver: Helheim. The moon and its light. The light in the night. The power of witchcraft and death. Dreams and hallucinations.

Black: Niflheim. The absolute concentration of force. The black hole. Death and utter coldness. Bearer of life and the hidden light. The all-potential.

White: Muspelheim. Pure energy. Total unlimited force, perpetually radiating and expanding.

4

MAN AND HIS SOULS

Nordic spirituality does not specify a clear separation between body and soul. The boundaries between the physical and the spiritual are vague, and when studying the myths one can get the impression that there were no such boundaries at all in the old days in the North. In the Nordic description of the human being, the soul has many aspects. A person consists of nine soul forms. Seven of these are connected to the seven worlds of Yggdrasil that are the actual creation, if we do not count the two primal realms of the thurses. Muspelheim and Niflheim represent the two polar extremes that cannot in themselves include any of these seven principles of the soul. The world and its inhabitants arise in the Ginnungagap between these two poles. Thus the two realms of the thurses must be omitted when discussing the contents of creation itself. This is illustrated in the Ur ætt where the worlds between Muspelheim and Niflheim are connected and united. This unity is man, and the seven worlds represent seven main aspects in a person.

Humankind was not created by the gods. It already existed in the form of two trees—Ask (ash) and Embla (elm). These two logs were found on a shore by the three gods Odin, Höner, and Lodur (Loki). The shore indicates that they had been cast out of the great primordial sea from which, according to the myths, everything originates. In the *Völuspa* it is written:

From the circle three Æsir appeared, powerful, benign, down to the house, found on dry land scarcely able, Ask and Embla, without destiny.

Breath they had naught, neither Hug they owned, no blood, no manners, no godlikeness. Spirit and Hug, Odin and Höner gave, Lodur gave manners and godlikeness.

From Odin, Ask and Embla are given life and breath. From Höner they are given understanding and movement. Lodur gives them senses and emotions. These three gifts and the physical form of the logs represent the division into four worlds, or levels, that is common in Western occultism.

The spiritual level is represented by the gift of Odin: Life and breath.

The mental level is represented by the gift of Höner: Understanding and movement.

The astral level is represented by the gift of Lodur: Senses and emotions.

The physical level is represented by the logs Ask and Embla.

In a more detailed arrangement of the different aspects of man, the seven forms connected to the seven worlds between the realms of fire and ice can be described in this way:

1. *Lik:* The physical body. Matter. The logs Ask and Embla. The skeleton and framework for the other aspects. In Old Norse the physical body was called *lik*. This term is still used in Swedish and denotes a dead body, a body without the other aspects. The lik is connected to Midgård.

2. *Önd:* The spirit, the breath. Breath and our spirit are closely connected. We have been given life through the breathing of nature—the

wind. The god of the wind is Odin. Önd is the essence of life; önd is the spark or the core. All life has a core of önd. There is önd in nature, and the stronger the önd is, the more powerful a place is. Stone circles, certain trees, and other formations in nature, as well as some people and animals, can have a higher amount of önd. There are three directions of önd: heavenly önd, earthly önd, and the önd of the underworld. Heavenly önd flows from above and down, earthly önd flows horizontally, and the önd of the underworld flows upward. Strong power places are a meeting point between these directions of önd force. Among humans the önd moves in the same way. The center is in the chest beside the heart or slightly below the navel. Both points can be connected to the Gifu rune. Önd represents the Sanskrit terms *prana* and *atman*. The word is etymologically related to *atman,* the spirit and the divine spark. Önd is connected to Asgård.

3. *Hugr:* The *hugen* or *hugr* is the understanding, the thought and the conscious qualities of the soul. The hugr is one-half of the couple *hugr* and *minni,* thought and memory. These are manifested in Odin as the two ravens Hugin and Munin. The hugr is analytical thinking, and it represents the functions of the left cerebral hemisphere. The hugr can make long journeys, similar to the journeys of the mind and the intellect. The hugr flies with ease, is characterized by clarity, and belongs to Ljusalfheim.

4. *Minni:* *Minni* is a very important aspect of the soul. Minni is the memory, but in a much deeper sense. It represents the ability to travel in the reservoir of deeds from the past and memories from ancient days. This magical memory is symbolized by the well of Mímir, which represents the akashic records. Odin sacrifices one of his eyes in the well to gain the ancient wisdom. This wisdom belongs to the giants, and the well of Mímir can be found in Jotunheim. Mímir is personifying the minni, which belongs to Jotunheim. Minni is the associative thinking that represents the functions of the right cerebral hemisphere. Hugin and the hugr fly into the future. Minni and Munin fly into the past: knowledge about the past is more important than thought about the future. In the *Grimnismal,* Odin says: "Hugin and Munin fly over the world every day; I fear for Hugin, lest he not return, but even more I fear for Munin."

5. *Fylgja:* Everybody has a guardian spirit and guide. This is called the fylgja and is closely connected to the Vanir and Vanaheim. The fylgja appears in three forms: as an animal, as a person of the opposite sex, and in an abstract form. Individuals have a fylgja as well as families, tribes, and the whole of humanity. It is said that the horse is the fylgja of man. Totem animals are inherited fylgjas. A clairvoyant person can see the fylgja in other persons. It is often reflected in the appearance of a person. The abstract form of fylgja resembles a glowing, geometrical, and ever-changing bundle of energy. The fylgja follows a person through life. It watches over birth and guides one in dreams and through death. A magician makes sure to have good relations with his fylgja and learns how to communicate with it. The conception of the fylgja has lived on in tales and stories about witches and their magical animals.

6. *Hamr:* The shape of our appearance is controlled by our *hamr,* also called *hamn* or *ham.* The word means "figure" or "garment." This principle is what controls the outer shape of all living things. This is the form-giving principle. The hamr is connected to Svartalfheim since the dwarves and the black elves are the ones who shape and form things. Powerful magicians can use the hugr to change their hamr, thus changing appearance and form. During an ecstatic trance or deep sleep they release their mind or soul and leave the body. They will instead take on the form of some animal, usually their fylgja. This is called changing hamr. This can be so powerful that other people will believe that they are really encountering the animal that the magician has chosen. But according to the myths, if the animal were to be hurt, the magician would also be hurt. This is the danger with such magical operations. One encountering a magician in another hamr usually becomes sleepy and might fall asleep. This indicates that the person is entering the same world of perception as the magician and sees what he is projecting. There are many examples of change of hamr in Nordic myths. Odin, Loki, and Freya are masters of this art. Freya is the master of sejd and hamr change. Her hamr is a falcon, and occasionally she lets other gods borrow this form. In later folklore, Freya and her devotees have been turned into witches riding on broomsticks. The broomstick is originally the tool that the female magicians used to enter ecstatic trance.

7. *Vard:* The soul double of a human is called *vard* or *vård.* Certain people can, during their lifetime, send their vard away on journeys to other worlds. For all people, the vard is disconnected from the body when the physical body dies. The vard is the same as the ghost or phantom. It belongs to Helheim.

There are two more aspects of the soul that are very important in Nordic spirituality but that can not be directly linked to any of the worlds. Together with the seven above they create the nine main aspects of man.

8. *Od:* The word *od* means "ecstasy" or "ecstatically raving" and gave rise to the name of Odin. Odin has an alter ego named Od, who is a lover of Freya. Od is the power of divine inspiration, the ecstasy that causes the mind to transcend itself. Odrörir, "that which causes ecstasy," is the name of the divine mead that symbolically induces the divine ecstasy. Odrörir is also the cauldron or chalice where this mead is kept. This is the original Grail. The later interpretation of the Grail as a container of the blood of Christ is a medieval misinterpretation. The original Grail in Nordic spirituality is the chalice that brings ecstasy. Odrörir is the spiritual intoxication of the poets and magicians. Od is expanded consciousness, in which one experiences the deeper meaning of the world and the coherency of the all. Od is the force that makes it possible to travel between the worlds. Od can be compared to the threads or the paths that connect the abovementioned aspects of man with creation.

9. *Hamingja:* This is the total amount of power and illumination a person is in possession of. The word means "happiness" or "luck" and is connected both to the fylgja and the hamr. The word is derived from *han-gengja*—a person who can change shape. The *hamingja* is a supernatural power that powerful persons can achieve. With this power, one can change hamr and have a good contact with the fylgja. The hamingja will make a person victorious and resistant. The hamingja is strengthened when the other aspects of the soul are awakened, conscious, and in balance. The hamingja is power and knowledge united. The hamingja can be viewed as a universal magical power that surrounds and empowers the other aspects of a person.

＊

There are additional principles of life and the soul in Nordic spirituality. An important term is *megin,* which denotes "power" and "magic" or "magical power." Gods, humans, and natural phenomena have megin. Thor has *asmegin*—divine power. The sea has *hafsmegin,* the earth *iardarmegin,* and so forth. Magne, the son of Thor, personifies this power. The term *megin* corresponds to *mattr*—power. Megin also corresponds to the Japanese term *ki* or the Chinese *chi*—terms that can be found in martial arts like aikido and tai chi chuan. The belts in Japanese martial arts not only indicate the grade of the person, but the knot focuses the practitioner's attention to the body's ki center, slightly below the navel. The belt is also central in Nordic magic and martial arts. Megingjord, the belt of Thor, focuses his gigantic force.

The Nordic word *ek* means "I" and denotes the individual self of the person. Ek also denotes the name of the person. For many people the self is focused on and in the physical body, the lik. When a person passes through the Odinic initiation the ek expands and includes all the aspects of the soul. The ek of the magician becomes one with his or her hamingja.

5

NORTHERN SORCERY AND PRACTICAL RUNE MAGIC

A s was the case in most ancient cultures, magic was important in the old Norse tradition. Magic was an actual force that influenced all parts of society and the life of both man and beast. The world was magical and filled with force, which is revealed in terms that denote the *megin,* or "magical power," of nature. Nordic spirituality was more magical than religious. There was no one-sided worshipping of the gods, but sacrifices offered in order to receive something in return. The respect for nature was great, and one of the most important elements in Nordic spirituality were the tree cults. All trees represent specific forces and functions. The universe contains the tree Yggdrasil that links the different worlds together. Yggdrasil is the world pillar that supports the sky. If the tree is cut down, heaven will fall, and the world will be destroyed. Man was created from ash and elm trees. An old thought is that the hamr and etheric body of a person together with parts of the önd and memory will pass into a tree after the death of the physical body. The memory and appearance of a person was thought to live on in trees and in other objects in nature. In the oldest cultures, trees were sacred and believed to be inhabited by the spirits of the ancestors. In trees the shape and faces of the ancestors were seen as shadows of the dead. The ancestor cult is the oldest form of religion and is connected to the cult around power objects in nature.

The robbing and devastation of nature that has characterized modern society is a result of our lost connection to history and our disconnection from our roots that link us to the nature around us. Materialism and the lack of respect for nature are a result of the influence of the monotheistic religions. When the divine is placed in a diffuse world beyond our own, the result will be that our soul and our focus are removed from the world. There is no state of opposition between Christianity and materialism; they share the same world picture, with the only difference being that materialism has realized the absurdity of the Christian theology. In the ancient religions the divine is everywhere, and man is also a part of it. Everything is power and magic—megin—in different forms and with different amounts of force. The magician learns how to direct these forces so that they work in accordance with his or her will and desire.

Nordic spirituality consisted of both magical and religious aspects, which are difficult to separate. The religious aspects have a more collective and social character, while the magical aspects are more connected to the development and will of the individual. This book is focused on the magical aspects. Unlike the later Western magical tradition, the Nordic magical tradition was not rigid and bound by laws but more intuitive and spontaneous. Nordic magic is related to shamanism, and Odin is often viewed as a shaman. The Nordic magical art consists of numerous methods that are more or less related. These are

1. rune magic
2. *uteseta,* sitting out, and meditation
3. sigils
4. galders and incantations
5. rituals
6. natural magic
7. sacred places
8. sejd
9. Odrörir

RUNE MAGIC

The runes can be used in an infinite number of ways. One's inspiration is the only limit. Through the *Edda* and Icelandic stories we can learn how to use the runes. The *Sigrdrífumál* especially gives concrete information about the use of certain runes. In certain cases it is obvious what runes are meant; in other cases one can guess or use one's discernment. In the *Sigrdrífumál,* runes of victory are mentioned first. They are to be carved on one's weapon while chanting "Tyr." In the next verse *ale* runes are mentioned, which are meant to protect against dangerous women.

> *On the horn thou shalt carve them*
> *and on the back of the hand*
> *and mark the nail Naud.*

Certain helping runes are also mentioned, such as those used to assist women with childbirth. They are to be carved on the arm while calling on the Dises. This is probably the Bjarka rune. Also *bränningsrunes* are mentioned to protect ships from storms at sea. They are to be carved on the mast or on the rudder and the oar. The water rune Lagu is the most probable choice here. Runes that belong to natural magic and the art of healing are mentioned in *Sigrdrífumál* as *kvistrunes* (branch runes).

> *Branch runes thou shalt know*
> *if skilled thou wish to be*
> *as a healer see the wound.*
> *Carve them on the bark*
> *and the tree of the woods*
> *whose branches lean toward the east.*

Here we might consider the Algiz rune, whose shape is associated with branches and which has been used for protection. Also certain *målrunor* are mentioned, which are to make a man speak with wit and for protection. The As rune can be one of these. Finally the *hugrunes* are mentioned, which are meant to strengthen the understanding and the hugr; these could be Ken or Dagaz.

> *Hug runes thou shalt know if greater wisdom*
> *than others you desire.*

In the *Hávamál* one finds a description of what is needed to become a master of rune magic. There are eight things to know.

> *Knowest thou how to carve them?*
> *Knowest thou how to read them?*
> *Knowest thou how to color them?*
> *Knowest thou how to test them?*
> *Knowest thou how to ask them?*
> *Knowest thou how to offer them?*
> *Knowest thou how to send them?*
> *Knowest thou how to sacrifice them?*

This list is the foundation of practical rune magic. We'll look at each one in turn. The Swedish words for each follow in parentheses.

Carve (*rista*): First and perhaps most important is carving the runes. One usually carves them on objects made of bone, clay, wood, or stone. Wood is the easiest material for carving, and this can be done according to specific knowledge about trees and nature magic that will be presented below. To learn practical rune magic one must of course know quite a lot about the runes. The ability to carve them correctly is included in this knowledge. The carving itself is a magical act in which the power symbolized by the rune is manifested.

Create twenty-four pieces of clay or wood and carve one rune on each piece. First, read about the rune and meditate on its shape and meaning. Let the carving become a powerful act where you experience the power of the manifesting rune. It is recommended that one carve one rune per day and place it under one's pillow to dream about it and its hidden symbolism. Many rune magicians have a special tool for rune carving, called a *ristir*. It resembles a pricker with a wooden handle upon which the name of the magician is carved in runes together with the runes *f, u, th, a, r, k*. If one wants to base one's workings in the Uthark system one can remove the Feh rune. The magician's carving is supposed to make an imprint in the web of Urd (Wyrd), the etheric web, and on the astral plane. The magician can carve with his ristir, wand, or with fingers in the air. The rune should be visualized in the air. This can be done over an area or object that is then purified and consecrated for magical work. A common form of rune magic is to carve the appropriate runes on wood or bone and to place them where the effect is wanted. Love runes were often placed under the bed of the object of one's love.

Read (*reda*): This line from the poem is also translated as "Knowest thou how to interpret them?" To read means being able to interpret and understand the runes, as well as to place the runes in the right order and to understand their influence on each other. It is important to use the right runes at the right moment and to interpret their meaning correctly. It is possible that the understanding of the Uthark is a way of "reading" the rune row from the normal Futhark. To read your runes, you should place them in the order of the rune row. Then place them in twelve circles, thus creating pairs of opposites in groups of four, six, eight, and twelve as previously described (alternative rune arrangements). Learn about the runes and how they relate to each other. The runes are symbols of forces that will react with each other when they meet. If one does not understand how the forces react with each other the result might be devastating.

Color (*färga*): Coloring the runes is done to activate their force. They are colored red because red is the color of magic (*megin*) and power. To color something red is to activate its force. Red represents the blood. The runes were charged through a sex-magic elixir created from menstrual blood and sperm. In the *Sigrdrífumál* it is written:

> *These counseled, these carved,*
> *these have been conceived by Odin*
> *through the drink, that he had drunk from the*
> *head of Heidraupner and the horn of Hoddrofner.*

Freya Aswynn has interpreted Heidraupner as a kenning for the menstruating womb and Hoddrofner as the male sexual organ. In rune magic, blood from menstruation and sometimes sperm is used, but also blood from the magician in symbolic amounts.

Many magicians choose to use red paint instead for coloring the runes. This paint should be made of natural ingredients only. Color all twenty-four runes you have made and visualize how they start to glow with magical power. Coloring them will give the runes a magical charge. In many traditions, the words for "magic" and "sorcery" are connected to the word for the color red. In German the word *Zauber* means "magic" and can be derived from the word *teafor*, which means "to color red." Many rune magicians use a small triangular object to color runes and magical sigils.

Test (*fresta*): *Fresta* means to test the runes. By testing the runes in magic and divination the magician will gain an increased ability to use them. In divination, answers are often obscure and hard to understand until the magician has used the runes for some time. The runes become charged, and their relation to the magician becomes stronger. The answers from the runes will become easier to understand and their power more tangible. For this reason, many rune magicians will not let others use their runes and will keep them in a bag of cloth or leather. By testing the runes often you will increase your ability to use them. To test properly you should not act like an opportunist thirsting for quick results and sensations. The runes represent powers that are beyond the limited will, understanding, and worldview of the common person. This must be respected and understood.

Ask (*bedja*):

> *Better is not to ask*
> *than to offer too much;*
> *gift demands gift in return.*

The runes correspond to forces in the universe. The rune magician asks different gods and powers to help out in the rune-magical work, as when Tyr is called twice when carving runes of victory. The magician must know, however, that everything that one receives demands something in return. Thus the magician understands that it is not wise to use the runes in a greedy way. The asking is connected to rune songs and magical calls. Create short invocations to suitable gods and to some runes that you wish to use. The invocations should be characterized by balance in relation to the powers. Show great respect but not submission. Odin is the most important god for the rune magician. The invocations should be simple and spontaneous, or rich in poetic qualities. It is possible to find short verses in the sagas that are possible to use. From Egil Skallagrímsson:

> *Good I was given*
> *by the spear god,*
> *confident*
> *I trusted him.*

Offer (*blota*): To offer means to sacrifice or to dedicate something. The magician sacrifices something to the gods or consecrates an area or an object by an offering. The offering in Nordic spirituality is more or less the same as conducting a ceremony. The magician conducts a suitable ceremony that connects an area or an object with the gods. One sacrifices something valuable to Odin and the runes in order to be given divine guidance in the rune-magical work. Balance is also very important here. The offering must not be exaggerated, and the demands must not be too high. The magician is not sacrificing because of a submissive attitude toward the divine but to create good relations. To offer is to make a small ceremony with the runes. It could be done simply by lighting a candle, burning incense, and reading an invocation.

Send (*sända*): To send also alludes to sacrificing. The magician sends the magical ritual to the world of the gods. The magician may burn rune staves and rune sigils where the will has been expressed. The smoke will reach the gods, and the wish is sacrificed to them. The magician must now cease to think about the ritual and the magical work. Only when the magician has sent away the energy and left it behind will the magical result be reached. For as long as it stays in the mind of the magician it will not be activated. The different aspects of the magician's soul, like the fylgja, will carry it away to the astral worlds, in the same way as Hugin and Munin fly for Odin. Another way to send is to visualize a rune and mentally send it away in the ether.

Sacrifice (*slopa*): This type of sacrifice is when the magician completes and finishes something and leaves it to the gods. In the old Norse society enemies were sacrificed with the words: "I give thee to Odin." Thus one let something be ended. For the magician it is all about taking matters to an extreme level. A magician should not send runes in a halfhearted way. The magician must learn to give himself to the magical work, like Odin in the world tree. The magician sacrifices himself to himself.

SITTING OUT AND MEDITATION

All magical processes are occurring both inside and outside. The magician must not focus solely on rune carving but also explore the magical dimensions in the inner and the outer world. The magician must not get stuck in a too-intellectual understanding of the runes. Meditation and vision seeking are also a very important aspect of Nordic spirituality. One common form of contemplation and meditation in the Nordic tradition is called *uteseta,* or "sitting out."

As the name indicates, it is a journey into nature in which one sits down and lets the knowledge come.

The place for a sitting out must be carefully chosen. It should be a place with a powerful aura. There are two main types of places that are suitable for different forms of sitting out. There are "light places" and "dark places." The light places are often on small hills or in natural open spaces with abundant verdure. These places are suitable for rest or for gaining energy. The dark areas are often in rocky landscapes or among dead trees, dry twigs, and strange vegetation. These places are suitable for vision seeking or communication with the dead. The magician will often feel what charge a place has. The light places feel safe and tranquil. The dark areas might feel threatening but also exciting and charged with great power. There are also areas that balance both aspects. No place is only dark or light. In dark places there is usually some very colorful plant that testifies that the presence of life is strongest in the vicinity of death. Beautiful natural areas are suitable for sitting out. It is always good to sit with one's back against a tree.

There is a complete system of runic meditation and rune yoga that will be discussed below. Sitting out is mainly about stopping the inner dialogue and opening to hidden wisdom. A sitting out may take some hours at dusk or dawn, a whole night, or many nights and days. During the sitting out the eyes are generally open, but relaxed. If one falls asleep it might be part of the magical work. The magician should not try to think about anything special but try to calm down the inner "talk" that characterizes the consciousness of modern man. But the magician should not force any thoughts away. The thoughts that arise should be ignored and disappear naturally. The magician should not observe anything in particular but see the wholeness. One should not be passive. All senses should be alert. The more a person thinks, the more disconnected he is from the surrounding world. During a sitting out one will see and hear things that one has never previously experienced. During a successful sitting out one will become aware of the "real" in the world, something from which modern people have isolated themselves.

Many sitting-out projects will be similar to making a pilgrimage. The magician travels to an ancient sacred place, a ship tumulus, a sacred spring, a historical place, or a beautiful natural area. The magician will then meditate on a chosen spot.

There are three main meditation positions documented in Nordic magic that are suitable for meditation. One is called *keltensitz,* a cross-legged position that can be seen in statues of the celtic god Cernunnos. The other position is on the knees with the feet under the body. This can be seen in Nordic statues. The third position is lying on the back with the arms on the sides of the body or crossed on the chest or belly. This position is used when meditating in a ship tumulus. It can be varied with the back leaning against a rock with the feet stretched out in front of oneself. During a longer sitting out the position is not as important as the inner silence. The sitting out can increase the magician's ability to see megin in nature and the web that links the universe together. This is one method of understanding the power of the runes.

SIGILS

Sigils and magical symbols are important aspects of Nordic magic. Many of the most significant artifacts are *bracteates,* medallions with magical inscriptions. Many of the rune row findings are on bracteates. Nordic sigil magic is often connected to talismanic magic, which is called *taufr* and also denotes magic and sorcery in general. This is the same term as the abovementioned *teafor,* which means "to color red." In talismanic magic the sigils and runes were colored with blood or red paint. There are two main forms of talismans, the *teinn,* which is a branch or a talisman made from wood, and the *hlutr,* which is any object used in divination or magic. The complete rune row was a common inscription. Other symbols that were used on Nordic talismans include the following, shown on page 76.

Hagal; the Scandinavian form of Hagal represents the complete rune row and protection. It is used as a frame for creating sigils (see below).

The *achtwan,* heavenly star of the eight winds. An eight-armed cross that represents the complete rune row, Sleipnir, and Yggdrasil. It is also used in sigils.

The ALU (As–Lagu–Ur) runes, which also represent the whole rune row and the sacred force.

The swastika, symbol of Thor, the sun wheel and the seasons, Midgård and agriculture. It is based on the numbers 9 and 4; the sun cross.

The hammer of Thor, a symbol of Thor and his power; megin and potency. This is both a hammer and a phallus. It is stylized as a T turned upside down and is used in consecrations.

The triskele, symbol of Odin and his trinity. It is based on the numbers 7 and 3.

The valknut, sign of Odin; three triangles that are intertwined. It symbolizes the trinity of Odin and the nine worlds.

The aegishjelmur, "the helm of dread." Four Algiz runes that create the perhaps most powerful symbol of protection. It can be traced to the dragon Fafnir and symbolizes the power of the dragon and the complete rune row.

One of the most important rune-magical methods to direct and activate the force of the runes is through *bind runes.* In a bind rune, different runes are combined in a symbol that represents the united and interacting forces of the chosen runes. A rune can also be charged if repeated in different directions, as in the helm of dread. Bind runes create very powerful sigils for magic and meditation. Create a bind rune of your name and use it for meditation.

Examples of bind runes:

ALU   ODIN

In *En Isländsk Svartkonstbok från 1500-talet,* we can find many advanced runic sigils. For example, to find a thief one should carve these staves on a box.

One should pour water into the box and then add millefolium to the water and say: "By the nature of this herb and the great power of this stave, may the shadow of the thief be seen in the water."

One shall also carve *iotunn villum* on a whalebone and carry it. One shall then say: "Odin, Loke, Frö, Balder, Njord, Tyr, Birger, Höner, Fröja, Gefion, Gusta, and all the gods and goddesses who have lived and lives in Valhalla from the beginning of time, may they help me to succeed in this matter."

En Isländsk Svartkonstbok från 1500-talet contains many sigils to kill the cattle of others, to win love, to remove anger, and so forth. There are even so-called *fjärtrunor,* which will cause terrible stomach pains. Even though the book was written in the days of Christianity, the influence from the old Norse tradition is very strong. The incantations reveal the old Norse worldview and have influenced modern rune magic.

Many rune-magical sigils are made of *lönnrunor,* or hidden runes. These hidden or secret runes are staves with branches that indicate the rune. In some forms of secret runes the branches point upward and some downward. One side of the stave indicates which ætt and the other which rune. Also here the Futhark is most common, but one can also use the Uthark. The branches to the left indicate the ætt and the right branches the rune's position in the ætt. The word *Odin* would thus be written 3:6, 3:7, 2:2, 2:1, and *runa* would be 1:4, 1:1, 2:1, 1:3.

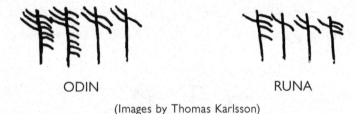

ODIN   RUNA

(Images by Thomas Karlsson)

Another form of magical sigil is built around the Scandinavian Hagal rune, or the eight-armed heavenly star, with runes, symbols, bind runes, or secret runes. The inscription ODIN RUNA could become a rune-magical sigil on the eight-armed star either with normal runes or with secret runes.

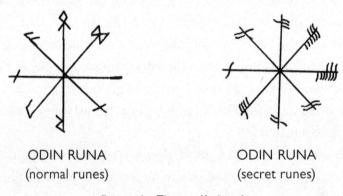

ODIN RUNA   ODIN RUNA
(normal runes)   (secret runes)

(Images by Thomas Karlsson)

Try making a magical sign in this manner using your own name. If your name contains more than six or eight letters you can make bind runes of the letters. If the name is very short, you can make an equal-armed cross or a magical sign, for example: T– O–R plus a stylized hammer.

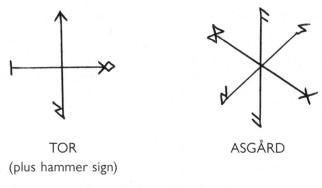

TOR
(plus hammer sign)

ASGÅRD

(Images by Thomas Karlsson)

The earliest Nordic sigils were the sun wheels and mandalas of the Iron Age picture stones. The Bronze and Iron Ages were periods of greatness and high culture, something these stones can verify. The picture stones are very common on Gotland, and they depict dragons, serpents, and multidimensional spiral forms. These symbols are very powerful objects for opening gates to other states of consciousness and other worlds.

They also reveal the basic conceptions of the Nordic worldview. The serpent and the dragon are the most common and basic forms on these stones.

The pagan cultures viewed the dragon as an ally. Only with the arrival of Christianity did the dragon-slayer myths become important. The archangel Michael or some other Christian hero kills the dragon, which symbolized the victory of Christianity over paganism. The cross is the sword thrust into the earth. The earth is the body of the dragon. On the picture stones there are dragons around whirling sun wheels, and they are often surrounded by four guardians representing the four cardinal directions. The picture stones are suitable as meditation mandalas and altar pictures.

GALDERS AND FORMULAS

When Odin hangs in the world tree he receives power songs. These songs are called *galders* and are a very important part of the Nordic magical tradition. The word *galder* is related to *gala,* "to crow," and *galen,* "insane." The galders are supposed to be able to heal wounds, control fire, make the weapons of one's enemies useless, and hypnotize people. A galder is a word of power that is sung or called in a high-pitched voice, outside the normal voice spectrum. The *jojk* and yodeling are related methods. Power songs can also be sung in a lower pitch, similar to Tibetan throat singing. The galders can be used together with a drum and should be sung rhythmically. The runes that denote the vowels are sung as they are, numerous times, emphasizing the vowel sound itself, like Ur:

Ur, ur, uuuuuuuuuur, ur, ur, uuurrrr.

The runes denoting the consonants are used together with the five magical vowels, *u, o, e, i, a.* The name of the rune should be sung three times, then followed by the consonant combined with the vowels. Reid would thus be sung:

Reid, reid, reid, ru, ro, re, ri, ra, reeeeeiiid.

There are other examples of the order of the vowels, either *u, a, i, e, o,* or *u, i, o, e, a,* or *u, o, a, e, i.* Use the first example to create and sing galders for every rune. It does not matter how it sounds, as long as the mind is one with the galder. One can contact the runes and their power through galders.

The galders denote the oral magic, and the runes denote the written or carved magic. The galders are connected to incantations and magical formulas. In Nordic magic, numerous magical words and names were used. The Nordic tradition is not a denominational religion where one dedicates oneself only to one force. One used the forces and forms that suited the situation. This pragmatic attitude is reflected in *En Isländsk Svartkonstbok från 1500-talet,* especially in this incantation for forcing a woman to keep silent: "Hereby may help me . . . all gods, Thor, Odin, Frigg, Fröja, Satan, Beelzebub, and all gods and goddesses who live in Valhalla. In your mightiest name, Odin."

We can observe here that a couple of the invoked names are late arrivals to Valhalla. In another incantation the invoked gods are, among others, Lord, God, Spirit, Creator Odin, Thor, Savior, Frö, Fröja, Oper, Satan, and Beelzebub(!).

The names are magical words of power. The art of incantation is undogmatic, but it is often constructed around a repetition of the galders in a rhythmic way with alliterations and rhyme.

RITUALS

There is no known ritual complex or ceremonial system in Nordic magic. It is indeed possible, however, that there once existed one around the religious cult at the temple in Uppsala. Nordic ritual magic is closely connected to the forces of nature, which are frequently invoked. The five elements in Nordic magic are the main foundation of ritual magic.

North
Ice

West   Midgård   East
Water   *Earth*   *Air*

South
Fire

Earth: Stability, presence, unity of different parts. Realization, actuality.

Air: Clarity, mental journeys, intellect. The wind of the east.

Water: Fertility, feelings, sexuality. The wind of the west.

Fire: Dynamic forces, pure energy. The wind of the south.

Ice: Stagnation, preservation, contains hidden aspects, potentiality. The wind of the north.

The altar represents Midgård. It is a miniature of the world of the magician. The altar is in the north since that is the magical direction of Thule, the outmost point in the north. *Thule* means "the place where one is forced to turn back"—the extreme north. *Thule* or a *thul* is also a term denoting a rune magician and a poet. The north is the area of potentiality, where all possibilities are frozen and can be actualized through the actions of the magician. It is good to place the altar before a big tree—an ash or a yew tree would be very suitable, but also a birch or an oak. In the north of the altar a picture of the Hagal crystal is placed, in the south a candle or burning incense. In the west a chalice or horn, and in the east a feather.

The Hagal crystal: Draw or carve the symbol on clay, wood, glass, or stone. During the winter it can be made of ice, which is very suitable. One can also use a bowl of glass and draw the symbol in it. A crystal or diamond can also symbolize the Hagal crystal.

The incense bowl: Here the magician burns suitable herbs or paper notes with runes on them.

The chalice or drinking horn: This represents the Odrörir of the gods. On the chalice or drinking horn you can carve the runes ODRÖRIR (ᛟᛞᚱᚠᚱᛁᚤ) and ALU (ᚠᛚᚢ). The chalice can be filled with mead or another suitable beverage.

The feather: A long swan feather is very suitable. The feather should be found in nature. All kinds of feathers can be used. The feather is used in purification.

✳

Other ceremonial attributes include:

The wand: The wand is called *gandr* or *ganden* and should be made of ash or hazel wood. It is used to direct forces and to carve runes in the ether. It was traditionally used in soul journeys and is related to the witch's broom.

The spear, sword, or hammer: The magician carries a weapon that is an expression of his power. The weapon is used to create the ceremonial room in the four directions.

The cape: A magician often chooses to use a cape for magical work. The cape represents the inner worlds.

The belt: The belt or power girdle (*megingjord*). Although many ceremonies are conducted naked, the magician uses a belt. It focuses the inner megin that is centered slightly below the navel.

Knife or sickle: This is used to cut herbs.

Ristir **or tool to color:** A tool, similar to a prickle used to carve, and a brush, piece of leather, or wood to color the runes.

A magical amulet: Hangs around the neck and represents contact with the forces that it symbolizes.

✳ Runic Ceremony

Stand at the altar and light the incense. Pour herbs on the charcoal (ordinary kitchen herbs can be used here). See the smoke rise and say:

Hell Odin and all gods and goddesses in Valhall!

Take your weapon and turn to the north and say:

May the Dragon and the forces of the north assist me,
in the name of Nordre!

To the west:

May the great bird and the powers of the west assist me,
in the name of Västre!

To the east:

May the powerful ox and the powers of the east assist me,
in the name of Östre!

To the south:
May the mountain giant and the powers of the south assist me,
in the name of Södre!

The watchers invoked are protecting the directions in the Nordic tradition. They are mentioned in the story about the Norwegian king Harald Gormsson. Continue the ceremony and cleanse your aura from all disturbing thoughts and feelings with the feather. Consecrate the drinking horn with the wand by drawing the sign of Thor (⊥) in the air above it. Lift the drinking horn to every direction and end in the north by saying:

To Thule!

Drink from the chalice or horn and feel its ecstatic power. After a while, speak again, when feeling the powers of Odrörir:

Runes you may take
and staves well read
very great staves
very strong staves
colored by the great Thule
and made by the powers
carved by a god rich in runes.

Then sit down in front of the altar and gaze into the Hagal crystal. Galder all the runes and feel how they are activated one by one through Hagal and are linked to you.

End the ceremony by standing up and saying:
To Thule!

NATURAL MAGIC

Trees were important in Nordic spirituality. Sometimes symbols of trees were used, in the form of a stave or a pillar. The tree represents the axis mundi, the world axis that links the worlds and unites heaven with the underworld. Sacred places were enclosed, and in their center stood a tree or a pillar. These places were called pole gardens (Old Norse: *stavgardar*) and functioned as sacrificial groves. When one entered the stavgardar one entered mythical time where the gods and the sagas were present. The sacred trees of the North symbolized paganism and were attacked by Christians. The Irminsul, the sacred tree of the Saxons, was cut down by Karl the Great in 772 when he was about to spread Christianity into central Europe in a bloodbath in which thousands of Saxons were killed. Irminsul and Yggdrasil are different terms for the magical tree of Nordic paganism. The tree can be found both in the

myth and in the cult. Irminsul denotes "the great stave" and is, like Yggdrasil, a key to other worlds.

Everything one needs for practical magic can be found in nature. Plants, herbs, and stones contain different forces that can be used for all purposes. This is a comprehensive knowledge that we will not deal with further here. We will here confine ourselves to the trees that are essential in Nordic magic.

Elm: The elm is equivalent to Embla, the first woman. The elm is associated with the female primordial force and represents both birth and death. The elm is the mother and the womb. Originally, coffins were made of elm, which symbolized how death was a new birth.

Ash: The ash is the tree from which the first man was created and is connected to the masculine force. Ash is used to create handles for tools and weapons. Magical wands can be made out of ash. The ash attracts lightning and is a good medium for önd and megin. Yggdrasil is often thought to be an ash or a yew tree.

Birch: The birch is the most important tree in feminine magic. The birch is a very powerful tree that was the first to return in the north after the ice age. Birchwood is filled with energy, and birch is often used to make magical objects. The birch brings luck and protects against negative energies.

Beech: The beech tree was used to write on and for amulets upon which one carved sigils. The beech represents knowledge.

Oak: The oak is perhaps the foremost tree in the Nordic cult. It represents the sky god Tyr and is connected to the All-Father. The oak tree is very strong and was used to build boats and houses.

The Elder: The elder is a magical tree. It is the favorite tree of the fairies. Its German name, *Holunder,* indicates the connection to Holla (Hel). The elder should be treated with respect. It will protect while outdoors but can have a dangerous influence indoors. Elder must not be burned since the fairies live among its branches. The juice made from the elder is a very powerful magical drink.

Fir: The fir represents the midwinter and the verdancy that can resist the powers of cold. The symbolism of the fir lives on in the tradition of the Yule tree. It originally was bad luck to cut down a fir during the winter, since it symbolizes the power that survives the winter. During the winter solstice a living fir was adorned outdoors.

Hazel: The hazel was used by druids and Nordic magicians to make magical wands. Hazel represents wisdom and magical power. Runes are often made of hazel.

Yew: The yew tree symbolizes both death and eternal life. It can become very old, and it is also extremely poisonous. From the yew one can extract certain hallucinogenic substances that have been used by shamans and witches. Perhaps it was a yew tree from which Odin hung, under the influence of its mystical wisdom-bringing poisons. The yew was called *barr-ask,* and Yggdrasil might be a yew tree.

Linden: The linden is associated with love magic and feminine magic. It is connected to the goddess Freya and was believed to be a tree where lovers met to receive a blessing from the tree. This was also the tree of justice and law.

Rowan: The rowan stands for megin and protection. The red color of the berries is connected to Thor, and in Nordic mythology the rowan saves Thor from being swept down in the underground river.

Apple: The apple tree is the Tree of Life in Nordic mythology. It is the tree of the goddess Iduna. Iduna is the goddess of eternal youth. It is she who gives the fruits from the Tree of Life to the gods to prevent their aging.

Become familiar with these trees and recognize their character and how they look. Meditate under them and feel their different forces. Trees can become powerful allies. Many magical initiations and illuminations take place under trees. Only a chosen few are mentioned above. Expand your knowledge to include additional trees and their characters.

SACRED PLACES AND NATURAL POWER

A sacred place is a place or area that is consecrated to the divine powers and that in itself has a special power. Often these areas are natural places, such as a sacred spring, a peculiar tree, a scenic lookout, or a rock. They can also be created areas like a temple or a grave. In the Nordic cult these places are in areas that have natural power. The universe consists of webs of önd and megin. On earth the burning core of the planet is the generator of this force. This generator has been called the dragon in the Nordic tradition. The dragon in the Nordic tradition is an actual being who transmits life force to the earth. With the arrival of Christianity and monotheism not only the old faith was attacked but also the spirit of the earth and nature. The old dragon-slayer motif illustrates this. As mentioned above, the cross is the sword that penetrates the earth—the dragon's body. The churches were built on top of the old sacred places. But unaware of this process, the church did not achieve the annihilation of the old powers; instead it included the pagan heritage. In the oldest churches, which are built on "dragon points," the presence of the pagan power remains very tangible. An important aspect of Nordic magic is the knowledge of the force fields and energy lines that are called "dragon lines."

Dragon lines can be seen by the clairvoyant and felt by sensitive people. They can be measured with tools like pendulums, divining rods, and so forth. This knowledge can be traced to the old Nordic tradition, and it still lives on in many areas of the Nordic countryside. One of the earliest documents concerning this topic is the black-arts book called "Le Dragon Rouge" from the sixteenth century. All old Norse sacred places are built in accordance with the dragon lines.

To investigate the energy lines of sacred places with a divining rod or pendulum is important in the process of understanding the Nordic tradition. Sitting out at these places can bring very powerful results. Many of the sacred places are constructed in such a manner that they create reactions in the force-web. It is thus possible to work magically with these power places without access to the original constructions. If one were to build a power place in accordance with the Nordic tradition, it would certainly have an effect on the surroundings. It would also have to be constructed at a point of power. We will now take a deeper look at three different forms of place-constructions: stone circles, labyrinths, and ship tumuli.

Stone circle: A stone circle illustrates the cyclic wheel of the seasons and of the day, the hours, and months. In the North these were used as local legal assemblies (*thing*) and as meeting places. Important stone circles were constructed in the form of the eight-armed star, with a great stone in the middle. At the end of each arm a big stone was placed and between these also two large stones. Together there were twenty-four stones in the circle. This construction can be very powerful as it embodies the functions of the complete rune row and the cyclic wheel.

The center stone is placed on a power point. Smaller stone circles can be constructed with eight stones and one in the middle. These stone circles will become centers for magical meetings, rune-magical workings, and invocations of the gods. The stone in the center can be used as an altar.

Labyrinth: In Scandinavia there are hundreds of labyrinths of different sizes. They were used in certain cultic ceremonies. They are called "serpent stones." These are not labyrinths in which one might get lost. There are two main forms of labyrinths. The most common has a path leading toward the center where a slightly larger stone is placed. One walks the same path in and out of the labyrinth. The less common labyrinth is one long serpentine path that brings one in and then out again. We shall here focus on the more common labyrinth. It is constructed for dance and trance states—in combination. These serpentine paths induce a hypnotic influence and represent the brain and consciousness.

The labyrinth is constructed on top of an energy vortex where there is a gate to "the other side." The labyrinth symbolizes Hel and

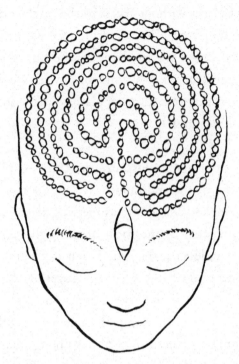

A common labyrinth influencing consciousness

the underworld, death and birth. To enter the center of the labyrinth is to reenter the original womb. To walk out of the labyrinth symbolizes birth. It is a very powerful magical act to enter the center of the labyrinth and meditate there. This is a way to contact Hel and to be initiated in the secrets of the runes. The exit will then represent rebirth. In the Nordic cult a young woman was often standing in the middle of the labyrinth. The ones who entered the labyrinth were supposed to save her and bring her back. This theme can be found in many myths and in magical systems where the divine spark is symbolized by a woman trapped in the middle of matter. In the center of the labyrinth there are possiblities to reach very powerful experiences of wholeness, to see the web of Urd (Wyrd), the runes and the önd, and to release the soul. The path through the labyrinth can be compared to the initiation process of the Uthark.

A classical labyrinth can be constructed in the following way:

Construction of a classical labyrinth

Ship tumuli: A ship tumulus is a craft for reaching the other side. These tumuli represent boats as well as wombs. They have a crystalline form and are built on places where the earth energy creates a sort of

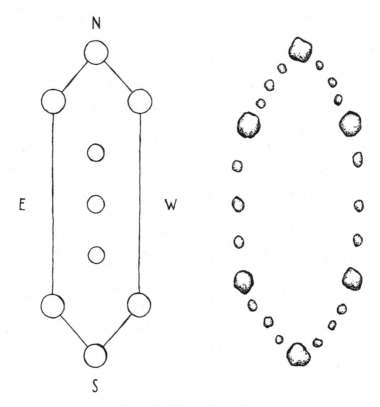

A ship tumulus

vacuum in time and space. These are sometimes called "crystal gates" and are believed to make journeys to other worlds and other states of consciousness possible. It is even more important to find the right place when creating a ship tumulus. The construction itself will create a positive energy structure for the opening of a gate, but they should be placed on a natural gate if they are to work perfectly. A ship tumulus is constructed in the same way as the symbol of the Nordic world tree. One can sit or lie down in a ship tumulus, and they are also suitable for a group of magicians. A ship tumulus is illustrated on page 91.

SEJD

The art of sejd is one of the most important aspects of Nordic magic. It is a dark tradition that resembles the sinister left-hand path. Sejd is a technique that includes ecstatic trance that releases the soul, or *vård*. Sejd can be compared to a "little death" in which the practitioner achieves the ability to see the future and the unknown. Sejd brings great powers and magical abilities and is connected to the art of shape-shifting (*hamfarir*). In the Nordic tradition there was "white sejd," which was concerned with knowledge about the harvest, the year, and the future. There were also a "black sejd," which was associated with death rituals and curses. The sejd was conducted by the *völvas*, the wise-women, as well as by a small number of men. In the old Norse society it was viewed as extremely unmanly for men to be associated with sejd. This did not stop Odin from learning this powerful technique. For this, Loki mocks him in the *Edda* poem *Loketrätan*.

> Also sejd it was claimed that you
> practised on Samsö.
> You the superstition of valor used;
> in the shape of magician
> you wandered the world;
> praise for shameful unmanliness.

The art of sejd was included in the feminine mysteries since it was connected to birth and death—the gates that the soul passes through. The goddess of sejd was Freya, and sejd is characteristic of Nordic witchcraft. The riding on brooms is a heritage from the art of sejd. The phallic broom was used in sejd as a tool for inducing ecstasy. Freya taught Odin sejd, and through sejd he could gaze into the future or strike people with madness, illness, or death. Sejd is related to the art of the ecstatic oracles in Tibet and other parts of the world.

A classical description of sejd can be found in the tale of Erik Röde. The wise seeress Torbjörg, whose nine sisters had also been seer-women, walked from house to house. People wanted to know about the future, about coming harvests. She arrived clad in a blue cape decorated with stones. The cape was strapped with leather, and a necklace of glass pearls hung around her neck. She had a lambskin hood, and on her hands she wore catskin gloves. The cat is Freya's animal and connected to sejd. She wore calfskin shoes with long straps with brass bells. In her belt hung a leather purse with her magical tools, and she carried a staff clad with brass and pearls. Everyone saluted her respectfully, and she was served "goat milk porridge," which was made from the hearts of certain animals. A tall sejd seat was arranged for her, and a number of women sat down in a circle around her. One of the women sang a magical song, a *vardlokkur*, which is required in sejd. The song was so beautiful that many spirits were attracted, according to the wisewoman. Most of her prophecies were also to come true.

A vardlokkur is a form of galder or magical song that takes the practitioner of sejd into the trance and guides the soul, but it can also be used to invoke spirits or find lost souls. The singing is important in sejd. A story from Norway tells us that a choir, consisting of fifteen young men and fifteen young women, was used at one occasion. In the story of the Laxdalingarna it is mentioned how a sejd man is sitting on the sejd seat and galders with such power that a storm hits the enemy. The art of sejd is described in the *Ynglingasaga* in relation to Odin:

Odin himself could practice the art that is most powerful and is called sejd, through this art he could learn the fate of people and what the future would bring, to destroy and bring death and illness. He could take the wit or force from someone and give it to another. But to practice this art was viewed as so unmanly that is was not suited for men, thus the women were taught this art.

Odin, the devoted seeker of truth, will not be stopped by any views about what was decent or suitable. He learns sejd through Freya, who also was his mistress. The art of sejd is connected to sex magic. By arousing a strong sexual excitement and instead of orgasm directing the energy upward to consciousness it is possible to free the soul. The same technique was used by the Indian tantrics to awaken the kundalini, to free the astral body, and to open the third eye. The word *sejd* denotes "inner heat" or "boiling" and is a method to activate the inner fire. The wand, drum rhythms, and vardlokkur are used to reach the ecstasy of sejd.

ODRÖRIR

In Western occultism the mysteries of the Grail have attracted the attention of many scholars and magicians. The Grail is often described as a cauldron or chalice. In the most famous version it is the chalice that Jesus shared with his disciples during the Last Supper. With this chalice Joseph of Arimathea gathered the blood of the crucified Jesus. The angels brought this chalice to Mont Salvatsch, where King Titurel built a temple for the Grail. An order of knights whose purpose was to guard the Grail was created. The Grail contains the divine power, and its present location is shrouded in mystery. Seekers of the Grail, like King Arthur and his knights, traveled all around the world to find it. Only one who is pure in spirit can find it, and finally the innocent Parzifal is the one who succeeds.

The Christian version of the Grail was formulated during the Middle Ages. It is heavily influenced by older Nordic myths. Originally the Grail did not belong to the Christian tradition but to the Odinic mystery cult. The mysteries of the Grail are one of the most important aspects of the Nordic tradition. The old Norse symbol of the Grail is the chalice or cauldron Odrörir. It contains the mead of ecstasy and inspiration, brewed from the blood of a dead god. The mead is also called *Odrörir,* which means "that which creates ecstasy." The ecstasy, or *od,* is the divine inspiration that is in fact the essence of the all-power of Odin. The odic mead has its origin in the peace between the Æsir and the Vanir. A bowl was placed in the middle, and both races spat in it. Saliva was used in ale brewing in the old Norse society. From the saliva of the two god races the wisest of all the gods arose: Kvaser. He was later killed by two dwarves, Fjalar and Galar. They collected the blood of the god and mixed it with honey. Thus the fantastic mead called Odrörir was brewed. The giant Suttung finally gains possession of Odrörir, and he keeps it in a mountain guarded by his daughter Gunnlöd. Odin makes a journey to steal the sacred mead. Under the name of Bölverk (he who causes evil) he makes Suttung's brother Bauge drill a hole in the mountain wall where Odrörir is kept. In the shape of a snake he crawls in through the hole. He seduces Gunnlöd and stays with her for three nights, and she promises him three sips of the mead. Odin swallows all the mead in three deep gulps and is transformed into an eagle. He flies back to Valhalla, where he spits out the mead. On the way he spills some drops of the mead. These drops are the small poetic gift that ordinary people and lesser poets might possess. Odin is the first Grail knight, and the myth about Odrörir describes an initiation process.

Odrörir is a brew that induces visions, similar to the Indian soma. Soma, like Odrörir, is both a god and a brew. Soma is connected to the moon and magical inspiration. Both Odrörir and Soma have been interpreted as brews containing hallucinogenic mushrooms, which could explain their use in the cult. We know from other cults that certain mushrooms are believed to be the flesh and blood of the gods. This could explain the outer aspect of the myth of Odrörir, Soma, and the Grail.

The chalice is the outer form of the Grail. In a medieval German minnesinger tale it is told that the Grail originally is an emerald in the crown of Lucifer. At the fall of Lucifer, the emerald fell into the underworld. Wolfram von Eschenbach, who wrote about Parzifal in the thirteenth century, mentions the Luciferian stone *lapis exillis,* which has divine powers and is the real Grail. Seekers of the Grail and alchemists are in search of this stone—the Philosophers' Stone. In certain versions of the Grail myth the chalice was born from this stone. The chalice would give man a possibility of contacting the divine power of the eye. The stone from the crown of Lucifer represents the divine eye, or third eye, which in India is called the eye of Shiva. In the Nordic tradition this is the eye that Odin sacrifices in the well of Mímir. The well of Mímir represents memory and the unconscious. The well, and the eye that Odin sacrifices, are represented by the moon. The sacrifice in the well of Mímir is related to the Grail myth and the initiation process that the legend of Odrörir describes. The most important aspect of the mysteries of Odin is to reach the state of ecstasy that awakens the divine eye.

6

RUNE YOGA

A recurrent thought in most esoteric traditions is that sounds, speech, numbers, letters, colors, gods, symbols, and so forth, share occult correspondences with each other. Thus the runes can be linked to galders, gods, symbols, and speech. If the runes are viewed as cosmic principles, it is important to expand their signification beyond their shape and function as writing letters. In German rune magic a system was developed in which magicians contacted the powers of the runes through different body positions. These positions can also be used to direct and control the rune powers. In Friedrich Marby's version this correspondence between runes and postures was called "rune gymnastics." Siegfried Adolf Kummer called it "rune yoga." After them, many rune magicians have worked with runes and body positions. There is no evident support, however, for rune yoga as an old Norse phenomenon. The Gallehus horn is often used to support these theories. This horn features pictures of people in positions that are reminiscent of certain runes.

If one studies the existing systems of rune yoga, one will find many long-winded arguments. Many rune magicians have dismissed rune yoga altogether. One could criticize the rune-yoga approach that tries to imitate exactly the shape of the runes with the body at any cost. The practice ends up reminding one of charades, and holding the positions often becomes uncomfortable. Thus imitating the shapes of the runes can feel far-fetched.

If we assume, however, that the runes represent cosmic principles, it is not as important to solely imitate their shape. Below we will present a rune yoga that has been developed into a rune dance in Dragon Rouge, but it can be varied to fit the personal experience of the runes. The twenty-four positions, or *stödhur*, do, to a certain extent, rely on the shape of the actual runes but also express their function and character.

TWENTY-FOUR RUNE POSITIONS

Several runes in the rune row are based on a stave that is shaped as a vertical line. Thus the ice rune denotes a starting point in rune yoga where one stands upright in concentration. The stave represents the spine, and the rune row is a description of different energy levels located on the spine in the body-mind complex. This model corresponds to Indian kundalini yoga. The Ur rune denotes the untamed primal serpent power that the magician learns to control through the rune row and the twenty-four rune positions. At the Feh rune the magician's will is able to control this force. The stave of the rune represents the world axis, Irminsul. The word *Irminsul* means "the great stave." The name *Iormundgandr*, for the great serpent that encircles the world, also means "the great stave." The serpent and the stave are two expressions of the

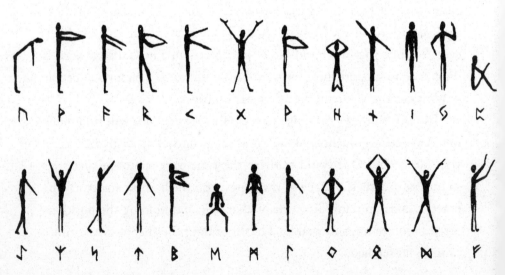

same principle: the force that rises up through the spine. In kundalini yoga Iormundgarndr represents the kundalini and Irminsul the spinal channel *sushumna* through which the kundalini arises.

Ur: Lean forward and feel the primordial power of Ur and the volcanic force that boils in the center of the earth. Most positions can be varied, including this one. It can be done with straight legs and the body bent forward with arms hanging down and the palms against the ground. But it can also be done with bent legs, or without the hands touching the ground.

Thurs: Stand straight with your arms stretched out and hands clasped. The arms represent the two Thurs realms. Feel how the right arm is fire and the left ice (if you are right-handed). The clasped hands represent the two extremes united, and the arms create the spike that makes the Thurs rune complete.

As: Stand straight with arms stretched out in front of you without bringing your hands together. Between your arms you can feel the power of the wind as it is brought back and forth through your breathing.

Reid: Stand straight with one leg in front of the other in a firm position. Hold your arms in front of you, one hand above the other. You are standing as if you were driving a carriage and holding the reins, or standing with a sword in your hand.

Ken: Stand straight with open arms. Feel the force from fire, heat, and expansion.

Gifu: Stand with legs wide apart and arms stretched above your head thus making an X form. The hands should be stretched upward. Experience how power is flowing down from heaven and up from the earth through your body. It flows through you in both directions.

Wynja: Stand straight with feet together and hold your arms in a wide embrace.

Hagal: Sit down on your heels with the legs slightly apart. Rest the elbows on the knees and keep the upper arms directed upward with the fingers inward to the head.

Experience how you are focusing your power and keeping it inside in the same way that the Hagal crystal contains all the runes and their power inside of it.

Naud: Stand straight with arms by your side. Then point one arm upward and the other downward. You can change the position of the arms in a wheellike motion, representing the wheel of destiny.

Is: Stand straight with arms by your side. You are focusing yourself and your force, and you are present here and now, though passive.

Jara: Stand straight with one arm in front of you, the forearm pointing straight up. The other arm should be behind you, forearm pointing down. Let the arms rotate clockwise to illustrate the wheel of the year and the work of the harvest.

Pertra: Sit on your heels with your feet apart. The arms should be pointing forward with upper arms pointing straight up. The fingers should point outward. This position is similar to the Hagal position but is striving outward and the elbows are not resting on the knees. You are the rock that gives birth.

Eihwaz: Stand straight with your left foot behind the right and your left arm pulled up at the side holding your hand at waist level. The right arm should point forward, slightly downward. You are illustrating the yew tree and an archer.

Algiz: Stand straight with arms raised above the head. Feel how you are standing like a tree, visualizing the trunk and the crown. Feel the force flowing through you and express reverence for the sacredness of your body.

Sol: Stand straight with the left foot behind the right and the right arm stretched forward and up. This is the salutation of the sun.

Tyr: Stand straight with the arms stretched outward from the body pointing slightly downward. You are Irminsul, the sacred tree of paganism. You are also illustrating the border between heaven and earth with your arms. You are experiencing the feeling of flying like the eagle.

Bjarka: Stand straight with fists clenched at the chest and the elbows pointing out. The position can illustrate two female breasts or someone holding a spear or wand close to the chest.

Eh: Stand with your legs spread wide and with knees bent. Hold your fists clenched at the waist. This position is called the horse stance and can be found in many martial arts.

Mannaz: Stand straight with arms crossed over your chest. You are the perfect man in balance with the planets, the stars, the web of Urd (Wyrd), and the runes. These different cosmic forces are interacting inside you.

Lagu: Stand straight with one arm stretched forward with the palm turned down to the earth. Feel moisture and water veins with your body and the hand.

Ing: Stand straight holding your arms above the genitals or lower belly. The elbows are pointing outward horizontally from the body. You are channeling the inherent sexual force in the seed and the Ing rune.

Dagaz: Stand with legs wide apart and arms stretched above the head, creating the shape of an X. Unlike the Gifu rune, the palms are here turned outward. You are beaming like the sun and are feeling the force of the rune flowing through you. Stand with the left hand turned to the west and the right hand to the east. The hands represent the day between sunrise and sundown.

Odal: Stand with your legs spread wide, hands clenched slightly above the head. The elbows should point horizontally outward. This position gives power and protection. It centers and limits the mind.

Feh: Stand straight with arms stretched outward. The lower arms point upward, hands clenched. The position illustrates the horn of a tame cow who is holding riches and runes.

Try every rune position and feel the force and character of the rune. This is an effective way to attain knowledge about the runes and their function. You will become one with the rune. You may galder the name of the rune while standing in the position. Make a series of "rune movements." Begin to learn how to "dance the runes." Make the whole rune row in a series of movements. When you have learned this, proceed to include the galders. A drum can indicate the rhythm of the dance. Try to dance your name. Move in runic positions that make magical words and incantations like RUNA, ALU, LAUKAZ, or the names of gods. There are a number of rune movements that can express magical processes. Dance the movement Is–Mannaz–Ken–Hagal–As–Gifu. This illustrates the process in which what is inherent in the ice is also inherent in man. Through the fire, parts of the ice are removed and fall down as hail. Through the breath of the gods man receives the soul gifts. Create your own series of movements describing magical processes.

7

RUNIC DIVINATION

The interpretation of omens and seeing into the future have always been part of magic, and in the Nordic tradition the runes have always been the most important divining tool. All forms of divination are based on a philosophy of existence and how it is constructed. The different symbols that are used in a divination are symbols of the different forces and tendencies in existence. These symbols, as in the I Ching, tarot, or runes, can reveal what forces are presently active. A divination will map the present tendencies and can thus present a picture of the future. Runic divination has ancient roots. Tacitus describes how a runic oracle was used by Germanic tribes: They took a branch from a fruit tree and cut it into little pieces that were marked with signs. The pieces were randomly spread over a white cloth. The oracle gazed up toward the sky and called on the gods, from which he picked up signs three times.

The runes are aspects of the web of destiny called the web of Urd (Wyrd). This web is connected to time. The three Norns, Urd, Verdandi, and Skuld, who weave the thread of the web, represent the three aspects of time: what was, what is, and what is to come. Skuld is the youngest of the Norns, and her face is concealed. Since she reveals the future, this concealing shows us that it is hidden from us. But the future is not only hidden, it is also indefinite. History and the present flow like a thread that disappears into the shrouded future, but where the thread finally will be cut lies in the hands of humans. By reading the web of Urd with the runes we can understand the present age and the past and also lift the veil of Skuld and see what is hidden in the future.

One of the most basic forms of rune divination is to draw three runes from a bag that will signify the three Norns. The first will signify the past, the second the present, and the third the future. By seeing the connection between the three drawn runes the picture will be clearer and the answer easier to understand. One can also employ the tarot Celtic cross way of placing the cards, but using runes instead. A suitable runic divination format is based on Yggdrasil. Nine runes are placed that represent each of the nine worlds. First, one places a rune in the middle, or Midgård. This represents the person who is seeking advice. The order of placing the other runes can be varied.

Midgård: The person who is seeking advice. It also represents the present situation in its obvious form, and possibly the question itself.

Jotunheim: Background, history, memories, and context; the background of the person or the question.

Ljusalfheim: Reason and the intellect; one's intellectual view and conception; the intellectual map.

Svartalfheim: Feelings, instincts, motive, and the driving force. Svartalfheim can also describe the persona.

Vanaheim: The companion, relationships, and the surroundings. The spiritual relations with the fylgja can be revealed here as well as earthly and sexual relations. Vanaheim can also describe the future and the seeds that one sows in the present.

Asgård: Ideals and goals.

Helheim: The unconscious, fears, dreams, and hidden instincts.

Muspelheim: Dynamic and active forces behind something; what makes someone expand outward and continue.

Niflheim: Forces that slow things down and bring them into focus.

If there appears to be an imbalance between Niflheim and

Muspelheim, there is a risk that the person either burns out (Muspelheim) or stagnates (Niflheim). According to the same principle the other worlds are balanced in pairs: feelings (Svartalfheim) should be balanced with the intellect (Ljusalfheim), ideals and the superego (Asgård) with the unconscious (Helheim), the fertile future (Vanaheim) with the past (Jotunheim). Midgård is in the center and any eventual balance or chaos can be revealed in the worlds around it.

Another divination method is based on the five elements of Nordic spirituality: earth, ice, fire, air, and water. Earth is in the middle, ice above, fire below, air to the right, and water to the left. The different elements can have different meanings in the divination, for example:

Earth: the one seeking advice and the question itself;
Ice: an obstacle or a focusing of energy;
Fire: what energizes or burns out;
Air: thoughts and ideas; and
Water: feelings and intuition.

In certain systems of runic divination special meaning is given to runes that appear upside down or reversed. Runes that appear upside down will have an inverted meaning. If the Tyr rune appears upside down, for example, it could thus be interpreted as disorder and lawlessness. Some runes cannot be inverted but can appear reversed. These can be interpreted as having a reversed meaning. Ken reversed might not mean water in such an interpretation but rather a fire that is declining instead of increasing. A third group of runes can appear both upside down and reversed. Lagu, for example, could then be interpreted as water leaking out, which then would lead to drought. Like all interpretations in divination the meaning is understood when considering the situation, the questioner, and the question. The only way to learn how to read the runes is to work with them often. Many rune magicians do not follow the system of interpreting the runes according to whether they are upside down or reversed. Then the runes will have the same meaning regardless of how they are drawn and placed.

AN INTERPRETATION OF THE RUNES

What follows are suggestions about how the runes can be interpreted in divination. These descriptions can be modified depending on the situation and the person asking advice. Feel free to expand the possibilities of interpretation as much as possible but without leaving the Nordic and runological core.

Ur: Primordial force. Return to the source. If you are facing a problem, you should go back to the beginning and for a moment leave your present plans and solutions behind. Let the situation be an unwritten page again and get ideas and energy from the many possibilities that this offers.

Thurs: Chaos and conflicts, which can lead to new possibilities. Thurs is the rune of the giants, and they live in a world outside the known world. The Thurs rune symbolizes the importance of daring to go out into the unknown to find something new. The unknown can appear frightening at first and force one into chaotic situations before it is understood and mastered. The Thurs rune is the rune of black magic and witchcraft, and it reveals the possibility of choosing unusual forces and solutions. Thurs also reminds us of the strength and learning that one can get from leaving the ordered life and entering wild nature or other new environments. In a life analysis, Thurs can advise one to balance old conflicts and oppositions. A new creation arises through the balance between the two primordial Thurs realms—Niflheim and Muspelheim.

As: Creation, life force, and the power to create. The rune of the gods symbolizes the possibility to create something new and enter a new situation. A creation is never a calm process. The gods slay Ymer to create the world, and the power of creation is closely connected to the storm. Creation demands that one leave the old behind and break loose from passivity and the unorganized to create something new. The rune can also reveal the possibility of bringing something old back to life and giving it new power, just as the gods give the logs Ask and Embla life.

R **Reid:** Order and structure. The rune of Thor advises one to be like Thor; that is, to use force and responsibility to gain control of life or a certain situation. The rune also denotes a journey. Not the loosely structured journey of Thurs but rather a journey in a wagon where one has full control. This is also a journey where one's purpose is clear and one has a certain goal in sight. The Reid rune advises one to do the right thing, even if one meets resistance.

< **Ken:** Fire and energy. The torch rune symbolizes the will and the energy that is your driving force. The will can bring both light and clarity but also burn the ground. Fire is both playful and dangerous. Ken can also indicate illumination, sometimes as a painful insight in a certain matter. Ken advises one to use the fire, but use it in the form of a torch, with control.

X **Gifu:** To give and to take. In the old Norse world, relations were based on gifts: in relations between people, in religion, and toward the ancestors. The gift rune advises one to be generous and willing to sacrifice. The gift rune illustrates a balanced relation between giving and receiving. It is a karmic rune that advises you to free yourself of debts and dependencies. The gift rune reveals the importance of giving to coming generations what you have been given, as well as the importance of giving respectful gifts in return to previous generations, the ancestors, and the gods. The gifts should increase in size but without exaggerating. The rune advises one to give but not to heap up gifts without careful thought. Giving should be balanced.

P **Wynja:** Joy and wishes. The joy rune describes how wishes are fulfilled; it is the force that arises in happiness. The joy rune describes the joy that can be found in the small things in life; it is the great happiness and harmony we can experience through good relations with the gods and the other worlds.

Hagal: The seed of knowledge. Wisdom through destruction. Hagal contains the secrets of the runes and thus of life. These are revealed when one confronts death and destruction. By confronting that which one would rather not see at all, one will reach the essential in life. One learns how to make the right choices when using death as an advisor. When we are gazing into the destruction brought by the hail rune, Hagal reveals that the water of life can be found inside it. We will realize that we do not need to fear the inevitable. We will rather see it as a source of wisdom, force, and joy. Hagal is the seed of possibilities. Hagal advises one to seek the essential in life—not to make small-minded choices because of laziness but instead to see everything in a greater perspective even though it might be difficult at first. Hagal is the rune of the dark goddess Hel, and through her wisdom one can see everything as a united whole.

Naud: Need and necessity. Time and fate. This rune can indicate difficulties and obstacles in one's path. These problems can be defeated only by great self-sacrifice. The rune corresponds to the nine-day sacrifice of Odin in Yggdrasil and to the goddesses of time and fate—the three Norns. The rune advises one to accept fate and see in it the possibility of reaching heightened knowledge and insight. This is the rune of initiation, and it teaches one to find the true will in the structures of fate. The rune represents necessity and the inevitable, and it advises one not to be scared by this but to find the strength in it to progress. The Naud rune also describes birth after the nine months of gestation—the inevitable pains of giving birth that lead to new life. In the same way, the Naud rune teaches us to work through other difficulties with the firm belief that they will lead to something new and better.

Is: Concentration and rest. Focusing and awakening. The ice rune describes the importance of resting and entering into lethargy and trance, just like the bear enters hibernation. Rest is a state where one preserves. Preservation is very important if one is to be able to create something. The ice balances the fire that symbolizes the will and its ability to constantly move on but also to burn. The ice rune advises one to be aware and present and to be thoughtful. The ice rune can also warn about things that might be frozen. At some point everything that lies frozen in the ice must be taken out.

Jara: The cycles of nature and the seasons. Return. The year rune reveals the cycles of nature and how day follows night, how spring comes after winter, and so on. This is the rune of the ecological cycles. It denotes good harvests and fertility. Jara signifies play, dance, and marriage. It reveals the marriage between Frey and Freya. It symbolizes harvest feasts and the festivals of the year. The year rune also represents the eternal return where the old is constantly reborn in new forms. This rune advises one to sow and to reap and to see everything in its cyclic form.

Pertra: Hidden treasures. The underworld. This rune is connected to the feminine mysteries and the female womb. Pertra corresponds to the well of Urd and represents both the womb and the grave. It represents the well that is hidden in the underworld, in the mountains, and in the rocks. Here in the hidden the seed of life and destiny can be found, and we will return here after death. In a divination the Pertra rune can signify a discovery of hidden treasures and new sources of power and inspiration. Pertra is describing the bag in which the runes are placed. It describes the play of fate, which we can all join.

Eihwaz: Hunting and journeys between the worlds. This rune belongs to the male mysteries and is connected to the masculine. It illustrates the world axis that stretches between the regions of life and death. The yew tree symbolizes life as well as death and dying. This is the rune of hunting and archery. In a divination, Eihwaz advises one to be goal-directed and to enter into one's hunting grounds. Eihwaz describes the regions of trees and wild nature where one can find knowledge about the unknown.

Algiz: Protection. The force of nature and the gods. Algiz is one of the most powerful runes of protection. It illustrates a horned animal, a tree, and a man with outstretched arms. Algiz describes how one is seeking contact with higher powers and how one receives protection from them. The Algiz rune can be interpreted as an awakening of the sexual forces and how that might activate the fighting spirit. In a divination about spiritual development the rune can be interpreted as the awakening of the inner force and how it strives toward the divine.

Sol: The force of the sun. The sun rune represents light and summer, awakening and energy. It can also promise victory and protection. The force of the sun gives warmth and life and can be used in healing. The sun rune is the fiery energy that, unlike the Ken rune, is not controlled by man. The sun rune can also warn about the burning power of the sun. We should not constantly stand outside in the light. We must balance the heat of the sun with the rest and thoughtfulness of darkness and coolness.

Tyr: Courage and victory. Law and order. The Tyr rune describes how one, through courage and self-sacrifice, can reach success and victory. This is no mere egoistical success but rather the joint success that demands that we give of ourselves. The Tyr rune illustrates the common laws and rules that uphold the common order and creates the structure that can preserve something. The Tyr rune advises one to be brave and to reach victory and success through self-sacrifice.

Bjarka: Birth and rebirth. This is the most important of the feminine runes. It is connected to Frigg and Freya. It represents strength and courage to bring life into what is cold and sterile, thus beginning a new and fertile epoch. It represents both love and witchcraft. The brushwood of the witch's broom was made from birch, and the birch rune can symbolize how one is entering the other worlds. The birch rune advises you that you have the power to bring life to where there is none.

Eh: Relationships and friendship. Journeys and communication. Trust as a foundation for entering the unknown. The horse rune describes the friendship and symbiosis between horse and rider. To dare to start a journey into the unknown one must have a deep trust in the companions of the journey. The Eh rune promises friendship and trust, but it demands that we should take care and responsibility for our relationships and answer with truthfulness and in the good spirit of comradeship.

Mannaz: Self-realization. The human in harmony with the divine. The male and female in balance. The man rune illustrates a person who is conscious and whole. To become a whole person without inner disunion and inconsistent living is the most important and perhaps the most difficult work for a person. It represents striving toward a self-realization that does not become small-mindedness and egoism but one that demands self-sacrifice and a great respect for the immensity that surrounds us—gods, nature, ancestors, fellow humans, and the future that we are creating. Mannaz advises you to strive toward an inner balance and an inner attitude of consistency and consequence where you are aware of your choices and take responsibility for your actions. You can grow by seeing yourself as part of a greater picture.

Lagu: Water, feelings, fantasies, and dreams. The Lagu rune describes the dreamy feelings as a contrast to the will-related feelings of the Ken rune. This is the rune of art, intuition, and visions. Just like water, these feelings can take many different forms. They can purl like a stream or spread out vast like an ocean. They can freeze and they can boil. The Lagu rune advises you to release the creative fantasies and explore the world of dreams, but Lagu also warns you about the risk of drowning in feelings and planless visions that never reach the shore.

◇ **Ing:** Creativity and fertility. Sow a seed for the future. The Ing rune illustrates a seed that contains the essential. Ing describes a concentration of the essential—the core of something. Ing also describes how one plants the essential to enable something even greater to arise in the future. Ing is the masculine generative power, and it illustrates the male seed. The Ing rune advises one to be creative and to focus on what is essential so as to make it grow into the future.

᛬ **Odal:** Relatives and ancestors. Safety and stability. Roots. The Odal rune describes our connection to our ancestors and the environment in which we grew up. It reveals our need to be rooted in tradition and history. To be able to grow and explore new areas, one must always have firm ground to return to. You are constantly creating this foundation and must never stop struggling to keep it. Odal can also warn us not to hide behind traditions or to renounce one's free will by referring to history. Odal also advises one to be a freeholder and to avoid situations of negative dependence.

ᛞ **Dagaz:** Awakening. A new day. Clarity and consciousness. The day rune describes how one is arising from the chrysalis and attains a new consciousness through rebirth. A new day is reached by leaving the old behind.

ᚠ **Feh:** Wealth and reward. Taming the wild. The Feh rune promises a reward for hard work. It describes how, by entering the unknown, one can tame it and gain control over it. Here one can find new riches. One must not stagnate, however, and merely sit on top of the newly acquired knowledge and wealth. One should use it wisely and with responsibility.

8

RUNOSOPHY
AND CABBALA

A deeper study of the runes and old Norse magic will reveal many similarities to the Cabbala. The deep and magical character of the runes was noticed by Olof Verelius (1618–1682), professor of native antiquities. According to the instructions of Olof Rugman from Iceland (1636–1679), Verelius created a structure for magical use of the runes. The runes were both *målrunor* (letters for writing) and *trollrunor* (magical signs). The trollrunor were the magical forms of runes and could be divided into twenty levels or alphabets with increasing power. In the first level the names of the runes indicated what they symbolized. The rune (ᛉ) was, for example, called *madher,* which means "man" or "human." In the second level a characteristic quality was added, as in this example: *madher moldar auki,* which means "man is the fornication of the soil." Level by level, the meanings of the runes were deepened, and at the seventh level one would need the wisdom of a seer to understand them. Here the really dark runes appear, such as *skaderunes, linrunes, speldrunes,* and so on. Those who were initiated in the highest levels of the runes could use them to "call forth the dead and conjure evil spirits." The deep and hidden meanings of the runes are reminiscent of the letter mysticism of the Cabbala and other similar traditions such as the magical use of Sanskrit in Tantra or the esoteric levels of the Greek letters. Verelius believed that the runes were dangerous pagan symbols used in black magic.

Johannes Bureus (1568–1652) was a predecessor to Verelius. On behalf of the Swedish king he traveled around Sweden and wrote down information about runic artifacts. Bureus was inspired by the Cabbala and alchemy and read the works of Agrippa, Paracelsus, Reuchlin, and other writers of occultism. Through a comparison with the Cabbala he became convinced that the runes had different dimensions. He believed that they were not only letters for writing but also esoteric, magical symbols. He called the secret dimension of the runes *adulrunes,* or "noble runes." Bureus removed the last rune in the Scandinavian rune row and described a fifteen-stave rune row divided into three ættir with five runes each. The ættir represented the principles of giving birth (SW: *födare*), the birth (SW: *födelse*), and the fetus, that which is born (SW: *foster*). Bureus believed that the runes had been created in ancient days by a mythical figure named Byrger Tidesson. Bureus wrote a runic ABC book and wanted the Swedish people to return to rune writing once again. This gained some popularity among Swedish officers who used runic writing in secret messages during the Thirty Years War.

Bureus created magical symbols of the adulrunes. They existed on something that he called "the falling stone," a symbol that consisted of a cubic stone three sides of which are revealed, each depicting five runes in the shape of a cross.

He also constructed a symbol that he called the Adulruna that contained the fifteen adulrunes. The symbol can be compared to the Monas Hieroglyphica of John Dee, which contains the symbols of all the planets. The Adulruna of Bureus is a map of the universe and of man's progression through different levels of existence. The symbol as an idea is related to the Etz Chaim of the Cabbala, the Tree of Life, and can also be a symbol of Yggdrasil. The Adulruna works both as a symbol of man and of the universe, the microcosm and macrocosm. At the center of the symbol is the Hagal rune that, according to Bureus, means "noble" and is thus a pivotal adulrune. The Hagal rune in this

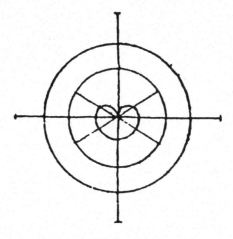

Adulruna
(Image by J. Bureus)

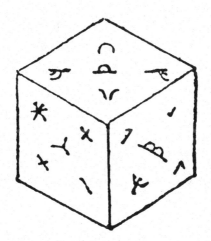

The falling stone
(Image by J. Bureus)

form (✳) is similarly essential in later rune magic. Hagal has been associated with hail or with a seed that contains the other runes. In the Adulruna of Bureus there is a path of Hermetic progression. He developed a cross of adulrunes in which the vertical line describes the progression of the adept. The adept is raised above the darkness of ignorance; *tenebræ* (ᛒ) through *splendor* (ᛀ), *lumen* (ᛁ), *lux* (ᛀ), *luminare* (✳), and *modus entis* (ᛉ) to *principum absolutæ primum* (ᚢ). The last principle is equivalent to the Ain Soph of the Cabbala. The highest is represented by the god rune (ᚢ), which represents the spirit and the One. This corresponds to the Thor rune (Thurs) in Bureus's system, and to Bureus, Thor represented the highest deity. The lowest level is the material and dualistic plane that is symbolized by the horizontal birch rune called Byrghal (ᛒ). The goal in Bureus's system is not to escape the lower level but to unite the high with the low, spirit with matter. The unification is symbolized by a rune in which the two principles have become one (ᛒ). Bureus constructed different runic sigils that described certain alchemical and occult processes. From his rune cross he developed a magical symbol that contains seven of the pivotal adulrunes.

The runes on the falling stone are constructed according to the same principle with five adulrunes, where one is in the center, two are at the sides facing each other and reversed, and one rune is above and one below. The symbol with the horizontal birch rune (Byrghal) with the rune Man below can be interpreted as man (ᛉ) and the divine archetypal plane (ᛁ) that has been separated by matter and the plane of duality (ᛒ). On each side is the upward-flowing (ᛀ) and the downward-flowing (ᚱ). The symbol corresponds to the cabbalistic and Hermetic worldview and the description of man in Tantra. The fact that Bureus with the (ᛒ) rune revealed that the secret of the goal with the adulrunes was the unity of the One and the level of dualities, makes his system correspond to the contemporary Draconian philosophy where the serpent and the eagle are united in the dragon, or where Shiva (the One) is united with Shakti (Duality) without the disintegration of any of the principles but rather enabling the creation of the third, the synthesis.

The system of Bureus is called the Gothic, or Götic, Cabbala as well as the Uppsala Cabbala, *Cabala Upsalica.* If we, like Bureus, would consider the thought that there were obvious connections between the old

Norse wisdom and the Cabbala, is it then possible to place the worlds of Yggdrasil on the *sephirot*? This can surely be done if in the same symbol we include its dark side, since the Nordic worlds are both light and dark.

Malkuth would correspond to Midgård, the material world of man. The rune that belongs to this level would be the rune of ecology and cycles: Jara (ᛃ). (See figure on page 118.)

Above Malkuth we find Yesod and it's darker "shell" and polar opposite, Gamaliel, representing the moon and the world of dreams. This level is connected to the astral plane and the world of the dead as well as to the dark goddesses. The old Norse world that could be placed here is Helheim, the realm of death, with the dark goddess Hel. The rune that corresponds to this level is Hagal (ᚺ) or (ᛡ).

Above Yesod we find Hod-Samael and Netzach-A'arab Zaraq. Basically, they represent the intellect and feelings, respectively. They are opposites and are constantly interacting. Here we can place Ljusalfheim (Hod), which rules thoughts and reason, and Svartalfheim (Netzach), which represents feelings and passions. The rune of Ljusalfheim and the intellect is the Dagaz rune (ᛞ). The rune of Svartalfheim is Eihwaz, the yew tree rune (ᛇ).

In the middle of the cabbalistic tree is the sphere of the sun, Tiphareth-Thagirion, which represents the self or the daemon. This belongs to the mental plane and the sphere of the heavens, and its symbol is the mandala, the sun cross (⊕). The Nordic world that can be placed here is Asgård and the Gifu rune (ᚷ). On each side is Gevurah-Golachab and Chesed-Gha'agsheblah. They correspond to the principles of suffering and lust.

The sphere of suffering can be represented by Jotunheim, the world of the giants and the Naud rune (ᚾ).

Chesed-Gha'agsheblah corresponds to Vanaheim. The Vanirs are the gods controlling fertility and sexual passion as well as witchcraft. The rune for this sphere is the seed rune Ing (ᛜ).

The highest level of the cabbalistic tree begins with a couple of counterparts representing nothingness and being, female and male,

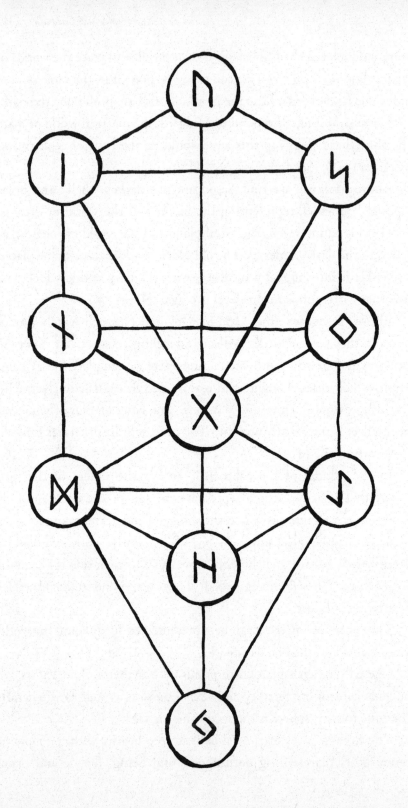

passive and active: Binah-Satariel and Chokmah-Ghagiel. Binah-Satariel corresponds to Niflheim, which is the extreme polarity of stillness, passivity, cold, and darkness. Its rune is the ice rune (|). Chokmah-Ghagiel is connected to fire and the sphere of extreme activity, Muspelheim. The rune belonging to this sphere is the sun rune (ᛣ).

So far we have placed the nine worlds of the Nordic tradition on the cabbalistic tree. The tenth level, which is the first and highest in the Cabbala, is Kether-Thaumiel. This level is the all-potential, the seed of becoming that unites being and nothingness. This level is connected to the state beyond the worlds: Ain Soph. In the Nordic myths this level corresponds to Ginnungagap, the great abyss where the worlds are created through a meeting of the polarities fire and ice. Ginnungagap is the pure energy that flows through everything. The first being that is created in the Ginnungagap is Ymer. He is a twin being, and we can here find a connection to Thaumiel, whose name means the "twin god."

If one is comparing, from a magical perspective, runosophy with the old Norse and Gothic magic, one will see that the parallels that Johannes Bureus found between the Cabbala and the runes are very interesting. This connection can be used to achieve a more complete occult world picture. Many rune magicians have found parallels between the runes and the Cabbala. The rune mystic Guido von List believed in this theory and saw himself as a reincarnation of the cabbalist Reuchlin. From a numerological perspective one can find many revealing keys that will point out similarities between the dark sides of the Cabbala and Odinic runosophy.

9

THE UTHARK
AND THE NIGHTSIDE
OF THE RUNES

An important and in many respects unique feature in runosophy and Nordic magic is its relation to the dark side. Most spiritual traditions focus mainly on the gods and principles of the light and tend to view the nightside of existence as something to avoid. In the Nordic tradition we rather can see an attitude where the dark is viewed as a prerequisite of illumination, a thought that echoes in the words of the psychologist C. G. Jung: "One does not reach illumination by visualizing the light but through exploring the darkness." This is the attitude that can be found in the mysteries of Odin's initiation. Through self-sacrifice and encounters with giants and powers of the underworld, Odin increased his knowledge. Odin attains illumination in the secrets of the runes through a journey to the dark regions. In the same way the modern rune magician must seek the wisdom of the runes in the nightside of existence.

What, then, is light and what is darkness? There are an infinite number of prejudices regarding these two intellectually and emotionally charged terms. A common thought is that the light represents good and the dark represents evil. This is a reflection of monotheistic dualism in which darkness and light stand in an extreme ethical opposition. In the Nordic tradition, creation is thought to have arisen through the meeting of two opposites, the realm of fire and the realm of ice. Existence is only threatened if the balance between these two extremes is in danger. The Nordic gods do not represent the infinitely good but are instead more nuanced and have both light and dark aspects. Odin, the most important god in runosophy, is a dark and demonic god who is feared by most people. He is a dark wanderer whose deeds are difficult to predict, and he is the god of the hanged and dead. Odin is surrounded by attributes, like ravens and wolves, which in the history of religions are usually connected to dark entities. He is spoken of as the all-father, but he has a dark function when seen beside the light god, Tyr.

In the myths, light represents order and harmony. The world of man belongs to the light sphere but is infiltrated and attacked by dark elements that are trying to break in and create chaos. The world of the gods is the highest, utmost light and represents a perfect order. This world is often viewed as being located high up in the skies or on top

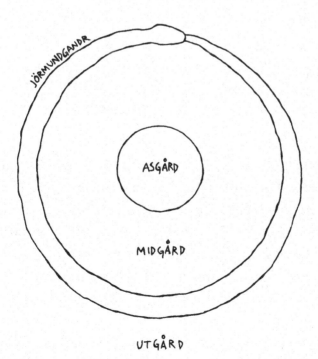

of a mountain. The world of the gods is in the center and at the highest point. The gods of light are usually worshipped through prayer or are called upon as ideals and protectors of order and structure. The gods of light are often pictured in a perfect anthropomorphic shape. The dark represents chaos. This is the wild nature and the cold infinity that surround the world of man. While the world of the gods has limits, the dark side is characterized by its limitlessness. The dark side is inhabited by powerful entities, which are often described as both brutal and extremely wise. They are older than the gods of light and are often non-anthropomorphic characters, in the form of mythological animals or bestial demons. Dragons and giantlike creatures are what usually inhabit the dark worlds. These worlds are outside and beyond the world of man. They might exist beyond the oceans or in the underworld. On a psychological level, the world of the gods of light represents our ideals and the superego, the world of man is our mundane consciousness with its limitations, while the dark side represents the unconscious. In Nordic mythology three strongholds illustrate the three different principles as follows:

Asgård: the world of the gods; the light; ideals and the superego;
Midgård: the world of man; mundane consciousness and the limited mind; and
Utgård: the world of the giants; the dark; the wild and limitless; the unconscious.

In the Nordic tradition the importance of the dark forces is evident. By traveling to the spheres of the dark, the gods are enhancing their power. The walls of Asgård are even built by a giant, which reveals how the gods need the dark forces to protect themselves from the very same. The giants are not mere primitive forces, as they are sometimes described to be. They are also in possession of ancient wisdom. The primordial giant Mímir is the most wise of all beings, and Odin sacrifices his eye in his well in Jotunheim to gain this wisdom. To reach illumination Odin is constantly diving straight down into the dark depths.

HELWEGR

While many spiritual traditions are striving toward the perfect heights of the light, Odin teaches us to seek in the dark. In the *Hávamál* the hanged Odin tells us that he sent his eye down into the depths and there picked up the runes. This is a journey into the roots of the world tree and the underworld. Hel is a central character in the Odinic initiation. She is the dark goddess of the underworld and the dark opposite to Odin.

Her name means "the hidden one," and she represents the dark and unknown parts of existence. Hel can also be interpreted as "whole" or "hole." She is the goddess of the tunnels and holes of the underworld. She is the dark mother, and her womb will give birth to reborn gods. She also represents the completion where death and life are united. The kingdom of Hel can be found beyond the two gates of life: birth and death. Life and renewal take place in the realm of darkness. The light god Balder is killed by the blind god Höder. During a game in which the invulnerability of Balder is tried, Loki uses his cunning to make Höder shoot an arrow of mistletoe against Balder. The mistletoe is the only thing able to hurt Balder, and he dies. But instead of going to Valhalla, he is pulled down into Hel. Hermod, the son of Odin, travels to Hel to try to bring Balder back. But only after Ragnarök will Balder return, together with his dark companion, Höder.

Hermod rides upon Odin's eight-legged horse, Sleipnir, down the pitch-black Helwegr, the road to Hel, for nine days. Here we can find interesting runosophical symbolism and numerology. The nine-day-long journey of Hermod represents the nine days that Odin hangs in Yggdrasil. Sleipnir is the steed of Odin, and the name of the world tree means exactly that, the steed of Yggr, or Odin. Here we find magical symbolism where the horse represents the tree. The steed is the same as the wand of the witches, with which they travel to other worlds. But the wand is more than just a witch's broom. This is the world pillar that runs between the worlds and that unites the dimensions of life and death. In man, this partly represents the spine that connects our instinct center to the brain and the thought functions; the unconscious and the subconscious to the conscious and the superego.

Sleipnir has eight legs. This is a symbolism that is recurrent in different shamanistic and magical traditions as a symbol of the possibility of riding both in this world and in the realms of death and the unknown. It is also interesting to note that at a funeral, the corpse was often carried by four men, which can be connected to the eight-legged horse who takes the deceased to the other side. Eight is also the number of runes in each ætt, and certain aspects of Sleipnir correspond to the Hagal rune. If we add the number of legs of the horse who takes the deceased to the other side, with the number of days that the journey takes, we have a key to the Helwegr. Nine is 3 × 3. If we multiply 8 by 3 we will get the number of runes of the rune row, 24. If we multiply 8 by 3 × 3 (9), we get 72: a very interesting number in runosophy as well as if we, like Bureus did, connect it to cabbalistic numerology. In runosophy it is interesting since the number 72 (or 3 × 24) stands for the fact that every rune in the rune row has three meanings. Every rune has a light, dark, and neutral aspect. The number 72 is also one of the most important numbers in the Cabbala, and it is the foundation of the black magic of the Goetia grimoire. The magical connections between Gothic and goetic magic are explored in the Dragon Rouge magical order. A central character in these traditions is the legendary magician Faust. In Faustian magic, elements of goetic demonology are united with Gothic runosophy.

Even without numerological speculation, we can draw the conclusion that the rune row is a *helwegr,* a "hel path." It can lead one down to the center of the underworld and back again. The rune row is a path of initiation where the magician, like Odin, gazes down into the dark depths and picks up rune after rune in the journey to and back from Hel. The secrets that the concealed goddess Hel keeps in her womb are thus accessed by the magician. The descent into the underworld can represent the journey of the sun to the darkest night of December and its rebirth in spring, but above all it represents a deep alchemical process of transformation where the initiate creates himself and reaches divinity. Odinic rune magic can be interpreted from numerous angles. To reach an explicit understanding of the descent to Hel, as illustrated by the runes, one should observe them positioned in twelve circles inside each other with the opposing couples on each side as described in chapter 3. The runes can be visualized or work as keys during a drum journey in which the magician should be in a room that is completely darkened and meditate to the monotonous rhythm of a drum. The Uthark has been interpreted as the dark and inner version of the rune row. It begins with two very dark runes that symbolize the descent to the dark worlds. The Uthark ends with the two exact opposites of these runes, which represent the ascent from the underworld and the illumination into the secrets of the runes.

Ur: With the Ur rune the descent into the underworld begins. The Ur rune symbolizes the gate to the underworld. The Ur rune is the rune of beginning processes. Here everything is yet unfulfilled and concealed. Ur belongs to Urd, the goddess of fate, and the rune represents how we are seeking to enter into the well of Urd during our search for the wisdom she keeps hidden and in the past.

Thurs: With the Thurs rune the gate opens. This is the rune of the biune that makes two into one, and it symbolizes how we are creating a crack in existence to gaze into the dark. Thurs is the opposite rune of Dagaz; they represent night and day, respectively. Thurs is the gate to darkness.

As: The As rune symbolizes the adept who, like Odin, lowers himself into the depths. The As rune is the breath that the magician inhales to enter the trance. As the third rune in the Uthark, it also represents the three ættir that the magician is on his way to explore.

Reid: The journey has begun, and the magician rides on the back of Sleipnir or Yggdrasil down the Helwegr, or like Thor to Utgård. The rune represents the rhythm of breathing, the heartbeats and the rhythm of the drum. It also keeps the magician from losing energy and helps keep order during the journey down to the realms of death or the forces of chaos.

Ken: With his will, the magician lights a torch in the dark tunnels. Ken represents the will, the knowledge, and the inner light that prevents the magician from being lost in the maze of the underworld.

Gifu: This is the rune that symbolizes the core of the initiation. Like Odin, the magician sacrifices himself to himself. By self-sacrifice the magician can reach illumination in the secrets of the runes. The magician must give himself to gain himself. Through a symbolic and magical death, the magician can arise as his own creation. Gifu also represents the soul gifts given by the three gods. On this level the magician sacrifices himself. The opposite rune is the man rune, Mannaz. On the Mannaz level the magician is reborn with all soul gifts in full power.

Wynja: Wynja represents not only joy and harmony but also the will and its power to make wishes come true. During the initiation, Wynja represents the magical will that makes the Odinic self-sacrifice possible on the way to deep insights. Wynja represents the will to cross the underworld river Gjöll. Wynja opens the Gjallar bridge, which is guarded by the maiden Modgunn, who asks all travelers about their name and family.

Hagal: This rune is pivotal in the initiation. It represents the seed to all runes. The runes are frozen potentialities inside Hagal. Through the magician, the runes can be made into actualities. Hagal concludes the first ætt of the Uthark and corresponds to the gate to Hel. Hagal symbolizes the first meeting with the dark goddess Hel.

Naud: The initiate is approaching the deepest parts of Helheim. The ninth rune represents the nine-day-long journey of Hermod or Odin's ninth and final day in the world tree. The magician encounters the three Norns, who are weaving the web of fate. The threads of fate are the foundation of the runes. At this stage the initiate can influence fate through the threads.

Is: Down in the deepest parts of Hel the dark and cold world of Niflheim opens up. Here one experiences the extreme cold, and everything is frozen. The darkest force of existence, the dragon Nidhögg, can be found here, gnawing on the roots of the world tree.

Jara: The eleventh rune in the Uthark represents in its cyclic aspect the well of Vergelmer, which can be found in Niflheim. This cyclic rune symbolizes the fact that eleven streams carrying the seed of creation and rebirth are flowing from the utmost cold.

Pertra: At Pertra, the magician finds himself at the center of the underworld. This is the bottom of the well of Urd and the deepest part of Hel. Pertra is the innermost hole of the underworld and the womb of Hel. This is the twelfth rune in the Uthark, and here the runes are born. This is the grave where the magician dies and the womb where he is reborn as his own creation. Pertra represents the winter solstice. Pertra is a dark goddess who rides together with Odin in the wild hunt, when the dead are raging in the woods on the darkest night of the year. Pertra is an alter ego of Hel.

Eihwaz: The rune Eihwaz also corresponds to the winter solstice and the night sky. This rune symbolizes Yggdrasil and the hallucinatory trance in which the magician now finds himself, deep down in the deepest levels of the darkness of the underworld. It also symbolizes the spear of Odin and a tool with which one can pick up the runes. This rune is also connected to the wild hunt and its ecstasy.

Algiz: This rune symbolizes the reborn magician who creates himself. He stretches himself up toward the sun and the heat. The darkest and coldest phase of the night has passed. The magician has visited the interior of Helheim and can now return. This rune represents sacredness and divinity, which characterize the magician after his rebirth. The magician has now made himself divine. The rune has been used as a symbol of birth.

Sol: The sun rune is the opposite of the ice rune. It represents the reborn, divine nature of the magician, where the higher self has been united with the conscious self. The sun rune represents the force of the magician that rises up like lightning or a snake from the underworld.

Tyr: The power rises up through the world tree or the magician's spine. The word *tyr* means "god," and the Tyr rune embodies the new nature of the magician, as a god. The magician formulates his law and creates a new order.

Bjarka: The birch is the first tree that returned after the ice age. In the same way, the birch rune symbolizes how the magician, through his force and power as a god, makes the world verdant again according to his will. This is also the rune of witchcraft, and it is connected to Freya's knowledge about the art of sejd, which is the prerequisite of Odin's initiation into the secrets of the runes.

Eh: The eighteenth rune represents the eighteen rune songs that Odin receives during his initiation. The horse rune is connected to Sleipnir and Yggdrasil and the journey out of the underworld.

Mannaz: The magician has united the hidden forces with his human nature. The magician has reached the state of the perfect man, where the hidden forces are controlled by the magician and his will. The magician can here fully use the soul gifts that he was given by the three gods but which were before unconscious to him and beyond his control.

Lagu: The water rune balances its opposite, Ken. Here, Lagu symbolizes Odrörir and the magical mead that brings inspiration and wisdom to the magician.

Ing: Ing is a sex-magic rune that symbolizes the ecstasy and orgasm that the magician experiences and channels. This orgasmic force is focused to the will center of the magician, and thus it awakes the all-seeing eye. The magician reaches, in a spiritual sense, a royal level and becomes a lord or a lady, like Frey or Freya.

Odal: The magician accomplishes and manifests his will in a magical kingdom. This can be the magician's temple or the group of magicians with whom he works. The magician reaches, in a magical sense, Valhalla.

Dagaz: We have now reached the opposite of the Thurs rune. Dagaz denotes the illumination of that which has previously been concealed in the dark.

Fehu: The magician has integrated and learned how to control the dark and wild forces. The powers of death and darkness can be used to serve the magician in accordance with his will. The magician has reached a state of completion and reward, in return for his self-sacrifice.

POSTSCRIPT

The runes are multidimensional. The magician should not overemphasize their physical forms. Only by studying and exploring the different aspects of the runes both in theory and practice will one be able to open the gates to the secrets of the runes. Runosophy is in itself a helwegr where the magician, through his work with the runes, step-by-step enters their dark depths. This is a long process that will reveal many different phases. When you believe you have reached the bottom, new depths are discovered. When you think you are at the end of a path, you will realize that the journey has just begun. The knowledge about the runes is not linear; it is cyclic. When you stand before the completion of Fehu, the gates of Ur will open.

This part was to a large extent written on the island of Gotland, the great island in the Baltic Sea that bears Odin's epithet, *got*. On this island, the oldest and most remarkable runic artifacts have been found. In an overgrown grove, the flat gravestone that, unlike other inscribed stones, had its carvings on the underside, hidden from the eyes of the world, was found. This stone is the only archaeological find that possibly reveals an Uthark. The unique picture stones that have revealed much about the old Norse tradition were also found on Gotland. One of these stones shows the ancient goddess holding a serpent in each hand. Perhaps she is illustrating something essential about Nordic spirituality.

A dark goddess like Hel is the key to the wisdom of the underworld. She holds the reptilian forces, concealed inside of us, that can take us into the world of the gods. If we, like Odin, gaze down into the depths, we can reach illumination in the darkest blackness; in the deep we can find the path to the highest peaks.

It is of course very rewarding to be able to live and work magically in an area like Gotland, where runes were carved in ancient times and that once belonged to ancient, mysterious gods. But the runes are not limited to any place or time. The secrets of the runes are accessible to all those striving with an iron will, like Odin, and dare to gaze down in the dark depths of the unknown and into the depths of themselves to find the force and wisdom of the runes.

PART 2

The Adulruna
and the
Gothic Cabbala

Translated by Stephen E. Flowers

JOHANNES BUREUS, MAN OF THE NORTHERN RENAISSANCE

By Stephen E. Flowers

For centuries, the life, work, and image of Johannes Bureus remained largely forgotten. Even over the past century he remained mysterious and often misunderstood. Such is often the fate of historical magi. Scholars such as Hans Hildebrand and Sten Lindroth, and more recently Susanna Åkerman and Thomas Karlsson, have begun to lift the veil on the contributions of this scientist and magician. To understand Johannes Bureus more clearly we must comprehend the historical and cultural milieu that preceded him and in which he lived—the Renaissance and the Reformation. Bureus was shaped by these cultural paradigms, but he also shaped them in turn. He was an active agent in history, and as such he can be counted as a true magus—one who through his personal effort and work, even if only subtly, to some extent transforms the world around him. As such Bureus was a consummate Renaissance man in Sweden who bridged the gap between objective science and subjective magic. That he accomplished this before the gap grew so wide between these two impulses that it seemed it could

133

never be bridged speaks directly to his genuine and enduring value as an intellectual and spiritual fountainhead.

The present sweeping study by Thomas Karlsson was originally written in Swedish for a Swedish readership—a readership presumably well aware of the historical background relevant to the study. As a general introduction to this work, it might be useful to review some of the historical context relating both to Swedish history and the history of ideas during the Renaissance and Reformation in Europe.

HISTORICAL CONTEXT

The country now known as Sweden takes up the bulk of the eastern part of the Scandinavian peninsula. This region had a rich Bronze Age (1700–500 BCE) culture that left behind many mysterious rock carvings that were precursors to later Germanic myth and legend. When the Germanic peoples articulated themselves linguistically and culturally from the rest of the northern Indo-European world around 700 BCE, at least the southern part of what is now Sweden was included in the original Germanic homeland. At that time the Germanic peoples were defined by one commonly intelligible dialect referred to by linguists as Proto-Germanic. The peoples of the region presumably shared most major cultural features with the other Germanic peoples to the south in what is now northern Germany. They all spoke more or less the same language, worshiped the same major gods and goddesses and shared a common system of values. However, theirs was a tribal, and not a nationalistic society. These small organically conditioned groups were fiercely independent and bore a tremendous sense of internal authenticity and solidarity.

Tacitus (56–115 CE), a Roman historian, wrote a remarkable ethnography of the Germanic peoples in 98 CE commonly titled *Germania*. In this work he mentions both the Gothones (Goths) and Suiones (Swedes). It is not unreasonable to conclude that the Goths emerged from the southern part of Scandinavia before settling first on the Baltic coast around the mouth of the Vistula River and that the Swedes were somewhat to the north of them. During the so-called Migration Age, when many Germanic tribes migrated across the European continent, the Goths wandered widely through what is now Russia and throughout the Mediterranean lands and even into North Africa. The Swedes, on the other hand, consolidated their position in Scandinavia during this period. However, many presume that the migrating Goths merely represented part of the whole Gothic world and that many of them remained behind, lending their name to regions in what is now southern Sweden (Östergötland and Västergötland) as well as to the island of Gotland.

This period of tribal migrations on the continent was well concluded by about 800 CE, by which time the still-pagan Scandinavians entered into a dynamic historical phase of raiding and trading with Christian countries to the south and west. This period is called the Viking Age by most scholars. Much of this activity for the Swedes was centered on the countries across the Baltic to the east, reaching as far as the Islamic world. It was a time of great power and wealth for all the Scandinavian countries—Denmark, Norway, and Sweden—all of which had developed their own individual identities by this period. As this age drew to a close the individual Scandinavian lands were at least nominally Christianized. Sweden was the last to fall in about 1100 CE.

It was at the very end of the Viking Age and at the very beginning of the Christian Middle Ages in Sweden when the bulk of the great runestones, which were to occupy so much of Bureus's scientific life, were carved. These are for the most part memorial stones that commemorate dead ancestors. The stones were usually commissioned by the survivors of the deceased. By the early modern period, when Bureus lived, these stones were between four and five hundred years old, and the runes with which they had been inscribed were largely forgotten, as was the original significance of the stones.

Christianity, and with it medieval European culture, was established relatively late in Sweden. In fact it was not firmly established until about 1200, and even then, pockets of the old traditional culture remained in the remoter areas of the countryside. The center of pagan culture had been Gamla Uppsala, just a few miles north of the medieval town of Uppsala. After the destruction of the pagan temple at Gamla Uppsala in 1100, the political and spiritual center of the country moved to the new town of Uppsala and the cathedral there.

The period following Christianization was characterized by civil wars in Sweden. Power began to be consolidated under the great Jarl Birger Magnusson, who ruled as regent after 1250. This was accomplished by organizing the ancient local legal assemblies (*thing*) into a network throughout the country. Centralized authority over the minor nobility and farmers developed only slowly and partially in medieval Sweden. Until the final consolidation of power by Gustav Vasa in the early sixteenth century, Swedish history was marked by prolonged times of internal strife and intermittent periods when the country was at least partially controlled by Denmark. In 1521 Vasa was elected king of Sweden by some two hundred farmers at Tuna near the ancient coronation stone of Mora, where the pagan and early Christian kings of medieval Sweden were invested with royal power. Vasa drove out the Danes with the help of the German Hanseatic League—a commercial cartel that dominated business interests in the Baltic and North Seas from the early eleventh to the sixteenth centuries.

The early 1500s saw another influence coming from Germany—Protestantism. The new king and national hero, Gustav Vasa, embraced the idea of Lutheran reform but moved slowly and wisely in its implementation. But a hundred years later all of Europe would find itself in an international war pitting Protestant against Catholic. This became known as the Thirty Years War (1618–1648). Gustav Vasa's grandson, known as Gustavus Adolphus, ruled as king from 1611, when he was only seventeen years old, to 1632, when he was killed in battle at Lützen in Germany. Gustavus Adolphus was a student of Johannes Bureus, and Bureus was later well supported by the king. The young king was a capable ruler and a brilliant military strategist. The tide of the Thirty Years War was turned by his numerous victories on the continent between 1630 and 1632. Northern Europe would remain Protestant and independent of Rome.

S. M. Toyne, writing in *The Scandinavians in History,* describes the death of Gustavus Adolphus as follows:

> On November 6th, 1632, the battle of Lützen brought the last victory in death to the Swedish hero. Cut off by a thick mist, he was shot by some Croats in the middle of the battle. As his rider-less white horse brought the news down the ranks, the Swedes were blinded with fury, and surged forward to revenge the death of their beloved leader. For once, discipline went, and the old "berserk" spirit took its place. Panic seized the Imperialists, who fled in disorder.

HISTORY OF IDEAS

The world of Johannes Bureus was one of ideas. The time period in which he lived was one of revolutionary change and a tremendous forward-looking spirit. However, Bureus himself, like so many of his fellow Europeans of the age, looked back to tradition, often secret tradition, as fuel for these changes. Beginning in the Florentine Renaissance of the fifteenth century new ideas began to emerge to challenge the intellectual hegemony of the Christian Middle Ages. But whereas the Renaissance in Florence was mainly characterized by the expansion of awareness to encompass previously rejected or unknown sources of knowledge, for example, the Cabbala, Hermeticism, and other non-Christian philosophies, north of the Alps a new wind was blowing.

Theophrastus Bombastus von Hohenheim (1493–1541), better known by his academic moniker, Paracelsus, introduced a revolutionary way of thinking and established it as a mode of intellectual operation. He would experiment and expose the results of his experiments to rational analysis. Although Paracelsus is considered a magician on the one hand, he is also known as the father of modern medicine and pharmacology on the other. His methods of operation called the authority of ancient and "received" knowledge into question. He wanted to prove the validity of theories and ideas based on experimental work. In this he was followed by the Welsh English magus John Dee (1527–1608).

This Paracelsian method quickly gained an international following and was applied to matters both exoteric and esoteric. The ideas of Paracelsus were especially well received north of the Alps in Germany, England, and Scandinavia. Esoteric topics such as Hermeticism, Cabbala, astrology, magic, and alchemy were fundamentally reshaped by Paracelsian ideas that called for a good deal less medieval faith in authority and a good deal more modern reason to be applied to the contents of these arcane traditions.

At the same time when Bureus was maturing intellectually there emerged from central Europe a movement known as Rosicrucianism. This movement was itself largely the spawn of Paracelsian ideas, especially as received by such men as John Dee and Francis Bacon in England. Early Rosicrucianism is principally known from the contents of three texts: the *Fama Fraternitatis* (1614), The *Confessio Fraternitatis* (1615), and the *Chymische Hochzeit* (1616). The Rosicrucian movement early on appears to have been a secret secular brotherhood of mainly Protestants who were keen to bring perfection to mankind and the sciences through the application of a system of previously hidden knowledge.

The central myth of Rosicrucianism, recounted in the *Fama,* tells of the travels of a German, "brother C(hristian) R(osencreutz)," to the East to seek true illumination. He sojourns in Damascus and Fez absorbing what the Arabic philosophers have to teach. Afterward he returned to Germany and gathered three students, thus founding the "Fraternity of the Rose Cross." Eventually brother C.R. died, at the age of 106, and was buried in a secret vault. After 120 years this mysterious tomb was discovered and opened—and thus the door was opened to a general reformation throughout the world. On the one hand Rosicrucianism was an exponent of the Protestant Reformation of Martin Luther and others, but on the other hand it was a continuation and expansion of earlier trends in esotericism north of the Alps.

The Renaissance and Reformation both in their own ways ushered in the Modern Age. The Modern is imbued with an optimism for the future not based on the faith of the Middle Ages that the return of Christ was imminent but rather on the reason of the ancients coupled with the burgeoning scientific method pioneered by Paracelsus and others. The young Johannes Bureus found himself in the midst of these volatile and exciting times.

Johannes Bureus was an esotericist and magician. His esoteric ideology is well outlined in the present book. His magical legacy is less well known owing to a lack of documentation. However, it must be said that his methods were intended to have an effect on the world around him and that they indeed had such an effect. Bureus was also a groundbreaking secular humanistic Paracelsian. He used the Paracelsian method of gathering data based on experiential observation and the subjecting of the results of this observation to rational analysis. Whereas many Paracelsians used this revolutionary technique in the field of "natural philosophy" (as the natural sciences were called then), Bureus applied it to what we would call the humanities. Of course, it must also be said that in the time around 1600 the distinction between *Naturwissenschaft* and the *Geisteswissenschaft* was not as great as it is today. This original close association is at the root of why Bureus could slip so easily between exoteric and esoteric approaches to runology, for example. That the distinction between these categories does in fact exist for Bureus is also emphasized by the tendency on his part to write studies that were either exoteric or esoteric in their tenor.

Johannes Bureus was interested in magic and Hermeticism at least from his early twenties. He studied the *De magia veterum* or *Arbatel,* which was originally published in Basel in 1575. It is very likely that Bureus read a version of the *Fama* that circulated in manuscript form in 1613 and that it affected him deeply; it was to this experience that he refers when he said that in that year he "received knowledge concerning the hidden truth." Although the identities of most early Rosicrucians are unknown, and that even the authorship of the early RC documents has been called into question, Johannes Bureus is one of the few men who actually signed his name to a Rosicrucian treatise—a Latin poem printed in 1616. It is clear that the underlying motives and temperament of Bureus were esoteric ones, although he focused almost exclusively on the idea of the communication of secret knowledge from an unseen, divine realm to the world of humanity. This spirit animated his runology, both exoteric and esoteric.

Bureus is sometimes compared to the Welsh English magician and philosopher John Dee. These comparisons are apt and quite profound. Dee created a system of symbolic magical communication ("Enochian tablets"), had a symbol that summarized his magical philosophy (the Monas Hieroglyphica), and helped guide his country in a time when it stepped upon the stage of world history as a great power. Dee is even said to have coined the term "the British Empire."

As Sweden assumed its place as a world power for a short time during the first half of the seventeenth century, especially during the illustrious reign of Gustavus Adolphus, Bureus assumed a leading ideological role. As John Dee sometimes used the myth of King Arthur to bolster his idea of a British empire, so too did Bureus utilize the preexisting myth of Gothicism to support Swedish national interests.

The historical Goths were tribes that probably migrated from what is now southern Sweden into eastern Europe around the second or first century BCE. During the third to fifth centuries CE, they continued to migrate through southeastern Europe and into the Mediterranean, where they did battle with the eastern and western Roman Empire, sacked the city of Rome itself in 410, and established powerful Gothic kingdoms in what is now Italy, Spain, and southern France. All the while they kept up relations with Scandinavia. But by the eighth century they had all but disappeared from history as a visible people; however, owing to their great achievements, they endured in Germanic and European myth, legend, and tradition. The mythic tradition surrounding the Goths, something known to the historians of ideas as "Gothicism," was especially strong in Scandinavia. It also remained important in Spain and England.

Gothicism is most usually seen as an interpretation of history and a model for political action or nationalistic identity on the part of the country in question, be it Sweden, Denmark, Spain, or England. However, as Thomas Karlsson points out, the Gothicism of Johannes Bureus was more profound. With him, Gothicism became a system for the esoteric education of the individual and for esoteric communication between the divine and human worlds. Ironically, yet fittingly, this approach had perhaps the greatest effect on history owing to the role it may have played in the education of Gustavus Adolphus, Sweden's most illustrious king, at the time when Sweden was a great world power.

Although this book deals with Bureus's work in the esoteric field, he was also a pioneer of scientific or academic runology—the study and interpretation of actual runic artifacts. Previously, the thousands of runestones scattered across the Scandinavian landscape, and especially in Bureus's own native Uppland, were seen as artifacts from before the Deluge recorded in Genesis and were created by "giants." Only isolated words were interpreted by humanists such as Olaus Petri (1493–1552) and Johannes Magnus (1488–1544). It was Johannes Bureus who first studied the runic artifacts in a systematic way. He was enabled in this endeavor by his "fieldwork" in the district of Dalarna, where runes were still being used by farmers for practical purposes. Bureus's method of decoding runic texts can be seen as an example of the Paracelsian method in the humanities. Bureus's first runological document, *Runakänlones lärospån* (1599), was a basic phonetic key to runic inscriptions. Eventually Bureus would record and interpret hundreds of actual runic texts. A short time later, similar, even more systematic work in runology was developed by the Dane and chief rival of Bureus, Ole Worm (Olaus Wormius). In this rivalry the roots of the two current approaches to runology can perhaps be seen. Bureus was a humanist and a spiritual man with interests in esoteric matters, while Wormius was a physician with a more empirical sensibility. Despite the fact that Bureus produced a number of works of scholarly value in the field of runology, it appears that his motivation for these studies remained something deeper and more radical. As such Bureus is the father of radical runology.

The works of Bureus bring the ancient gods and goddesses of the North once more into esoteric religious consideration as entities to be venerated and honored. Although his runology places the ancient Germanic gods in the forefront, Bureus does not, however, see the esoteric meaning of these gods as being anything essentially different from the esoteric meaning of Christianity. For him, Christ and Odin are one. As such he shows himself that he is an adherent of the perennial tradition, one of the true magi who, although outside the conventional understandings of the exoteric church, nevertheless honors Christ without abandoning the hidden truth. This secret knowledge is used to interpret Norse myth as well as the Bible and harmonizes their meanings. Unfortunately, during Bureus's lifetime relatively little was known of the deep and rich mythic lore of the ancient North. If he had had time to synthesize the contents of the *Poetic Edda* into his work it would have been far richer in Norse content. But the chief manuscript of this work was only discovered toward the end of Bureus's life. As his work stands, it can be seen as reflective of an initiated Hermetic-Rosicrucian understanding of the perennial tradition underlying a spectrum of mythic models typical of the best thinkers of his day.

Johannes Bureus is the father of modern esoteric runology and the first "high priest" of a renewed spiritual tradition that places the old gods of the North back in their natural and rightful place at the center of the spiritual life of the Germanic peoples. As such, he is worthy of our respect, and his work is deserving of our further attention. The present offering by Thomas Karlsson provides us with many tools to help us understand and honor this valiant pioneer.

INTRODUCTION TO
PART 2

Gothicism is associated by many people mainly with the Swedish fantasies of great power expressed in Olof Rudbeck's *Atlantica*, where it is maintained that Atlantis was situated in Sweden, or with the Götiska Förbund (Gothic League) and the bombastic nationalistic and Romantic poetry of the 1800s. Gothicism is a cultural movement that projects its origin back to the Goths, whose legendary great deeds the movement's followers wanted to ascribe to their own history. In Sweden the Goths were connected with the Geats, or in exceptional cases to the inhabitants of the island of Gotland, while in Denmark it was thought that the Goths and Jutes were related. Gothicism was characterized by grand fantasies and speculations and came to be meaningful in both cultural life and propaganda. Gothicism in general, and Swedish Gothicism in particular, lived in a close relationship with the esoteric currents that thrived throughout Europe. Ideas of Paracelsus and later the Rosicrucian awakening would influence Gothicism as much as anything. From this quarter came along apocalyptic predictions and prophecies that were useful in Gothic propaganda, but with this intellectual material also came Hermetic speculations of a significantly more individualistic character that emphasized humanity's gradual ascent toward a higher state of being. The foremost representative for the meeting between Gothicism and esotericism was the antiquarian Johannes Bureus, who was the teacher of King Gustavus Adolphus. Bureus was a pioneer in runology and Swedish linguistics and is acknowledged as the father of Swedish grammar, but Bureus himself thought that it was within the sphere of mysticism that he made his most important contribution.[1]

Bureus represents what we would call an esoteric Gothicism. In him the motif of Gothicism coalesces with the esotericism of his age, with such things as alchemy, Cabbala, Hermeticism, astrology, and magic. Bureus himself called his esoteric system for Nordic Cabbala a *notaricon suethia* or a *Cabala Upsalica*.[2] Bureus also applied the methods of the Cabbala to his runological research.[3] In speaking of an esoteric Gothicism we can differentiate this tendency in Gothicism from the nationalistic chauvinism that we normally associate with it. With Bureus the Gothic themes with runes and ancient Nordic themes appear in an equally imaginative way as with Rudbeck, but what is particular to Bureus is that he utilizes these themes to describe a highly individualistic initiatory path that leads to an alchemical and cabbalistic coalescence with God. Usually Gothicism, both the older and younger, is restricted to using the theme of the mystical Goths to support the kingdom or nation in a mythologized version of history. Esoteric Gothicism utilizes Gothic themes for individual initiatory purposes. In speaking of an exoteric Gothicism we can also include persons and groups that, in a way partially independent of Bureus's "Gothic Cabbala," incorporate elements in their Gothicism (or Gothic elements in their esotericism). That this is not merely to be thought of as esotericism in the most general sense is due to the importance placed on the myth of the Goths in the esoteric speculations. The Goths were thought to be the mystical exponents of the forgotten truth that mankind stood on the verge of reviving again.

This part is concerned with the esoteric elements in Gothicism as they are expressed in the writings of Johannes Bureus. The focus is on a description of Bureus's most important esoteric work: *Adulruna rediviva*.

As I approached the ideas of Bureus, I tried in the main to proceed from the source material that I read in Stockholm, Uppsala, and Linköping.* The most important source materials were the six manuscripts of Bureus's esoteric work titled *Adulruna rediviva*. Four of these are found in the National Library of Sweden in Stockholm, and two are found in the Carolina Rediviva in Uppsala. Bureus drew up seven versions of *Adulruna rediviva,* one of which disappeared from the National Library of Sweden in 1812. There is also a manuscript in the National Library of Sweden titled *Antiquitates Scanziana* that in part has contents similar to that of *Adulruna rediviva*. *Antiquitates Scanziana* is more comprehensive, and one finds in it a significant amount of valuable information about Bureus's esoteric thought. Bureus's runic account mostly describes the linguistic implications of the runes but reflects certain esoteric trains of thought as well. Printed texts such as *Runa ABC-boken, Runa redux,* and apocalyptic writings such as *Nordlandalejonsens rytande* (Roar of the Nordic lion) give an insight into Bureus's intellectual values. In Linköping's diocesan library I studied Bureus's highly interesting, but muddled, notebook titled *Cabbalistica,* which reveals much of his own references and those esoteric thoughts that characterize his works. In Linköping is also found the linguistic *Om språkens uppkomst* (On the origin of language), which describes his mystical view of language. Two aids that were indispensable as I studied Bureus were a sketchbook and a pocket calculator. Only by drawing Bureus's Hermetic symbols and calculating his cabbalistic numerical values did his ideas become fairly intelligible.

To complete the picture of the Gothic ideas I also looked at writings by Stiernhielm, for example, a manuscript by him that also had the word *Adulruna* in the title but that has different contents than Bureus's work. Additionally, later Rosicrucians such as Erik Julius Björner and Johan Göransson were of interest—as, for

---

*See the descriptions of sources in chapter 13, "Esoteric Gothicism after Bureus," and in the list of sources in the bibliography.

example, Göransson's *Is atlinga* (1747)—as well as writings from later Gothicism such as the periodical *Iduna* of the Götiska Förbund (Gothic League) and Jonas Love Almqvist's description of the degrees of the Manhem League.

Besides these source materials, I found Hans Hildebrand's biography of Bureus of 1910, Sten Lindroth's classic treatise of 1943 titled *Paracelsismen i Sverige till 1600-talets mitt,* as well as Susanna Åkerman's treatise *Rose Cross over the Baltic* (1998) extremely useful. Susanna Åkerman has written several scientific articles on Bureus. Hildebrand, Lindroth, and Åkerman have written the most detailed descriptions of Bureus and his esoteric work. Bureus is noticed many times mainly for his contributions as a linguist, as in Hjalmar Lindroth's *J. Th. Bureus: Den svenska grammatikens fader* (1911). In his role as a typographer Bureus is described in *De yverbornes typografi* by Nils Nordqvist (1964). Bureus is mentioned in a more popular scientific context in Sten Lindroth's collection of essays *Fru Lusta och Fru Dygd* (1957) and in Mats G. Larsson's *Sveahövdingens budskap* (2000). An article about Bureus's apocalyptic speculations by Henrik Sandblad is found in *Lychnos* (1959). In Björn Anderson's dissertation, "Runor, magi, ideologi: En idéhistorisk studie" (1997), which focuses on Sigurd Agrell, there is a chapter on Bureus that mainly seems to be based on Lindroth's treatise. The Texan Stephen Flowers wrote a short booklet on Bureus partially based on Hindebrand.[4] Bureus's name surfaces in a few different books, but any more detailed studies are rare. Bureus appears in a literary context in Erik Lundberg's *Vid språkets rötter* (1994).

A good deal has been written about Gothicism in general, such as A. Blanck's *Den nordiska renässansen i sjuttonhundratalets litteratur* (1911); Kurt Johannesson's *The Renaissance of the Goths in Sixteenth-Century Sweden: Johannes and Olaus Magnus as Politicians and Historians* (1991); J. Mjöberg, *Drömmen om sagatiden 1–2* (1967–1968); and B. Grandien *Rönndruvans glöd: Nygötiskt i tanke, konst och miljö under 1800-talet* (1987). Johan Nordström's *De yverbornes ö* of 1934 is a classic study. Johan Nordström also published Stiernhielm's

Den Svenska
A B C Boken/

På thet enfalligeste så stält / at de
vanlige bokstavarne lämpa sigh efter Runerne/och bådhe semias
medh wår vanlighe Pro-
nunciation.

Visdoms början san/ är vist Gudz
alvara fruchtan:
Vis migh visan man / dän i yngskone
ratadhe fruchtan.

Trykt i Vpsala/ af Eskil Matzson/
år / 1624.

philosophical fragment with a detailed introduction to Stiernhielm's esoteric world of ideas. Mats Malm's treatise, *Minervas äpple: Om diktsyn, tolkning och bildspråk inom nordisk göticism,* which came out in 1996, is a further contribution to research concerning Gothicism. Ingmar Stenroth published *Myten om goterna* in the year 2002 and took up Gothicism both in Sweden and abroad from antiquity up to Romanticism. Gunnar Eriksson published the extensive and prize-winning biography *Rudbeck 1630–1702: Liv, lärdom, dröm i barockens Sverige.* At present the author of this work is writing a doctoral dissertation about Johannes Bureus and the Gothic Cabbala.

10

GOTHICISM AND
WESTERN ESOTERICISM

Within the history of religion, Western esotericism has developed into a new field of research and become one of the most conspicuous areas of study seen internationally.[1] The research into Western esotericism spans areas such as Cabbala, alchemy, ritual magic, Rosicrucian movements, Freemasonry, seventeenth-century occultism, and contemporary phenomena such as Wicca and the New Age. For a long time esotericism was observed with skepticism from academic quarters. Theologians conceptualized esoteric teachings as being heretical, and natural scientists viewed them as superstitious and reactionary.[2] The researcher Frances Yates (1899–1981) maintained, contrary to contemporary understanding, that esotericism, or what she called "the Hermetic tradition," was entirely derived from the development of the modern sciences.

The concept of Western esotericism is a methodological construction that researchers developed to cover several different movements, thinkers, and traditions that, despite great differences, have meaningful common denominators. Western esotericism can be viewed as a third stream of thought alongside Greek rational thought and Judeo-Christian faith, the two great intellectual traditions upon which Western culture rests. Within Western esotericism there is a resistance to both rational thought and dogmatic faith. Humanity and the universe are seen in a holistic way as reflections of each other, which implies that humans can obtain knowledge about God and nature by studying their own interior worlds, and also, on the other hand, that investigations of nature and theological studies help humans to discover truths about that interior world. Furthermore, esotericism is characterized by this development in understanding occurring gradually through different stages of initiation. The basic traits of Western occultism are to be found throughout Gnosticism and Hermeticism, even though the concept of Western esotericism most designates the thought that developed during the Renaissance, when Cabbala, Neoplatonism, medieval magic, and Hermeticism were combined.[3]

Western esotericism got its special stamp from Renaissance thinkers such as Marsilio Ficino and Pico della Mirandola. Ficino, who was commissioned by Cosimo de' Medici to found a Platonic academy in Florence in the 1450s, was asked ten years later by Medici to put his work aside and instead devote himself to the *Corpus Hermeticum.* This text had been rediscovered in Macedonia, and in 1471 the first Latin translation was finished. It was circulated in no less than twenty-five editions up to 1641, not counting all the other translations that were also done. The mythical author of the text, Hermes Trismegistus, was thought to belong to a remote time, and his writings were thought to present the *philosophia perennis,* the perennial philosophy. This *philosophia perennis* had been formulated from all the ancient doctrines of wisdom, and through the idea of an original doctrine of wisdom different traditions could be combined and correspondences established.[4] These ideas were collected under the designation Hermeticism, which is often used synonymously with esotericism. Regarding the concept of Hermeticism, Antoine Faivre writes that it can designate (*a*) esotericism in the most general sense, (*b*) alchemy, and (*c*) the Greek writings from the beginning of our era that are ascribed to Hermes Trismegistus. Faivre suggests that a new verbal construction—namely, "Hermetism"—ought to be used to designate the broader interpretation of Hermeticism, which includes esotericism in its different forms.[5]

The esoteric tradition maintains that it is primeval or even timeless. Among scholars of religion one finds various conceptions of the history of the esoteric tradition. Olav Hammer indicates in his treatise *Claiming Knowledge: Strategies of Epistemology from Theosophy to the New Age* that there are two main conceptions among historians of religion.

> One group may delineate the historical development different than the adherents would, yet still agree in drawing parallels with older traditions. Not infrequently, the Esoteric Tradition is seen as a modern manifestation of a tradition dating back to renaissance hermeticism, or reaching back still further to the Gnostics, or even to pythagoreanism and orphicism. There is a good case to be made for a different view of history, espoused by a second group of scholars, in which such links to premodern epochs are seen as more tenuous due to a radical modernization of these earlier traditions.[6]

The adjective *esoteric* goes back to antiquity and was introduced around the year 166 by Lucianos of Samosata. The word *esotericism* as a noun is of a later date and was popularized by the Frenchman Alphonse Louis Constant, also known under the pseudonym Éliphas Lévi, and the word was introduced into English by the Theosophist A. D. Sinnet in 1883. Lévi even introduced the concept of *occultism,* a word that was probably invented by him, with inspiration from Agrippa's *De Occulta Philosophia* of 1533.[7] The concepts of occultism and esotericism have often been thought to indicate the same phenomena, but many scholars have thought it useful to keep these concepts separate. Wouter J. Hanegraaf argues that the concept of occultism ought to be used to designate a specific development within esotericism.[8]

A classic definition of esotericism comes from the sociologist

Edward E. Tiryakian. He defines it as the belief system or the theoretical knowledge upon which the practices that constitute occultism are based. Occultism is the practice, and esotericism is the theory. Tiryakian writes:

> By esoteric I refer to those religiophilosophic belief systems which underlie occult techniques and practices; that is, it refers to the more comprehensive cognitive mappings of nature and cosmos, the epistemological and ontological reflections of ultimate reality, which mappings constitute a stock of knowledge that provides the ground for occult procedures.[9]

Antoine Faivre has accepted Tiryakian's application of the concepts but has indicated that they contain certain weaknesses, as there are practical sides of esotericism and theoretical ones in occultism.[10]

In his *Access to Western Esotricism,* Antoine Faivre writes that esotericism is not a field such as art, philosophy, or chemistry but rather a way of thinking. Faivre explains that

> the etymology of "esotericism" clarifies the idea of secret by suggesting that we can access understanding of a symbol, myth, or reality only by a personal effort of progressive elucidation through several successive levels, i.e., by a form of hermeneutics. There is no ultimate secret once we determine that everything, in the end, conceals a secret.[11]

Faivre actually thinks that six criteria have to be met before one can speak in a useful way about anything specifically esoteric (among other things to differentiate it from non-esoteric initiations), of which four are the most important. The criteria he enumerates are (1) universal correspondences, (2) living nature, (3) imagination and mediation, (4) experience of transmutation, together with (5) traditional concordance, and (6) transmission.[12]

(1) Correspondences involve the idea of hidden connections between the visible and invisible parts of the universe, in accordance with the Hermetic motto "As above, so below." Connections exist between minerals, the human body, plants, and so on.

(2) The idea of a living nature proceeds from the view that the cosmos is a complex, manifold, and hierarchical unity where nature occupies an important place along with God and man. Nature is permeated by a light, or a fire, and is rich in potential revelations and could therefore be read like a book. But Faivre also thinks, which is important, that since the beginning of the 1900s there also arose a monistic spiritualism, inspired by Oriental mysticism in which nature is disregarded or even denied.

(3) Imagination and mediations. Esotericism is differentiated from mysticism by the emphasis on intermediary levels between the terrestrial and the divine. The doctrine of angels and other intermediary beings is important in this context, as is the idea of gurus and initiators. Where mysticism sees the imagination as an obstacle, esotericism sees it as a means to an end. Faivre expressively describes this:

> Understood thus, imagination (*imaginatio* is related to *magnet, magia, imago*) is the tool for knowledge of self, world, Myth. The eye of fire pierces the bark of appearances to call forth significations, "rapports" to render the invisible world visible, the "*mundus imaginalis*" to which the eye of the flesh alone cannot provide access, and to retrieve there a treasure contributing to an enlargement of our prosaic vision.[13]

(4) Experience of transmutation. Without the experience of transmutation as an important component esotericism could be mixed up with some form of speculative spirituality. The word *transmutation* comes from alchemy and indicates a transition or transformation from one plane to another, the subject's metamorphosis to higher levels.

To these four basic components within esotericism can be added two related components as follows:

(5) Concordance is found between different religions and doctrines, and it is possible to discover common denominators that unify them.

(6) Transmission. Knowledge can or must be transmitted from teacher to pupil according to a given model, often through initiations. Conditions for this "second birth" are that (*a*) the teachers are respected and not called into question, as one becomes part of this tradition, and (*b*) that initiation occurs though some teacher or master.

Hanegraaf indicates that it is important, as historians of religion, to differentiate Faivre's application of the concept of esotericism from the popular use of the term that can be found in New Age contexts, where the concept of esotericism has taken on new implications. Hanegraaf cites Christoph Bochinger, who describes how the concept of esotericism came to be applied within the New Age, where it is

> first and foremost a concept referring to Individualkultur according to the motto "You have it all inside yourself, check it out!". . . . Thus Esotericism changes . . . from a special tradition of knowledge into a special type of "religion," the "journey within.". . . Similar to the word "spirituality," "esotericism" thus became a surrogate word for "religion," which accentuates its subjective element focused on inner experience.[14]

Faivre's method of investigating Western esotericism has come to be the one most commonly used in the field. Faivre succeeded François Secret, who, until 1979, had the first professorship in the subject called "the history of esoteric Christianity," which was founded in 1965 at the École Practique des Hautes Études, Sorbonne. When Faivre took over, the title of the professorship was changed to "esoteric and mystical currents in modern and contemporary European history." In 1999 another professorship was founded in the subject at the University of Amsterdam with the title "the history of Hermetic philosophy and closely related currents" and is held by Wouter J. Hanegraaf. Two full-time scholars are connected to the institute: Olav Hammer and Jean-Pierre Brach. The latter left the institute to take a professorship at the Sorbonne. The institute in Amsterdam offers courses from the under-graduate level to doctoral studies.[15]

Henrik Bogdan, a scholar of religion at Göteborg University, opened a Swedish department of Faivre's research organization, ARIES (Association for Research and Information on Esotericism), and now conducts a course on esotericism at the University of Göteborg. In an article on Western esotericism Bogdan writes:

> The study of Western esotericism does not merely deal with the obser-vation of earlier forgotten or suppressed aspects of Western culture, or the understanding of the historical context for modern phenom-ena such as the New Age, but rather it deals above all with the wid-ening and deepening of our knowledge about, and understanding of, Western culture in its totality. The topic of Western esotericism does not simply comprise an isolated group of traditions exclusively of interest to historians of religion, but rather this is also of impor-tance for an interdisciplinary understanding of our history and con-temporary world. Literary historians, art historians, and musicologists increasingly make their presence felt in the forum where Western eso-tericism is discussed, which testifies to the cultural anchoring that the esoteric currents had—and to a great extent still have. The study of Western esotericism promotes a reinterpretation and a suggestion of the conceptions we have about what composes our culture.[16]

If we want to have a deeper understanding of the driving forces and the fantasies that nourished Gothicism, it is also useful to investigate its points of contact with Western esotericism.

INITIATION

The third (imagination and mediations), fourth (experience of transmutation), and sixth (transmission) criteria for esotericism, according to Faivre, all point to to the idea that there are different levels of reality that the adept is to investigate and penetrate. This investigation occurs through initiation. Initiation is a key concept within esotericism. The goal of initiation is to reveal the hidden kernel that is concealed behind the outer appearance of phenomena. Through initiation the adept comes into contact with the interior part of religion and myth and receives knowledge about their concealed truths. The classic initiatory theme is based on a symbolic death, descent into the underworld, and rebirth and return. The initiate leaves his old life and his old ego behind and is reborn, often with a new name that represents the new person.[17]

Mircea Eliade explains initiation in his *Rites and Symbols of Initiation* in the following way:

> The central moment of every initiation is represented by the ceremony symbolizing the death of the novice and his return to the fellowship of the living. But he returns to life as a new man, assuming another mode of being. Initiatory death signifies the end at once of childhood, or ignorance, and of the profane condition.[18]

Concepts such as ascent and descent and that opposites merge into one another recur constantly in the description of esoteric initiation. One's old life is represented as a cage or a prison of ignorance, from which initiation and esoteric enlightenment provide liberation. Johannes Bureus equates the lowest rung on his runological ladder toward enlightenment with a cage.[19] The same ideas are found in the initiatory system of the Manhem League in which the first degree represents humankind in its state of darkness. In the lowest degree the adept in Manhem is supposed to realize that impurity and ignorance characterized the world and his earlier life.[20] Even if much distinguishes Bureus's Hermetic runic initiation, with its apocalyptic character, from the educational and socially aware initiatory system of the Manhem League, both are nevertheless influenced by the initiatory mysticism of the esoteric tradition. Bureus emulated the Hermetic and Rosicrucian models that were widespread during his lifetime. The Manhem League was given shape by the surrounding secret orders during the 1800s and emulated the Freemasonic order structure, almost in a Gotho-Nordic form.

THE PROPHETS
OF GOTHICISM

The year was 1434, and there was an ecclesiastical conference in progress in Basel. Representatives of the Christian nations had been assembled to discuss the business of the church. It was not long before a clamor arose among the delegates who could not agree about how they were to arrange their seating. Everyone wanted to sit on the right side, as it was the most distinguished, and everyone wanted to be seated in the most advantageous position as possible. The lesser nations realized that they would find themselves seated in the less prestigious places, but large nations such as England and Spain could not agree about who it was who deserved the best seat. In the midst of the dispute Sweden's envoy, Nicolaus Ragvaldi, suddenly rose and openly declared that it was Sweden that deserved the most distinguished place. In a speech that caused amazement among the other delegates Ragvaldi explained that Sweden had at one time been the most powerful and most meaningful nation of all. The Goths originated in Sweden, of course. This people had subdued the world, and all the European nations were well acquainted with their history.[1] The Castilian delegates used their Gothic heritage as an argument to receive a favorable placement at the church meeting.[2] Ragvaldi wanted to remind those gathered that the Goths came from Götaland, which was in Sweden, and that they were a powerful people who vanquished Persian kings, such as Cyrus and Darius; took part in the Trojan War; made themselves known for their warrior women, the Amazons; and last but not least, subdued the powerful Roman Empire. He also reminded them that the Spanish kings and the Spanish aristocracy stemmed from the land of the Goths in the north. The Spaniards grumbled and asserted that it was much more distinguished to be descended from the brave emigrants than from the cowards who stayed behind. Despite his speech Ragvaldi had to be satisfied with a more ordinary place within the church meeting, but his speech was of great importance and was used as a diplomatic means of exerting pressure whenever the Swedes wanted to assert their historical rights. Over time the speech almost became a document of the rights of the state and is the most important source for early Swedish Gothicism.[3]

Ragvaldi actually provided nothing new. The history of the Goths was well known and accepted. One of the oldest portrayals of Swedish history is Ericus Olais's *Chronica regni gothorum* (History of the Gothic Kingdom) from the 1400s. As the title of the book shows, it was considered quite obvious to speak about the Goths in connection with Swedish history. In the *Fornsvenska legendariet* from the latter half of the 1200s we meet Gothic history being seen as the same thing as Swedish history.[4] Already in 1081, Pope Gregory VII uses the word *wisi-gothi* for Sweden's *west-götar*.[5] Sweden's linkage with the Goths has its most important source in the *Getica,* a text by the Romano-Gothic historian Jordanes. Jordanes wrote his chronicle about the Goths in 551. Jordanes was of Gothic extraction and wanted to give prominence to the Goths as a people who loved learning, contrary to Roman opinion.[6] They were not only the people who conquered Rome, but he also wanted to indicate all of the good traits that characterized the Goths. At one time they had emigrated together with their king, Berik, from the island of Scandza; that is, Scandinavia. They fared forth on three ships from Scandinavia, and the crews of these gave rise to the three tribes: Ostrogoths, Visigoths, and Gepids. In a few lines often cited by Gothicists, Jordanes describes the exodus: "It is related that the Goths once emigrated with their king, Berig, from that island, like unto from a workshop where peoples are created, or as if out of a womb of nations."[7]

Jordanes gives an account of the attack of Italy and the plundering of Rome that happened under the leadership of the Visigothic king Alaric. He also reports about the great Ostrogothic heretic Theodoric the Great as well as the different battles in which the Goths were involved. Jordanes's chronicle is the most important document for Gothic history. In the year 98 CE the Roman historian Tacitus had already written about the Goths, the *gotones,* in his *Germania.*[8] The Goths and the other Germanic peoples north of Rome were seen by Tacitus as noble savages with upstanding morality and ability in war. They are contrasted with a culturally weary and decadent empire, such as Rome. Both Greeks and Romans idealized the barren frontiers in the north where peoples lived a simple but vital and free life. They were of the opinion that the climate shaped hardy people with superhuman powers.[9] The Greeks thought that both their gods and they themselves had their original roots in the faraway lands in the north. The Greek historian Herodotus thought that the goddess Leto came from the land of Hyperborea in the outermost north and came to Greece, where she gave birth to Artemis and Apollo.[10] This so-called Hyperborean motif, with its roots in ancient Greece, would be the other very important pillar within Gothicism: the myth of the Hyperboreans and the history of the Goths.[11] It is where the Hyperborean motif is melded to the history of the Goths that Gothicism becomes especially interesting for the historian of religion. Gods and other entities became an important component of Gothic speculations.

THE BROTHERS MAGNUS

The early Swedish Gothicists had certainly not come to utilize the possibility of uniting these motifs. Johannes Magnus and his brother, Olaus Magnus, are among the most important personages within early Swedish Gothicism. A good century after Ragvaldi's remarkable speech came the next important event in the history of Swedish Gothicism. In 1554,

Johannes Magnus published a history of the kings of the Goths and Swedes, *Historia de Omnibus Gothorum Sueonumque Regibus.* It followed in the footsteps of Ragvaldi and represented Swedish history as something unique and magnificent. Johannes Magnus was a Catholic archbishop who found himself in exile in Rome and there encountered many questions concerning his homeland. He wanted to report concerning his homeland's fantastic history and to give Sweden a place beside the great European nations. Despite the fact that he took the opportunity to criticize Gustav Vasa (King Gustav I), Vasa saw great advantages in the book, and it was circulated widely, as through it Gothic ideas became even more useful. The book was translated into Swedish in 1620.[12]

Johannes's brother, Olaus Magnus, published a complementary history of the Nordic people, *Historia de Gentibus Septenrionalibus,* in 1555.[13] Olaus Magnus and his brother saw the runestones as a proof for the antiquity of Swedish culture. When the Romans were still a barbaric and illiterate people, literature and culture flourished in the North.[14] They were convinced that the great runestones must have been dragged into place by giants in the primordial ages, apparently at some point before the Deluge.[15] The brothers, who lived in exile, wanted to describe the North because in discussions with learned men on the Continent they discovered that old geographical and ethnological descriptions of the North were inadequate and unsatisfactory.[16] In 1539, Olaus Magnus had the *Carta Marina* printed. This was the first fairly accurate map of Scandinavia. High up on the map stands the mythical warrior Starkader with a rune tablet under each arm. These runes are of the same type that the brothers published fifteen years later in their "Gothic alphabet," a runic alphabet in ABC order with explanatory Latin letters over every rune. Olaus Magnus wrote that the Nordic people had had their own language since time immemorial and that they wrote to each other on pieces of wood, something he maintained was still done during war since wood is more durable than paper and was more available. The two brothers honored the country from which they were exiled, and in one of the many illustrations in Olaus Magnus's book there appears the phrase "preserve the ancient monuments" in Latin.[17]

In spite of the fact that it was close at hand, the brothers Magnus did not connect the history of the Goths with the myths of the Hyperboreans. This is remarkable since Johannes Magnus was very familiar with Jacob Ziegler's text *Schondia* (1532) in which this connection is made.[18] The high point of Swedish Gothicism was achieved in the 1600s, and it was then that the connection between the Hyperboreans and the Goths was seen as being obvious. Hyperboreans became Goths, and Greek myths became Swedish ones. Most consider Olof Rudbeck as the great representative of Gothicism, but one of the most important personages of Swedish Gothicism in the 1600s was Johannes Bureus. Even if he is relatively unknown to the general public in comparison with Rudbeck, Bureus has been called the father of Swedish grammar, the first pioneer of runology, and the high priest of Gothicism.

JOHANNES BUREUS

Johan Bure (1568–1652), or Johannes Bureus, the name by which he is best known, is one of Gothicism's most singular figures. In his works the Gothic myths would be reinterpreted so that they did not exclusively emphasize the history of the Swedish kingdom but could also be used as a path of individual enlightenment. With Bureus, older Gothicism and his runic and linguistic research were blended with his interest in the occultism of his time.

In an annotation under a picture of a runestone Bureus mentions the point in time when his runic investigations began, as he noted, "*Denna lärde migh först läsa runor 1594 widh lagh*" ("This first taught me to read runes around 1594").[19] The works of Johannes Bureus were decisive for the birth of a Swedish grammar.[20] He was also a great pioneer of runology and the one who reshaped the Gothic ideology in a very personal way. In 1599 he completed the first-ever printed work on runes. It was a large copper engraving in folio format called *Runakänslanes lärospan,* which was also called "The great rune table of Bureus."[21]

Bureus's Little Rune Table

☞ All Wijsheet är af Herrans Gudi/och är å när honom/Hans wijsheet är för all tingh. Gudz Ord är Wijsheetz/ ...de bennm. Herren hafwer genom sin Anda förkunnat henne. Han hafwer vthgutit henne öfwer all sijn werk.

Svenska ABC BOKEN medh RVNOR.

SVEA ARVN

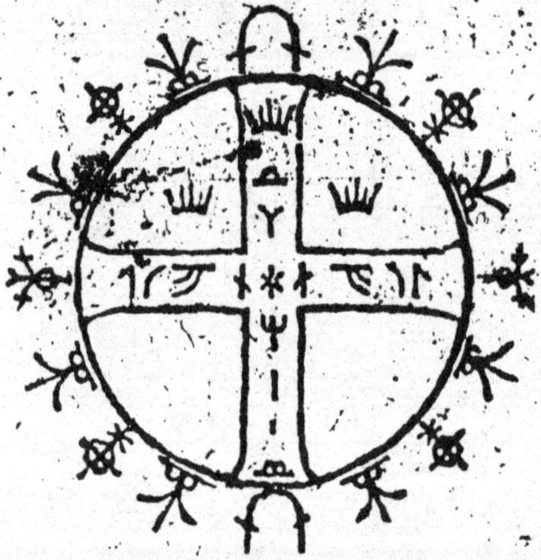

VPSALA RVNA

☞ Gudhz fruchtan är början til Wijsheet.

Stockholm/ 1 6 1 1.

medh tije åra frijheet.

The word *känsla* ("sense") characterizes the time and the science of the time. In this work Bureus illustrated many runestones and showed different types of rune rows with the phonetic values of the runes.[22] The runic investigations of Bureus were seen as so meaningful that the Swedish king forbade him to travel outside the country since the history of ancient times might be lost if anything happened to Bureus.[23] Bureus thought that Christianity and Latin had displaced the runes, and he wanted to make an attempt at reintroducing knowledge of them, so he published *Runa ABC-bok*. One of Bureus's greatest accomplishments in the burgeoning science of runology was his comprehensive survey of runestones. He managed to document 663 runestones. That is approximately a fourth of all those known in Sweden up until today.[24]

A runology was developed by Johannes Bureus that both maintained itself within a linguistic framework and drifted into deep esoteric speculations. Bureus, who was active in Uppsala, was inspired by the Cabbala and alchemy and read Agrippa, Paracelsus, Reuchlin, and other great names in occultism.[25] In a comparison to the Cabbala he was convinced that the runes also had different dimensions, partly as written signs but also as esoteric and magical symbols.[26] He developed a Gothic Cabbala, which he called the *Cabala Upsalica*. He called the secret dimension of the runes *adulrunor* or *adelrunor*. Moreover, he constructed a symbol he called Adulruna, which also contains the fifteen adulrunor. As noted above, the symbol has similarities to the Monas Hieroglyphica of the Welsh English occultist John Dee, a symbol that contains all the planetary symbols.[27] Bureus's Adulruna is a map of the universe and of man's development through different levels of existence. The Adulruna functions both as a symbol of mankind and of the universe, of the microcosmos as well as the macrocosmos. Bureus's most important esoteric text was titled *Adulruna rediviva*, "The adulruna revived."

With the birth of Gothic runology during the time when Sweden was a great power, one could say that a certain type of runic rebirth took place. The runes were used among many Swedish officers during the Thirty Years War (1618–1648) to encode communications.[28]

What is special about Bureus's Gothic runic research is that the runes are not merely seen as age-old written signs that demonstrate the ancient Norseman's literary qualities but that they were primarily symbols for an individual path of initiation and enlightenment in which the adept attains contact with God. Bureus's esoteric runology was also known about outside Sweden, and he received visits from long-distance guests who wanted to be instructed in the secrets of the adulrunor.[29] On his deathbed Bureus declared that it was his investigations into mysticism that he was most proud of, despite his meaningful contributions in linguistics.[30] His successors as royal antiquarians, such as Stiernhielm and Verelius, were to take up some of Bureus's ideas. At the same time they distanced themselves from his most occult and cabbalistic speculations.[31] The ideas he was probably most proud of, and which he worked out in several editions of *Adulruna rediviva,* appear not to have won any larger following. The thoughts were perhaps so personal, difficult to grasp, and occult that they had difficulty in receiving a more widespread distribution. This is at the same time quite remarkable since many mystics after Bureus appear to have developed similar trains of thought in ways independent of him, regardless of whether we speak of the Manhem League's Gothic initiatory grades or the runic mysticism of the Aryosophist Guido von List. Despite many similarities, it appears that these others developed their systems without direct influence from Bureus.

OLOF RUDBECK

With Olof Rudbeck's *Atlantica,* Swedish Gothicism of the 1600s reaches its zenith. It is also called *Atland eller Manhem* and consists of four thick volumes, the last of which is unfinished. Rudbeck is inspired by Snorri's *Edda,* which had a great distribution at this time and which is one of Gothicism's most important sources of inspiration. Rudbeck elevates Snorri's principles of substitution to a hermeneutic principle with which he can prove that a number of accounts in Greek mythology really deal with Sweden. When Rudbeck tries to explain why Plato talks about elephants in his portrayal of Atlantis it is because this is a circumlocution referring to wolves, which proves that nothing is to be found that contradicts his basic thesis that Atlantis was actually Sweden.[32] Despite the fact that *Atlantica* was already controversial in its own time, it enjoyed a significant influence. Several points of contact are to be found between Bureus and Rudbeck, even though they represent two different conceptual models of Gothicism. Rudbeck is a representative of an extreme form of nationalistically self-assertive Gothicism, while Bureus represents a Gothically colored esotericism that penetrates into the individual's experiences of the supernal plane.

Olof Rudbeck has become somewhat of an introductory figure when it comes to describing Gothicism. He gave rise to his own current, which is called Rudbeckianism and which had many adherents. But there is a reason to keep Rudbeckianism and Gothicism apart. As Mats Malm indicates in his doctoral dissertation "Minervas äpple," many disassociated themselves from Rudbeckianism during the 1700s without necessarily abandoning the basic principles of Gothicism. Dalin's *Swea rikes historia* is usually thought of as a revolution in the writing of Swedish history, but as Mats Malm indicates, this work calls Rudbeckianism into question, but not Gothicism. Dalin still has the basic attitude of Gothicism and is of the opinion that the Gothic language is the mother of all Germanic languages. What he distances himself from is the fantastic assertion of Rudbeckianism that the Gothic language was spoken before the confusion of languages at the Tower of Babel. Rudbeckianism can be seen as the outermost pole of Gothicism, where it serves national and historical demands.[33]

Over time Rudbeckian authority would diminish and adherents would become even fewer. Two gentlemen who stubbornly defended Rudbeck's ideas were Erik Julius Björner (1696–1750) and Johan Göransson (1712–1769). Björner was in a bitter feud with lesser scholars of a Rudbeckian bent, such as Olof Celsius. Björner could, among other things, not stand the fact that they wanted to de-emphasize the antiquity of the runes. Many times he found himself having his Rudbeckian theories shot down, but occasionally he came away from the fray victorious, as when he was able to prove that the Hälsinge runes were younger than the normal runes and not the other way around, as Celsius maintained.[34] Björner published a series of Old Icelandic sagas in *Nordiska kämpa dater,* which would become his most important literary work and one that would come to inspire the circle around the Gothic League.

Johan Göransson, who was somewhat younger, wrote patriotic books about runes and history. In 1746 he came out with a translation and interpretation of Snorri's *Edda* and published it under the title *De yverborna atlingars eller sviogötars ok nordmänners Edda* (The super-patriots: Edda of the Atlings or Sveagoths and Norsemen).[35] It contained only Snorri's prolog and the *Gylfaginning.*

Johan Göransson was an esotericist and was intellectually close to Bureus.[36] Göransson developed ideas in the spirit of Bureus about the spiritual content of the runes. He thought, "Wherever there is a rune there is a sermon."[37] The basic stave (|) signifies the initial letter of Jehovah and indicates ice and *J;* that is, As, or God. The rune row's first sign, the Feh rune, indicates the trinity, and the rune Madhur shows the crucified Christ.[38] According to Göransson the runes were created by Jephat's son, Gomer. Since his time the true teaching of the North was embraced, a teaching found concealed in the *Edda.* The Gothic kings, such as Bore, Odin, and Thor, were adherents of the true doctrine. These kings were elevated to the level of gods by other people. Thor was identical with the Egyptian Thoth and the Persian Zoroaster (Tor-As).[39]

Göransson received the commission from the king and the royal estate for collecting and publishing the great body of runic material that, since the time when Sweden had been a great power, had been stored in the archive of antiquities. The members of the college of antiquities strongly objected to the upstart Göransson receiving this commission. They effectively restricted his freedom and proposed that Göransson's prospective commentaries should be approved by Olof Celsius. Göransson was not at all aware of the esteemed runologist's antipathy toward the "disorderly" speculations of the kind Göransson was prone to making.[40] Göransson nevertheless finally published his last and most important work, *Bautil,* in which 1,173 runestones were cataloged and ordered according to geographical area. Despite the resistance, Göransson was successful in including a good part of his Rudbeckian theories, such as that the runestones were raised immediately after the Deluge and that the *Edda* is concerned with a Hyperborean theology in which Balder was the equivalent of Christ.[41]

THE GOTHIC LEAGUE AND LATER GOTHICISM

Later Gothicism began during the early 1800s. It had been preceded by a period of decline for Gothicism and a time of disinterest in things Nordic. The earlier form of Gothicism and Rudbeckianism had disappeared, or been scoffed at in learned circles, and only a few people such as Björner and Göransson had dared to be representatives of Gothicism during the 1700s. As a reaction to this disinterest the Gothic League was founded in 1811, and Geijer, Ling, and Tegnér were among the prominent figures. The aims of the league were literary as well as cultural, and patriotic in general. Inspired by Danish nativistic Romantics such as Grundtvig and Oelenschläger, they wanted to revive the "spirit of freedom" and "manly courage" of the Goths. They read Björner's *Nordiska kämpa dater* and wrote poems inspired by Norse mythology. They extolled the old Nordic myths and Icelandic sagas. They hoped that these would inspire a Gothic awakening. Atterbom published the mythological poem "Skaldar-Mal" in 1811 with commentaries in which he explained that the Nordic gods represented abstract principles. For example, Thor was "the symbol of the masculine principle of Divinity, the Light or Intelligence that stimulates the natural basis or the original imagination."[42] In the journal of the Gothic League, *Iduna,* each of the runes is presented furnished with a little poem that harkens back to the procedure we found practiced by Johan Göransson.[43]

Johan G. Liljegren (1789–1837) was a member of the Gothic

League who played an important role in giving runology a place in science again. He was awarded the medal of the Academy of Antiquities for his work *Anmärkningar öfver Runorna och Runminnesmärken i Norden*. In contrast to most earlier runologists, Liljegren did not get into the problem of speculating about the origin of the runes but instead restricted himself to demonstrating why he did not consider himself able to determine their origin.[44] In 1832 Liljegren published his important *Run-Lära* which would be decisive for all of runology during the 1800s.[45] He refers to the ideas of Verelius about the magical powers of the runes, which are based on the same concept as that of Bureus; namely, that the runes have many concealed levels.[46]

Although the Gothic League admired the *Eddas* as fine examples of "folk poetry," it was not just anyone who was accepted as a member. The league wanted to gather a small number of prominent poets and academic experts in old Nordic culture.[47] A somewhat different direction was taken by the Gothic Manhem League, which in part shared the same membership, but it was oriented more toward youth and focused on gymnastics and rites of initiation.

Gothicism can be divided into some main phases. These coincide to a great extent with phases within literary history. In the article "Den fornnordiska musan: Rapport från ett internationellt forskningsprojekt" in *Myter om det nordiska—mellan romantik och politik* by Margaret Clunies Ross and Lars Lönnroth, the history of the reception of old Nordic literature is divided into the following five phases.

1. From Snorri's *Edda* to Laufá's *Edda* (ca. 1230–1600)
2. Scandinavian Gothicism and the Baroque (ca. 1600–1750)
3. The Nordic Renaissance and Pre-Romanticism (ca. 1750–1800)
4. National Romanticism (ca. 1800–1870)
5. The Decline of National Romanticism (after ca. 1870)[48]

The first phase is where we find the early manuscripts that connect Sweden and the Swedes with the Goths and also with the Hyperboreans in certain contexts. To this period belong Ragvaldi, Ericus Olai, and the brothers Magnus.

The second phase is the period with which we most strongly associate with Swedish or Scandinavian Gothicism. To this period belong Johannes Bureus, Georg Stiernhielm, Olof Verelius, and Olof Rudbeck. During this period an extreme form of Gothicism arose that was developed by Rudbeck and is therefore called Rudbeckianism. We can count Erik Björner and Johan Göransson as later successors to this period.

The third period is most often called the Nordic Renaissance, which is a concept coined by the literary historian Anton Blanck in his book *Den nordiska renässansen i sjuttonhundratalets literature* (1911). Blanck described this as a Pre-Romantic literary current inspired by Eddic poetry and Norse mythology that was introduced by the Swiss historian Paul-Henri Mallet and that was developed by such predecessors of Romanticism as the Englishmen Thomas Percy and Thomas Gray and the German Johann Gottfried Herder.[49] During this phase ideas were developed about the sublime, something that is not the same as the classical ideals of beauty but rather something essentially different from beauty. The sublime is that which simultaneously awakens fascination and horror. Myths and archaic or ancient poetry are extolled as examples of the sublime.[50] The concept of the sublime becomes an important ingredient in the assessment of the Goths and things Gothic.

The fourth phase, identified as National Romanticism, coalesces with later Gothicism, which has its most important representatives in the circle around the Gothic League and the Manhem League—men such as Almqvist, Geijer, Ling, Atterbom, and Tegnér.

The fifth phase signals a decline in National Romanticism as well as Gothicism in the forms that were found during the early 1800s. That which we call Gothicism and Gothic literature and art occasionally do coalesce, for example in the assessment of the archaic and sublime. In many respects this actually constitutes two separate genres, as when the Gothic contains elements of Romantic horror. This latter genre lives on within art, literature, and music.

It was not only in Sweden that Gothicism occurred. In most European nations one could claim some sort of origin from the Goths. Besides Sweden, Gothicism was strong in Spain. In both Denmark and England ideas about a Gothic origin flourished. While Sweden equated the Gotar, the people of Gotland, with the Goths, the Danes pointed to a connection between the Jutes and the Goths. Several peoples have been associated with the Goths. The English poems *Beowulf* (ca. 700–1000 CE) and *Widsith* (ca. 700 CE) have been interpreted as Gothic histories. In England, as well as in other large parts of Europe, the Goths would become synonymous with the struggle for freedom. Celts and Goths were often juxtaposed. The Goths were seen as a free and powerful people who were able to smash Roman tyranny. Ingmar Stenroth writes in his book *Myten om goterna: Från antiken till romantiken:*

> Moral qualities also play a role in the new way of evaluating the Goths. Sweden was one of the few countries in Europe where serfdom did not take root. The English, who already in the 1600s were keen supporters of democracy as a mode of existence, think that it is here in the north where the Goths, the champions of freedom, originally lived. It is when the Goths leave Scandia that they were gradually able to liberate the European peoples from the Roman grip of imperialism, it was thought.[51]

When the Goths migrated out over Europe they took Russia and Poland and finally surrounded the Black Sea. The Goths were divided into the eastern and western Goths. The western Goths sacked the city of Rome and then went into Spain, where they would come to form the Spanish monarchy and aristocracy. The eastern Goths founded their own dynasties in Italy. The historian Rodrigo Toletanus wrote a book about the history of Spain in 1243, which he called *Goternas historia.* Spaniards became increasingly interested in their original homeland in Scandinavia. In the Spanish-speaking countries the myth of the Goths was widespread. Spaniards interpreted the struggle against the Muslims in conjunction with the Gothic heritage. Stenroth writes: "From the first moment the Spaniards see the struggle against the Arabs as a *reconquesta,* a reconquest of the old Gothic realm, culturally, geographically, and politically."[52]

The Goths are by no means always interpreted in positive terms. For the most part the Goths have been considered a dark, dangerous, and destructive people in European history. The Goths were barbarians, and the word *gothic* was synonymous with something primitive and barbaric. The Swedish forefathers were also sometimes divided with regard to the Goths. The history of the Goths would indicate the glorious and powerful past of the nation, but at the same time the Goths were also heathens.

The Bible contains prophecies that indicate that it is in the north that wickedness has its origin, but also it is the quarter out of which God's punishment will come. When the Goths attack Christian Rome, it is interpreted in terms of biblical prophecy. The Goths are conceived both as a manifestation of chaos and the powers of darkness as well as God's instrument with which he punishes the world, and this allows doomsday to come. During the Protestant Reformation the Goths were referred to as the people who punished Rome and the sinful Catholic Church. The Goths and other northern peoples are interpreted by the early church fathers as God's tool of punishment. Stenroth writes:

> Antiquity sees the Roman Empire as the center of God-given world order, and the attack of the Goths upon the empire could be conceived of as meaning that the final Judgment was close at hand. In his *History of the Jews* (80 CE) the Jewish historian Josephus already tries to identify the menace from the barbaric peoples of the north as a corroboration of Ezekiel's prophecy in the Old Testament.[53]

The church father Ambrose asserted in the fourth century that "*Gog iste Gothus est*"; that is, the biblical "Gog is the same as the Gothus."[54]

During the Renaissance the Goths come to represent the decline of culture during the Middle Ages. The Gothic is seen as the counter-pole of ancient civilization and classical ideals of beauty. The conflict between the Gothic and classical ideals continues throughout the cultural history of the Western world. Classical ideals are based on clarity, reason, light, and regularity. Gothic ideals are metaphysical and are based on archaic visions, dreams, the obscure and dark, inspiration, and possession. In poetry, classicism is marked by a pragmatic poetic vision that emphasizes rules and craftsmanship, while the Gothic merges with a metaphysical poetic vision in which the content is more important than the form.[55] In architecture *Gothic* became a pejorative term for a medieval church style that characterizes the cathedrals of Cologne, Strasbourg, and Notre Dame, among others, with its grand and pointed style. Despite the fact that the style is thought to have had its origin in France in the 1100s, it is called German or Gothic in what is a condescending nomenclature. Gothic architectural fashion, with its pointed style, has been associated with wild nature. The structures seemed similar to icicles, immense ancient trees, as well as grottoes with their stalactites and stalagmites. According to classical taste, the Gothic represented something tasteless and overgrown, menacing and terrifying. But with Germans such as Herder and Goethe, the Gothic would be reevaluated, and Gothic architecture would be appreciated once more.

In spite of this, the Gothic would become synonymous with wild nature and that which is ghostly. In art during the 1800s there developed a romanticism connected with ruins in which graveyards and ruins of Gothic churches are shown entangled by an untamed nature under the glow of a full moon. Caspar David Friedrich was one of the foremost representatives of the romanticism of ruins. Ruins became such a fashion that some people were obliged to construct ruins, because the supply of genuine ones was insufficient. The Gothic ideal would be connected with the Romantic idea of the sublime. The sublime was something magnificent that inspired dread but was fascinating at the same time.

The word *sublime* comes from Latin *sublimis,* which means "high," "exalted," "of a high order or magnitude." The sublime is an important category in classical aesthetics. A work about the sublime, which for a long time was erroneously ascribed to the third-century Greek philosopher Longinus, was translated into French in the 1600s. It inspired analyses and discussions about the sublime in art and the experience of art. Edmund Burke and Immanuel Kant were the philosophers who pondered and wrote most about the sublime, and their ideas proved significant for the concept. The sublime touches upon experiences that move beyond a rational explanation of the world. The sublime resembles the experience that the artist Kandinsky calls *"das Unheimliche,"* "the uncanny." For Burke beauty and the sublime had become distinct as definite formal qualities: beauty was round, soft, graceful, and often in pastel colors; the sublime was sharp, hard, grand, and in dark, strongly contrasting colors. Classical ideals were connected to the ideas of beauty, while the Gothic was linked to the sublime. Stenroth describes the differences between classicism and the Gothic in the following way:

> Classicism is supposed to be an imitation of simple nature with the geometrically constructed garden as its pattern. For this conception of reality the irrational ideal of Gothicism appears to be in bad taste. When the view of nature changes, when humanity perceives all the wild windings of vegetation and begins to investigate the uninhabited cliffs and precipices of the mountains, respect is once more found for the aesthetic qualities of the Gothic. . . . Now the architects of palaces abandon classical geometrical order in favor of a liberation from the constraints of rules. Formally pruned trees become overgrown, the lawn a meadow, the basin a lake, and the garden pathway a twisting trail for the lone philosopher, where he wanders submerged in melancholy thoughts.[56]

Among the English Gothic Romantics an "enthusiastic terror" was spoken of, and they tried to get away from the pure, bright, ordered ideal of classicism. Instead gods, demons, hell, spirits, human souls, enchantments, magical arts, thunder, torrents, monsters, fire, war, plague, and starvation were sought.[57] Sublime horror would be able to give mankind knowledge of a greater reality that did not allow itself to be captured within the limits of reason. Writings that formed this style included titles such as Edward Young's "Night Thoughts" from 1742 and Robert Blair's poem "The Grave" from 1743.

The connection between the romanticizing of terror and Gothic literature on the one hand, and the Gothic and dark, mist-shrouded lands of the north on the other, was a constant feature in the genre. H. P. Lovecraft, an influential author of Gothic literature, wrote:

> At heart I despise the aesthete and prefer the warrior—I am essentially a Teuton and barbarian; a Xanthochoric Nordic from the damp forests of Germany or Scandinavia, and kin to the giant chalk-white conquerors of the cursed effeminate Celts. A son of Odin and a brother to Hengist and Horsa . . . Grr . . . Give a drink of hot blood with Celtic foe's skull as a beaker![58]

After the destruction of Second World War, and with the misuse of old Nordic symbols and myths by the Nazis, the use of runes and old Nordic mythology for ideological aims came under heavy suspicion. In the forward to the book *Myter om det nordiska—mellan romantik och politik,* which was published in the context of the project *Vägar till Midgård* (Ways to Midgård), Catharina Raudvere wrote:

> The general interpretation that everything that makes use of old Nordic imagery implicitly carries with it undemocratic ideas confirms certain prejudices about religion in the pre-Christian North. Nordic mythology appears to be able to be washed clean of political contamination only with the greatest of difficulty.[59]

During the time of the hippies and the growing New Age movement, the old Nordic myths began to be taken up again, but most often with completely different political implications than during the Nazi period. Ásatrú and pagan groups inspired by old Nordic myths would be able to use these for anti-racist aims. Contemporary groups, however, can manifest several different tendencies—everything from extreme racism to a pronounced anti-racism. Mattias Gardell has divided the Ásatrú groups he has studied in the United States into three main categories: (1) anti-racist Ásatrú, (2) racialist Ásatrú, and (3) ethnic Ásatrú. The first group believes that Ásatrú has nothing to do with ethnicity. The racialist or radical racialists believe that the gods are found in human biology in the form of Jungian archetypes, and they think that Ásatrú is an exclusively Aryan religion. Between these positions we find the ethnic Ásatrú, who are critical of what they on the one hand consider to be "New Age–ism" and on the other hand consider to be "reverse racism."[60]

In England the Goths and Gothicism were used by liberals in the argument for parliamentarianism, and during the 1600s there occurred a century-long debate over parliamentarianism. The liberal Whigs extolled the Goths as a model, while the severity of classical culture was idealized by the conservative Tories. The liberals believed that it was in the north where freedom was originally found and that the land was originally inhabited by free tribes who were the descendants of the Goths. The power of the king was limited back then, and so must it be again.[61]

Swedish Gothicism could probably best be described as conservative, while the Danish form had many radical elements. The conservatives in Denmark were concentrated in Copenhagen, and during conflicts with Germany at the end of the 1800s, the conservatives wanted to focus their resources on Copenhagen, which the liberal farmers, who belonged to the Left, opposed. The Left started rifle clubs that had the ambition of being able to defend all of Denmark against the Germans. The activities of the Left were also found at the popular colleges (*folkshögskolor*) that were inspired by Grundtvig's ideas and Ling's gymnastics program. Nordic mythology, as interpreted by Grundtvig, was identified with the Left, while the classical images, which Grundtvig's followers scornfully called too "Romanized," were identified with the Right. In the Gothic polarization between the Nordic-Gothic and the classical-Roman, the Romanizers were associated with formality and conservatism, centralism, and rulership by an elite. Conversely, the same polarization was used to criticize Gothic ideals as being overgrown and barbaric. In Denmark mythic interpretations in the spirit of Grundtvig continue to be used, especially among Leftists and in the environmental movement, where the heritage of the idealistic popular colleges is sometimes preserved today, even in polemics against the political establishment in Copenhagen no less.[62]

Before we go further this may be the time to reflect on the meaning of the word *got,* which gave the Goths and Gothicism their names. The word can have many original meanings and is derived from the Indo-European root **gheu-,* which gave rise to the Germanic word for "god" and also the Icelandic word *geysir* (geyser).[63] The word has been connected with the meanings "spring," "to gush forth," "to pour out," which can give rise to interesting speculations with links to ancient Nordic religion and customs. The words for the Geats, Gotlanders, and Goths all go back to a Proto-Germanic word, whose root is **geut-/*gaut-/ *gut-.* The meaning of this root is "the one who pours out" and could indicate a man with an allusion to ejaculation. Another interpretation is that it indicates "those who live where the waters pour forth"; that is, people who live next to springs or water courses.[64] Gotland could, for example, mean "the land rich with springs."[65]

When Swedish Gothicism reached its culmination during the period when Sweden was a great world power, it existed under different conditions than it did during Gothicism's first phase. The older representatives of Gothicism, such as the brothers Magnus, were Catholics and belonged to a circle of men that was in its demise as Sweden was becoming increasingly Protestant. Johannes Bureus belonged to the new epoch and enjoyed the patronage of the powerful Protestant king.[66] The successes of Gustavus Adolphus caused Sweden to become a world power, and this created the circumstances whereby Swedish Gothicism found itself in fair winds, and its grandiose claims seemed more reasonable than they had earlier in history. It is above all during this period that we find strong points of contact between Gothicism and esotericism in its various forms.

Throughout the history of Christianity there have always existed groups that asserted that heavenly existence will be preceded by a thousand-year paradise on earth. The Antichrist would rampage at the end of times, but the church and the Christians would emerge victorious from the battle and establish a kingdom of glory that would endure until the eternal kingdom begins. This chiliasm, or belief that Christendom would be victorious at the end of human existence and prepare a heavenly kingdom, was widespread during the first centuries of Christianity but was condemned as heretical during the Middle Ages. During the religious upheavals of the 1500s these chiliastic ideas once more won a great many followers.[67] In these circles the book of Revelation and other prophecies were studied, and people looked for signs and made astrological predictions. During the decades around 1600 a great many ideas were disseminated right alongside the official teachings of Lutheranism. These were different forms of esoterically colored religiosity that at times merged with Lutheran teachings, but that many times found themselves in completely different ideological spheres. Often this concerned Neoplatonically inspired religiosity with points of contact with alchemy, Hermeticism, and Rosicrucianism. These free, spiritualistic, and unorthodox forms of religion gained great numbers of followers from all social classes in the Protestant world. Influential thinkers were persons such as Valentin Weigel, Johann Arndt, Jacob Böhme, and Johan Valentin Andreæ. Their most important common source of inspiration was the sixteenth-century Swiss physician Philippus Aureolus Theophrastus Bombastus von Hohenheim, better known as Paracelsus.[68]

Paracelsism would become an important undercurrent in the Protestant world, but it often found itself in a marginalized position. Nevertheless Paracelsian ideas were very influential in many areas. One of the central parts of Paracelsus's mission was to call into question Aristotle and the scholasticism that was then dominant in European seats of learning. Paracelsus was a revolutionary thinker who wanted to overthrow established teachings and replace scholastic rationalism with his natural doctrine, which is stamped by occultism and empiricism. Paracelsus and his followers felt that Aristotle and his logic were un-Christian, and they mounted an attack on the exaltation of the Christian world by this heathen. Instead they emphasized Plato, Pythagoras, Zoroaster, and Hermes Trismegistus (that these were supposed to be in any way less heathen certainly seems curious).[69] In his central esoteric document, *Adulruna rediviva,* Johannes Bureus writes that these ancient sages possessed knowledge of the secrets of the adulrunes.

During the time of Gustavus Adolphus, Paracelsism would gain great influence in Sweden. The king was under the influence of the Ramist Johan Skytte and the occultist Johannes Bureus, both of whom were opponents of Aristotelianism. In 1640, Johan Skytte delivered an oration to the students in the academy in which he praised and idealized the example of Gustavus Adolphus of opening wide the doors of the university to the true philosophy of Trismegistus and Theophrastus (Paracelsus).[70] Paracelsism, with its empirical method of experimentation that would become meaningful for all the alchemists of the time who were trying to produce gold from ignoble metals, had the intention of manufacturing miracle-working mixtures and discovering remedies for all diseases. Out of this heritage modern natural science also developed some of its most important points of departure.[71] The influence of Paracelsism on Uppsala University would above all put its stamp on the physics (natural philosophy) and medicine done there.[72]

During the early 1600s the occult traits within Paracelsism were enhanced, and cabbalistic concepts would become an important ingredient in the new Paracelsism. Paracelsus had not immersed himself in the Cabbala in the same way as Pico della Mirandola, Reuchlin, or Agrippa, but successors, such as the Leipzig physician Heinrich Khunrath, would be instrumental in explaining that Paracelsism was intimately connected with this form of Jewish mysticism. Through Reuchlin and Mirandola the Cabbala received a Christian stamp that made it easier to be received into the Christian world. The Paracelsian Crollius was of the opinion that the purpose of the Cabbala was to show how God dwells in our innermost soul and that this means our salvation.[73] Johannes Bureus is a meaningful representative of Paracelsian Cabbalism, and we again find the idea of an immanent divine aspect in his work where it is furthermore united with Nordic mythology.

THE PROPHECY OF THE LION

Perhaps the strongest influence of Paracelsus on the status of Sweden as a great power, and the Gothicism of that period, came from one of the prophecies of Paracelsus. In one prophecy Paracelsus proclaimed that there are three hidden treasures that would come to revolutionize the world when they were discovered. The first would lie buried in Weida in Friaul, the other between Swabia and Bavaria in a place he does not want to name so as to avoid a great evil. The third treasure would be found between Spain and France. These treasures were supposed to consist of incredible riches of gold and jewels, but above all they will relate to the writings of Paracelsus on the secrets of the transmutation of metals and the universal medicine. Someday three men will find these treasures. The first one is supposed to be thirty-two years old at the time, the second fifty, and the third twenty-eight.

This prophecy was supposed to be fulfilled when the Austrian Empire fell. The most influential part of the prophecy relates that at the same time there would come a golden lion from the North, from the land of midnight, and that this lion, *"Der Löwe aus der Mitternacht,"* would shatter the eagle; that is, the Austrian emperor. The prophecy warns that the time before the arrival of the lion will be marked by many plagues and afflictions. The dream of a lion from the North who is supposed to overcome the eagle flourished in chiliastic and reformist circles. Among the Rosicrucians, Paracelsus's prophecy was referred to and people were expecting the lion who would come from the North and save the righteous. The lion would establish the terrestrial kingdom of glory that was to precede the heavenly kingdom.[74]

At the time, tensions were increasing between Catholics and Protestants. In 1608 the Evangelical Union was formed, and as a counter to this the Catholic League was established the following year. Bohemia experienced a short time of freedom but was crushed in 1620 by Austria. Denmark entered the conflict, but the Danish troops are beaten down in 1626. Nothing seems to be able to vanquish the emperor and the Catholic League, which has all of northern Germany in its grip. The Roman eagle rules over the Protestant regions, and the Protestant population is desperately seeking a savior. Through Rosicrucian literature, people read the prophecy of Paracelsus concerning the lion from the North and turned their attention northward. At first it was believed that this lion was perhaps the Danish king Kristian IV, but after his defeat people's attention was drawn farther north. Could it perhaps not be that the successful king of Sweden, Gustavus Adolphus, was the midnight lion people were expecting? Johan Nordström describes the spirit of the time in *De yverbornes ö* of 1934.

Never before in the Protestant world had people abandoned themselves—despite the warnings of the professional theologians—to more fervent and romantic expectations of an incipient age of bliss than during these years of such terrible reality. Nothing betrays the strain of enthusiasm within this generation more than its preoccupation with the Rosicrucian mysteries. The message of the Rosicrucians concerning the prospective general reformation, since after the vanquishing of pontifical tyranny mankind should be united with the true religion of Christ and be in possession of the revealed secrets of nature to live in paradisiacal bliss, this message, itself a child of the spirit of the times, everywhere found faithful and dedicated hearts, penetrated into the palaces of the princes and

Aracelsus, Ariel.

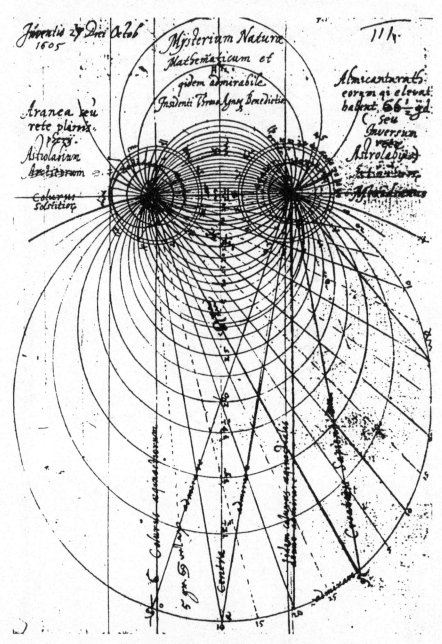

Bureus's "Astrologiska uträkningar"
(Astrological calculations)

the homes of the common man, won the support of the learned at the universities and the townsmen in the commercial centers, condemned by many, defended by still more, including by Lutheran pastors, discussed by all.[75]

One of those who would devote much attention to the prophecy of the lion was Johannes Bureus himself. Despite his closeness to Gustavus Adolphus, he would express his uncertainty as to whether it was really the Swedish king who was the predicted midnight lion, who many believed he was. Through his detailed reading of the book of Revelation, Bureus realized that the lion of the tribe of Judah, who opened the sealed book the Lord holds in his hand, must be the same lion that Paracelsus spoke about. That the lion in the book of Revelation referred to Christ was not a satisfactory explanation for Bureus. If it was the same lion that Paracelsus prophesied about and that was discussed so much in the time of Bureus, then the lion would come from the North. Besides, was it not so that it was Bureus himself who received the key for opening the apocalyptic age upon his enlightenment in 1613? No, that the lion in the book of Revelation and the prophecy of Paracelsus were intended to indicate Christ or the Swedish king appeared to be untrue. For Bureus the image became clear, and he came to realize that it was he himself who was the lion.[76]

THE ADULRUNES

Bureus composed seven manuscripts of *Adulruna rediviva*. One of these, in the Codex Holmiensis (F.a. 16), which disappeared in 1812, was written in Swedish. That it disappeared during the zenith of neo-Gothicism is worth noting. The manuscript F.a. 16 that disappeared could have been identical to F.a. 21. On a page of a catalog in the National Library of Sweden dated 1864 it is noted that whether these two manuscripts of *Adulruna* were identical is uncertain but that the cronogram "aDILrVnaMaL" indicates that F.a. 21 was written in 1640.* Of the four manuscripts in the National Library of Sweden, two are written in Swedish and two in Latin. Codex Holmiensis F.a. 21 and F.a. 23 are written in Latin, while Rål. 9 8° and Rål. 6 12° are in Swedish. Of the two manuscripts, Codices Upsalienis *Adulruna rediviva* R 551a and R 551b, that are found in the Carolina Rediviva in Uppsala, the former is in Latin and the latter is in Swedish.

The different manuscripts vary somewhat in content and dedications, but the basic structure and principal contents are generally the same. *Adulruna rediviva* consists of the following parts.

---

*This catalog page was extracted and copied for me by the manuscript unit at the National Library of Sweden.

The first section: The recumbent stone
The second section: The falling stone
The third section: The rune cross
The fourth section: The shepherd's royal office
The fifth section: The treasury of the Adulruna
The sixth section: The three crowns

Alphabetum Scanzianum ordine ptoprio.'

Υ	*Frey.*	F. Ρ /v confona.	1
ʔ	*Vr.*	h/u. Π/v. Π/y. Π/å.	3
ᛞ	*Tors.*	I / th. þ /dh.	5
ᛡ	*Odhes.*	Ⱶ/ð. Ⱶ/å. Ⱶ/Ⱶ/ð.	7
ᚱ	Rydbur.	R/r. ᚼ/ r/ er fin.	9
Υ	*Kyn.*	Ρ /ſ/c. Ρ /Υ/g. Ψ/q.	10
ᚯ	Haghall.	H/ Gh / Ch.	30
ᚾ	*Nadh.*	N. Ⱶ/n fin. Ⱶ/dn.	50
I	*Idher.*	I voc. J/j. Ⱶ/Ⱶ/e.	70
ᚬ	*Æru.*	Æ.. Ⱶ/a. Ⱶ/ an.	90
ᚱ	*Sun.*	S pr. Ⱶ/s. Ⱶ/ſ/ ss.	100
ᛁ	*Tidhr.*	T. Ⱶ/ tt. Ⱶ/d.	300
ᛞ	Byrgbal.	ᛞ/b. Ⱶ/ B/ p.	500
ᚱ	*Lagher.*	L. Ⱶ / ll.	700
Ψ	*Man*	M. Ψ / mm.	900

Ordide Latino.

Ι. ᛞᛞ. Ρ. Ⱶ. Ⱶ. Ρ. ΡΥ. Ⱶ. Ⱶ. ΙΥⱵ. ᚱ. Ψ. Ⱶ
a bb c d e f gg h i kk l m n n

ΨⱵ. ᛒ Β. Ψ. ᚱΒᛡ. 'ΙΙ. Ⱶ. Ⱶ ᛡ. · Π. Ⱶ Ι.
o o p p q ſ r r ſſ s t u u y x ȝ

ΠΡⱵ ᛁΠ. Ⱶ. ᚱⱵⱵ Ⱶ. Ⱶ. Ⱶ. ᛞ Ⱶ
v v   åå å ö ö ck dh gh th.

Runes and their numerical values from *Runa ABC-boken*

The first section, the recumbent stone, describes the exoteric significance of the runes. The second section, the falling stone, places the runes in three crosses of five runes each and describes their spiritual esoteric dimension. The third to the fifth sections continue with this. The rune cross is an arrangement of all the runes in the form of a cross heavily laden with meaning. The shepherd's royal office is a short piece with an illustration accompanied by an explanation that shows a king dressed in vestments decorated with runes. The treasury of the Adulruna is perhaps the most essential part that attempts to indicate the origin of the runes out of simple, original geometrical forms. The sixth section describes the mystical origin of the three crowns and does not deal with runes.

THE FIFTEEN ADULRUNES

Bureus divides the rune row into three groups of 5 runes each. This arrangement does not correspond to the traditional division of the rune row into the families of Frey, Hagal, and Tyr. Bureus removed the last rune in the rune row of 16.* Out of this the derived a symmetrical rune row with 3 × 5 runes. In the usual case, the rune row of 16 has three families, where the initial Frey family consists of the runes *f, u, th, a, r, k,* which caused the rune row to be called "futhark." The two subsequent families consist of 5 runes each. In the usual rune rows *m* comes before *l,* but Bureus reverses these and has the rune row conclude with the letter *m.* He undoubtedly derived this from the 19-figure rune calendars in which the runes also have this order. That he calculated using the runic calendar is apparent since he makes note of it when certain of the runes are "golden numbers"; that is, they mark a year within a nineteen-year cycle of time. Bureus's so-called *femter,* or "quintets," begin with the runes for *f, k,* and *s;* that is, Frey, Kyn, and Sun (Bureus's spellings in his *Adulruna rediviva*). He calls the first quintet the *födarefemt* (progenitor

---

*That the last rune should be removed was also the opinion of Magnus Celsius, who at the end of the 1600s studied the so-called Hälsing runes subsequent to Bureus. See *De stavlösa runornas tydning* by Sven B. F. Jansson (1983), 322.

quintet), after this comes the *föelsefemt* (generational quintet), and last comes the *fosterfemt* (generated quintet). Bureus developed speculations about this triplicity in connection with the adulrunes. His first group of runes is not a futhark. The rune *a* indicates an *o* instead, which it started to do toward the end of the Viking Age. Thus Bureus's first group of five is *f, u, th, o, r;* that is, *futhor,* which in his adulruna stands for "father," "progenitor," "creator." Bureus also had the runes represent numbers. In the first quintet the runes stand for the odd numbers between 1 and 9, in the next group of five they have the same values multiplied by ten to make 10–90, and in the last *femt* they are multiplied by a hundred; that is, 100–900. This forms the point of departure in his adulrunic gematria and his apocalyptic calculations. The symmetry of the rune row and the correspondence in number between the runes and various principles are of the greatest importance when Bureus develops his runology. In this he prefers to represent the runes *u* and *r* in their shorthand forms as they appear among the so-called Hälsing runes. In this way these two runes become mirror images of each other. Bureus renders the runes so that they appear to the greatest extent possible as mirror images of one other. The symmetry of the rune row is important for his esoteric speculations.*

The descriptions that follow of the interpretations of the runes by Johannes Bureus are taken from *Runa ABC-boken, Runaräfsten,* and the esoteric *Adulruna rediviva.* The etymological discussions are those of Bureus himself. The numerical values are from *Runa ABC-boken* and the etymologies from *Runaräfsten* and *Adulruna rediviva.* The rune images that follow were drawn by T. Ketola.

---

*The Hälsing runes are surrounded by a good deal of mysticism. The philologist Johannes Schefferus sent illustrations of two runestones with Hälsing runes to Athanasius Kircher, who asserted that these signs could not be interpreted as any script but were only ornament without meaning. Later he altered his opinion and asserted that they were carved to protect the inhabitants against attack by serpents. This was clear from the serpents depicted on the stones. He came across similar stones in Constantinople and in Arabia, where these are found among diabolical conjurations and superstitious songs of magic. See Jansson, *De stavlösa runornas tydning,* 7.

THE PROGENITOR QUINTET

(Födarefemten)

Frey: In the *Adulruna rediviva,* Bureus calls this rune the stave of Freyja. In ancient times the word *Freyja* (Sw. *fröja*) meant "lady" (Sw. *fru*). The word comes from "seed" (Sw. *frö*) and thus refers to fertility. In this instance, the word *fröken* (unmarried woman) is derived from this word. The rune is called *fä* (cattle) for the sake of abundance in the same way that the Hebrew letter *alef* means "ox." In *Runaräfsten,* Bureus calls the rune *fre, frö, fröj, frägh, frigg.* The farmers call it *fä* or *fähysing.* It is called *frö* (seed) or abundance because of the branches that come out from its main stave. Friday has its name from the same word as this rune. The rune signifies both the letters *f* and *v.* Bureus gives the rune the numerical value of 1.

Ur: This rune indicates original motion and expression. It corresponds to (1) the Latin *a, ab, e, ex;* (2) the *ur* in *urväder* (drizzly weather); and (3) the *ur* in *urverk* (clockworks), "on account of movement." *Yrka* (demand) is derived from it. Ur corresponds to the letter *u* along with *y* in the pointed form (with a point inside *u*) or *å* in a double-pointed form. Ur has the numerical value of 3.

Tors: Bureus writes in *Runaräfsten* that the Thor rune has the same name as Thursday, Thor's month, and *torsk* (codfish).

It remained in books of the Middle Ages longer than the other runes, perhaps due to some mystery it concealed, Bureus thought. According to him Tors can be compared to the Hebrew *tora,* which means "law," "correction," "instruction," "God's word." The name of the god Thor could have been derived from this. This rune is the sign of the highest freedom, because it means "to dare" or "venture" as well as "strike," "to turn back." Bureus uses as an example the river Torne, "where the Gulf of Bothnia turns back," Tören—Södertören—"where the countries of the three peoples meet," and Törnby, "where the inlet of Mälar, Skafven, turns back." As an adulrune this rune indicates Thor, God, unity, the Ain Sof of the Cabbala, and the highest spiritual level. Tors is the rune of God, and Bureus's interpretation of the name Thor (Sw. *Tor*) corresponds more to the Old Norse name of the sky god Tyr, whose name means "god." In the manuscript *Cabbalistica,* Bureus renames this rune *unitas Deus.*[1] Because Tors is the third rune in the row, Bureus thought that he could connect it to the trinity. The Tors rune signifies *th* and *d* and has the numerical value 5.

ᚺ **Odhen:** This rune is called Odin's stave (*mercurii litera*) or the *ödenstav* (*fata litera*)—"the stave of fate." This goes together with *od, öde, aud,* and *öud,* which, according to Bureus, mean possession. He compares it with the words *Svidiod* (Sweden), *månad* (month), *härod* (jurisdictional district), *klenod* (jewel). *Odhen* can indicate *o, å,* and *ö* in Swedish. The Swedish word for Wednesday, *Onsdag,* belongs together with the name of this rune. Bureus attacks those who call Onsdag such things as *woensdag, wendisdagr,* and so on, and is of the opinion that they have forfeited their right to use the runic script. According to him the Icelanders preserved the ancient and correct name of the day and call it *odensdagur.* In *Runaräfsten,* Bureus writes that Odin was the greatest of the heathen idols. Frigga was the wet nurse and foster mother of mankind, who fostered man and helped him during the time of his growing up. Thor rules over man's grown-up life. On the other hand, Odin rules over man's "end," or *fatum,* and corresponds to Mars, Pluto, and Mercury. Odin is connected to man's destiny (Sw. *öden*). The rune has the numerical value of 7.

ᚱ **Rydhur** or **Redh:** This is connected to *rede* (advice), *ride,* and *rudder* (with which one rules over a ship). Rydhur is a sign of dominion and justice (the "right"). It corresponds to the Latin *dominium.* Bureus complains that the rune *r* in one of its forms was displaced and put at the end of the sixteen-rune row. There it lost its venerable chivalric name and was instead called quite simply *Stupmadher* (inverted man). Rydhur has the numerical value 9.

THE GENERATIVE QUINTET

(Födelsfemten)

Y **Kön** or **Kyn:** Bureus gives the rune many alternate names such as *kaghn, gaghn, kaghvänd, gaghnum, göir, geir, käir, git,* and *kan* (*naturæ kön, notitiæ, nosce*), as well as *generosæ naturæ litera,* "the generous or noble stave of nature." The name of the rune means "the reproductive power of nature," but it is also related to the word "can"; that is, "to be able" (Sw. *kunna*).[2] The rune can also indicate "sex" (Sw. *kön*), with the meaning "boil"; that is, sore. Whenever this rune is on the golden number, animals and men will be struck by boils, Bureus warns. The rune name Kyn also stands for being knowledgeable and authoritative. When the rune splits in two directions (Y) the better side corresponds to the meaning "king," German *König,* which comes from *kön, kyni,* and *kunna.* The rune corresponds to the Pythagorean Y, which symbolizes man's choice between the evil leftward path or the good rightward path. The three lines in this Y in this form of Kön also indicate *intellectualis, animalis,* and *corporalis.* The rune corresponds to *c, k,* and *g* as well as to *ch, gh,* and *q,* even though Bureus takes note that *q* is not found in proper Swedish and that one should stick to Swedish inasmuch as it is as good as any other language. Bureus is of the opinion that languages should stand on their own and be "undiminished and unbloated." The rune corresponds to the number 10.

Haghal: This rune describes "that which encloses (Sw. *hagar*) or accomplishes everything and which is favorable." The name of the rune can be compared to a word such as *haglek,* which means "art" and "craft." Bureus thinks that this rune is formed from a combination of the runes *n* and *a,* which stand for grace and honor, respectively. Haghal embraces these two principles and corresponds to the Latin *grando.* The rune corresponds to the letter *h,* and the numerical value of Haghal is 30.

✝ **Nådh** or **Nodher:** This rune is also called Nodh and Nödh. The name of the rune means both "grace" (Sw. *nåd*) and "distress" (Sw. *nöd*). It is grace because one side of the sloping line is raised, but distress because it slopes down on the right side, Bureus explains. The rune indicates the letter *n* and has the numerical value 50.

| **Is** or **Idher:** This stave is "completely naked" and therefore received the name *poenitentiæ litera,* "stave of repentance." It is also called Idstav (*studii literi*). According to *Runaräfsten* the name *idher* comes from Edher, who first devised the runes. From this comes the concept *idingar,* "learned in writing," and *idh,* which means "study." It stands for *i* and, when pointed, the letter *e*. This rune has the numerical value 70.

✦ **Ar:** This rune sometimes indicates *a* and *ä* and sometimes *å*. Therefore it has different names such as *ära* (honor/glory), *ärv, är, ar, ari* (eagle), *are, år* (year), *årstav, Gloria* (honor), *perpetua requises* (perpetual rest), *littus, aquila* (eagle), *annus* (year), *annora,* and *sufficientia*. The rune symbolizes honor (Sw. *ära*) and the eagle (Sw. *örn*). The appearance of the rune best fits the names *gloria* and *perpetuo requises,* according to Bureus, because the slanting line is raised at the end. This is also what honor and perpetual rest does after experiencing distress. The rune concludes the second group of five and has the numerical value 90.

THE GENERATED QUINTET
(Fosterfemten)

| **Sun** or **Sol:** This rune is called "the highest sun in heaven" and also has the designation sun stave, of the sun, and *sön,* which gives its name to Sunday (Sw. *söndag*). Sol could have been one of the highest Gothic gods, and some people call the rune Sel instead, which means "soul" (*beatus, animus*). The sun is named after light, which was created on Sunday, and the sun is likened to the son of light. The words *son* and *sun* correspond to each other in this way. Connected to this rune are

the words *sona, suna* ("to forgive through the son"), and *ransuna* ("to recover what has been stolen"). This rune indicates the letter *s* and has two forms: ' and Ⴤ. The first is, according to Bureus, the more correct and is called "hanging sun" because it hangs from the top line of the serpent in runic inscriptions. The second form is, however, most common and is called "kneeling sun." The rune's number is 100.

Tidher: This rune has the same name as Tuesday. Some call it Tyr, and in Dalarna it is called Tijr. It is called the stave of time and it marks out time as well as times of celebration and solemn services. In ancient times the priests were called *tidmän* (time men) and *tijar,* Bureus reports. The foremost of these, according to Bureus, may have been Byrger Tidesson, the mystical originator of the adulrunes. Time is likened to a *skäkt,* a *armbågspil,* due to its hastiness. The appearance of the rune reminds us of an arrow. The rune is also called Tak (roof) because of its appearance. It is called Tyri, which means *tjärfakla* (tar torch), because when this rune is a golden number many conflagrations occur. Tidher represents the ascension (*ascensus*) and the elements of air and fire. The Tidher rune signifies *t* and sometimes *d*. The rune has the numerical value 300.

Byrghal: It is also called Birka, Birke, Birkal, and Björk. In *Runaräfsten,* Bureus writes that some think that this rune got its name from Berik. Berik is the legendary Gothic king about whom the Roman historian Jordanes writes in his work *Getica*. The Goths left their motherland, Scandza, in three ships and traveled out into the world under the leadership of Berik. The rune is also called Byrkal after *byrkarl,* "he who is lord over the homestead," as well as *byrgal,* "containing everything contained in everything." The name of the rune is also connected with *börja* (to begin), "the one who begins." The name of the rune is a compound word made up of *byr* and *ger* or *kär,* since this is the patron of the house, fatherland, and towns, and *bur* means "townsman," Bureus reasons. Some use the word *burgeir,* meaning "the son of war," in the same way that *ger-man* means "war man."[3] Because one of the names of the rune is Byrger, the rune gives its name to the mystical creator of the adulrunes. This rune represents mankind, the spirit submerged in matter and the microcosm. Byrghal is the opposite of the Thors rune. While the Thors rune, or the rune of god, represents the highest plane of unity and enlightenment, Byrghal symbolizes darkness, opposites, twofoldness, matter, and the material world.[4] In *Cabbalistica,* Bureus names Byrghal as the *binarius dæmon* in contrast to the Thors rune, which represents the *unitas Deus*.[5] In the same work Bureus shows how this rune in its twofoldness consists of the sun and the moon, day and night.[6] It is important to indicate that Bureus did not view this rune as evil or negative. The goal is to raise this rune to the level of the Thors rune; that is, that mankind and matter are to be made divine. Byrghal indicates *b* and *p* and has the numerical value 500 (while Thors has 5).

ᛚ **Lagher:** This rune is also called Lag and Lauger and is formed from the same name as *lördag* (Saturday). The name of the rune comes from *läkkia,* which means "to drip" or "pour," and *laug,* which means "bath" (Sw. *lög*), also a name for Lakes Mälaren and Luugen. The rune is also connected with water. The rune name Lag (*lex*) comes from the verb *laga* (to arrange). The name is also connected with "layer" (Sw. *lag*) as well as the word "lay," as in the sexual connotation; see also Swedish *samlag* (sexual intercourse) and *hjonelag* (concubinal union). Besides being connected to water this rune represents the law and often turns up paired with Tidher. This represents time and law; that everything has its time and place.[7] Lagher represents descent (*descensus*) and the elements water and earth. Lagher corresponds to the letter *l* and has the numerical value 700.

ᛘ **Man:** This rune has the same name as Monday and corresponds to the moon. Some call it Madher (man), and it is seen illustrating a man with outstretched arms. It indicates the sound *m* and therefore as the last rune indicates "the one that shuts the mouth." The rune Man can be connected with Stiernhielm's letter—and adulrune—mysticism in which the letter *m* corresponds to the lowest and last part of the Neoplatonic series of emanations that begins with the vowels and ends with the consonants. *M* is the lowest and indicates the earth, mire, darkness, and silence (cf. "the one that shuts the mouth").[8] For Bureus *m* corresponds to the moon as the light of the night. Bureus also calls Man the *manestav* for *mani* (moon). In a variant of the rune (ᛘ) a man scratching his head is shown. Bureus explains that this is actually the last rune but that the last rune is also often considered to be *stupmadher* (inverted man) (ᛢ), which signifies *r*. According to him it is thus degraded from its original place together with the fifth rune, Rydhur. Bureus equates the rune Man with "the human being as the measure of all things" and with the center of the world.[9] Man has the numerical value 900.

THE HIDDEN LEVELS OF THE RUNES

For Bureus language and words are mediators between man and the divine. Bureus explains that among the foremost gifts with which God honors mankind so as to differentiate him from the animals, belong "reason and rationality" along with the two sensory mediators, language and writing. Of all the natural powers, language is the most wondrous of all the arts and writing, "*dedh wirkeligeste och vnderligeste*" (the most true and wondrous).[10] In the introductory sections of *Adulruna rediviva,* Bureus gives an account of the meaning of the runes, words, and writing. The spoken word is a mediator between writer and reader; similarly, writing is the mediator between writer and reader. The son of God is the mediator between the creator and the created world, and therefore he calls himself Alpha and Omega, the first and the last letters in the Greek alphabet. The son of God is holy scripture, holy writing. This scripture is found in three forms: the divine, the macrocosmic, and the microcosmic.

Divine scripture can be revealed, as when Moses received the Ten Commandments from God, or it can be deciphered as divine signs in natural objects, as, for example, mystical inscriptions upon fish in the sea. Written signs are found engraved in nature and constitute fundamental patterns for humans to observe.

A similar idea is found in a remarkable account in runology in which the linguist and Icelandic historian of ancient times Finn Magnusen (1781–1847) enthusiastically described bold bind runes and runes with common main staves on a rock wall in Runamo in Blekinge. He manages to read a Nordic heroic epic into this feature and described his revelation in a written work of seven hundred pages.[11] But it actually turned out that these runes were merely natural fissures in the rock, and Magnusen met with devastating criticism. His book, *Runamo og Runerne,* is nevertheless a learned book with much factual runological information.[12] Finn Magnusen's revelations about the rock have fascinated many rune mystics, especially since he described how he understood the runes and translated them in a state of ecstasy and trance.[13] The esoteric runologist Nigel Pennick took up for Magnusen by comparing his experience with Artur Artaud's universal esotericism in which people interpret local natural symbols that express eternal hidden realities.[14] Pennick writes in his *Secrets of the Runes:*

> From the Runamo experience, as with earlier traditions, it is clear that natural runic patterns have a great deal to tell us. They have their own geomythic content, from which we can learn.
>
> This approach is the same as Bureus advocates when he writes about the divine script. This script is called macrocosmic and constitutes nature and the great world outside humanity. It is the book written by God *vtan synliga stavar*—"without sensory staves." The microcosm and man are God's third book.[15]

The runes are the first original signs that mediated between the creator and creation, between the writer and the reader. The runes are found in two main forms. There is the outer, exoteric form that Bureus calls "the evident" or "the known and sensible" runes that were of great interest but not the most important. These outer runes can teach us to read. But of significantly greater importance are the inner, esoteric dimension of the runes, called adulrunes, which relate to the usual script the way the Cabbala does among the Hebrews or the hieroglyphs among the Egyptians.[16] Additionally, there is an innermost, third runic dimension called the *alrunes*. Therefore the runes have three dimensions as follows:[17]

1. Evident runes
2. Adulrunes
3. Alrunes

THE RECUMBENT STONE
AND THE FALLING STONE

Scripture and God's son are one, and Christ reveals himself as a stone that communicates the message of salvation and enlightenment to mankind. Hildebrand explains Bureus's view of the mediator: "In the same way he does not equate this mediator exclusively with a shepherd or father, as the best servant of all by office, but also with a stone as the oldest thing of all and the most permanent."[18]

The stone that corresponds to Christ, and that transmits the communicative language, is one of Bureus's most important symbols. The stone is portrayed in *Adulruna rediviva* either as a recumbent or falling one. The recumbent stone represents the runes in their exoteric "evident" form. It is flat and square or rectangular and shows the runes standing in three vertical columns one beside the other. The recumbent stone represents "the scorned human form of the mediator." The falling stone signifies "the powerful divinity of the mediator" and the esoteric dimension of the runes. This stone falls from heaven into the world of men, where it takes the form of the recumbent stone. The falling stone is a cube, the three visible sides of which each bear one of the three quintets of runes. The runes in these quintets are arranged in the form of a cross with a rune in the

The recumbent stone

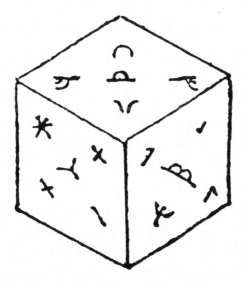

The falling stone

middle and two to the sides and one above and one under the central one. That the runes are placed in the form of an equal-armed cross shows that this involves spiritual, esoteric runes and not ordinary written signs.

In the first quintet, which is on the top face of the falling stone (see the image on page 199), the runes Odhen, Thors, and Frej stand in a row. These runes signify Wednesday, Thursday, and Friday, but as a group Bureus calls these runes TOF, and they are said to represent the original Nordic trinity. Bureus thinks that the original true religion maintained itself undefiled for a longer time in the North than it did in the southern lands. But over time an Asiatic master of witchcraft found his way up into the North and called himself Odin. His wife was called Fröja, and they declared that people should worship Thor during their lives—Fröja in connection with birth and the beginning of life, and Odin during old age and death. Heathenry and the worship of idols made of wood began with the advent of the false Odin. With this, the people turned away from the true trinity TOF, and the wisdom of the adulrunes was stifled.

The rune Thors represents the thing that is most free, effective everywhere and in everything. Bureus explains that the Northmen worshipped Thor from primeval times. The word *thora* indicates that the wisest people had the highest power and authority in the beginning, before the languages were confused.[19] Thor is immortal and both masculine and feminine. This is demonstrated, according to Bureus, by an image of Thor in the church at Gamla Uppsala that is bearded above and feminine below. This image is now thought to be a badly damaged picture of Christ. Thor corresponds to other sky gods such as Jupiter and Jehovah. The Thors rune illustrates an open door that rises up over the horizon and leads to a "shelter." Thor is the great invoker, and Odin and Fröja (represented by runes) are his messengers. They stand on each side of the door with their hands humbly stretched below the horizon, which Bureus shows in one of his illustrations, rendered here by T. Ketola:

At Thor's right side is found Odin, and the day before Thursday is Wednesday (Sw. *onsdag*). Odin is Thor's son. Odin is destiny, *fatum,* divine providence, which is the origin of everything as well as the one that destroys. As the destroyer, he is Odem, "the second blood-red Adam, who in the rage in his blood destroys all his enemies."

At Thor's left side is found Fröja, and the day after Thursday is Friday. Fröja was Thor's daughter and Odin's sister. She is the holy woman and corresponds to the Holy Spirit that in the beginning hovered over the water in the first book of Moses. She was worshipped in the North as the true spirit of sacrality and that which provides all good gifts. This is interesting because the rune is also called Feh, which is used to indicate riches, livestock, and property in other interpretations of the runes.

The two runic signs below the Thors rune (on the top face of the falling stone) are called the twins by Bureus, and he equates them with two ram's horns and an *oro* (*uru*) in a clock's works. The signs consist of the runes *o* and *r,* and together they form a word that characterizes the world outside and below the god Thor; that is, *or* or *oro* (agitation). These two runes signify perpetual motion and expanse. The twins are paired above the Thors rune and its horizon. They have, so to speak, passed through the "door" (the Thors rune). Now they form the Swedish word *ro* (peace) and represent eternal rest and inscrutable union with the highest god. Bureus cites Hermes Trismegistus: "Those chosen by god are of two kinds, the one are those who migrate, the other those who are still, and these are the highest holiness of souls."[20] Below and outside the door are also the two runes *u* and *r* in the form of Hälsing runes that Bureus most often uses for these two. They form the word *ur* or *or,* which is supposed to signify life, twofold/manifold, motion, *oro* (agitation), and divine activity. Above and inside the door they form the word *ru* or *ro,* which signifies eternity, the beyond, and God's world, unity, peace, and eternity.

In the second cruciform quintet, located on the left face of the falling stone, "the quintet of generation," are the runes grace (Nåd), sex (Kön), and glory (Ar) in a row. For Bureus these form the word NotArKon, which signifies the administration of the three realms of the sustainer, or God. This also corresponds to the three crowns in the Swedish royal coat of arms.[21] The word *notarikon* is derived from the Cabbala, where it indicates one of the cabbalistic letter codes. Sometimes this concept is synonymous with the Cabbala itself, and Bureus also called his runic Cabbala *notaricon suethia*.[22] The *n* rune on the left side is that of "glory in the Promised Land." While the *k* rune is the governance of the kin (*kyn*) of the realm, "which no eye has seen."[23] The *k* rune is split in two on top, but on bottom has only one stroke: "the single Tree of Life stands on both sides of the river that flows from God's throne." In this figure the rune looks like a Y and can be connected to the Pythagorean "Y" that symbolizes the life of a person where the foot is the innocence of the child and the two outstretched arms are the choice between good and evil, the right and left, virtue and vice. Bureus explains the runes above and below in the following way:

> The twins are, according to their name, placed with the Hagal (hail) above and Ider (repentance) below. They can also form boundaries between the aforementioned three realms, thusly:

$$4$$
$$1 \quad 5 \quad 3$$
$$2$$

> 1. 2. 3. 4. 5 so that one emerges from the valley of distress (1) into the plane of honor (3) over the passage of repentance (2), and the one who proceeds from there has to go through a torrent of hail (4) and on to the summit of character (5). This corresponds to the people of Israel's migration over the Red Sea into the wilderness, where they were nourished with manna and then through the rocky Jordan into the "redemptive land of peace," where they dwelled permanently, as well as to the movement of the high priest of God, first from the outer court then by the brazen altar (2), into the holy temple (3), and from there to a place before the golden altar (4),

and into the holy of holies (5). He who understands this, only he understands this quintet and the journey together with the fact that the mediator's priestly office is here equated with N, the recumbent stone with I, the royal government with A, the falling stone with H, and the office of the judges with K.[24]

The third quintet, the quintet of the offspring, which is located on the right face of the falling stone, can be read in two directions. Either (1) horizontally with the runes Tidher, Byrghal, and Lagher, or (2) vertically with the runes Man, Byrghal, and Sun. The three horizontal runes represent the three offices of the crowns (the priest, the king, and the judge) that mediate between Sun, the powers of the sun and heaven, and Man, mankind. Byrghal in the middle is the most important of these triplets. It represents the prince or king. On the king's right side stands Tidher with his priests, and on the left side stands Lagher with his judges. This arrangement is reminiscent of the two sephirot Chesed and Geburah in the Cabbala, which are situated to the right and left of Tipharet, respectively. Chesed to the right signifies reconciliation and mercy, and Geburah to the left has the power of judgment.

The vertical interpretation of this quintet shows Sun, Byrghal, and Man. Sun is the sun that illuminates the day and therefore is called "the most splendid of all sensible things." The man rune, which is also called Måna, is the light of the night; that is, the moon. Both represent the celestial world. In the middle is found Byrghal, which represents mankind and the cage in which mankind is trapped. Humanity sits in the cage of physicality and waits for redemption. The twins Tidher and Lagher on each side remind humanity that everything has its time and law. In *Cabbalistica* this cruciform quintet illustrates the sensory world: Byrghal represents humanity and the microcosm, Sun represents the archetype, Man stands for the macrocosm, and Tidher and Lagher for the elements. Tidher represents the ascending elements air and fire, while Lagher stands for the descending elements earth and water. Byrghal has the ambiguous role of representing the king, the foremost mediator between above and below, in the horizontal reading of this quintet, but in the vertical reading Byrghal stands for the cage (Sw. *bur*) that separates humanity from the heavenly world. This illustrates the dualism in Bureus's view of humanity.

The first section of *Adulruna rediviva* deals with the recumbent stone, or the scorned humanity of the mediator. The second section deals with the falling stone and the powerful divinity of the mediator. The third section takes up "the priestly office of the shepherd" and proceeds from Bureus's rune cross.

THE RUNE CROSS

Bureus's rune cross is constructed from the fifteen adulrunes. Seven vertically placed runes represent the ascending and descending path between heaven and earth. The two arms of the cross consist of four runes each, which are mirror images of one another. Out of the rune cross Bureus interprets seven "discernments" or contemplations, which he also calls clusters. These consist of groups of runes or so-called rune courses (here "course" refers to a row of stones set in a wall).

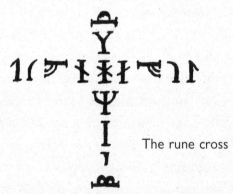

The rune cross

1. The first triplets of the cluster: A course of seven and two courses of four.
2. The second triplets of the cluster are (*a*) the shepherd and defender of four staves, (*b*) the herd of seven staves, and (*c*) the ravager of four staves.

3. The third cluster: Nine staves of outspread arms and its seven-stave summit.

4. The fourth flock: A cluster concerning the reckoning of time.

5. The fifth flock: Two realms and their governor.

6. The sixth flock: The staves in the quintet of the offspring that became the five wounds of the crucifixion.

7. The seventh flock: The imminence of the guide of law. The runic bow and arrow.

The first cluster is led into with a "course of seven," thus a group with seven runes from the rune cross. The Haghal in the very middle is removed, and this course of seven consists of every other rune in the rune cross. These seven runes correspond to the seven weekdays and the seven planets of alchemy.

Course of seven
(Image by T. Ketola)

	På	står			märkiandes här	
1	hufvudet	⌂		þ		♃ Jovis
2	v. armen	⤙		⼁		♀ Veneris
3	v. handen	↑		↑	dag	♄ Saturni
4	fötterna	⼁	Staf	⼁	diem	☉ Solis
5	bröstet	Y		Y		☽ Lunæ
6	h. handen	⼁		⼁		♂ Martis
7	h. armen	⼌		⼌		☿ Mercurii

The correspondences of the course of seven
(The second column, rows 1–7: head, left arm, left hand, feet, breast, right hand, right arm.)

The course of seven illustrates Christ on the cross, as well as Odin or Byrger as the crucified. To explain why the third section concerning the shepherd's priestly office begins with this symbol, Bureus cites the Gospel of Matthew (16:24): "If any man will come after me, let him deny himself, and take up his cross and follow me."[25] The course of seven illustrates the crucifixion of the body. The bearing of the cross should occur every day.

Bureus explains that Thursday is the Northmen's holiest day. This comes before the Sunday of the Christians or the Saturday of the Jews. Thursday as the holy day originated, according to Bureus, when King Ninus of Babel lost his father, Bel, who is called Jupiter (Jove, Jehovah = Thor) in the chronicles. Thursday became a holy day in memory of his father.

The two "courses of four" in the first cluster are formed by the eight runes that do not make up the body of Byrger or Christ (= the course of seven) and the seven days of the week. Four of these (ᚱᛏᛣᚾ, *r, n, a, u*) are found on the horizontal line of the cross and make up the first of these two courses of four. These runes from the word *RUNA* (ᚱᚾᛏᛣ). Bureus explains that the word *runa* means "experience" (Sw. *rön*) and signifies a "test" or "experiment." We can add to Bureus that the meaning of the word *runa,* "secret," "hidden wisdom," and such, fits well with the meaning he gives the word. The runes RUNA and AURN that form the word *runa* can be depicted as a gateway (see images below). This is the gateway of grace (Nådh) and honor (Ar) to eternal peace (the

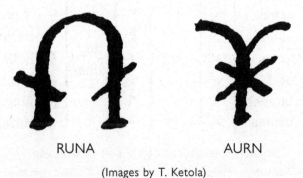

RUNA   AURN

(Images by T. Ketola)

runes *r* and *u* or *o* = *ro* ["peace, rest"]). The word *runa* itself makes up the gateway to the higher worlds. The four runes can also be composed in another way so they form the word *AURN* (Sw. *örn*), eagle, *aquila,* the double-headed symbol of the Gothic warriors of the Roman emperor Tiberius. This is the "mocked, scourged, stripped, and crucified mediator."[26] Bureus writes that the Haghal rune stands in the midst of the crucified staves that a thrall sold for thirty pieces of silver. The number for Haghal is 30, and for Bureus it symbolizes Christ and the Holy Spirit.[27]

The second course of four consists of the four vertical runes that do not indicate days of the week, or the crucified body. These four runes (ᚱᛁᛉᛏ) can be read as *PIGKynd, virginis filius,* "the virgin's son." The Swedish word *pig* relates to *piga,* a young woman or maiden. *Kynd* relates, for example, to the German word for children, *Kinder.* This son of the virgin can lead mankind out of bondage (Byrghal) through the rune Idher (repentance) and the embrace of grace and honor (the embrace is an expression of the equation of Haghal with the union of the Nådh and Ar runes) through the gateway of RUNA to the divine Thors, which is reached through Kyn, the son of the virgin.

The second group of triplets of the cluster or flock are the "four-stave shepherd and defender," "the seven-stave herd," and the "four-stave ravager." The four-stave shepherd, or defender, is equated to a spiritual sheep pen where the sheep are enclosed in a protective wall or fire. It consists of the trinity TOF and Byrghal, which corresponds to the humanity of the shepherd. The Odhen rune corresponds to his divinity. TOF is the trinity and Byrghal is humanity. Due to its appearance, Byrghal is equated with the Holy Virgin's breasts with which she nurses the shepherd when he becomes a human being in the quintet of the offspring. Byrghal can also be equated to a double-door that functions as the entrance and exit for the sheep. Byrghal is also the basis or foundation upon which congregation rests. The name can therefore also be interpreted as *bärg-all* (save-all).[28]

The seven-stave herd is made up of the five runes in the vertical line between Byrghal and Thors (between Christ as man and God), together with the two innermost ones on the horizontal line, Nådh and Ar. These runes represent the multitude of the congregation with the sevenfold unity of the spirit of holiness.[29] Bureus ties these runes together in a special symbol or bind rune that occurs often in his works. The symbol is called *signum foederis,* "sign of the covenant." As one example, he places this symbol upon the Rosicrucian altar he illustrates on the cover of his early Rosicrucian pamphlet, *Ara Feoderis Theraphici F. X. R.* The runes in this stave can be arranged so that they

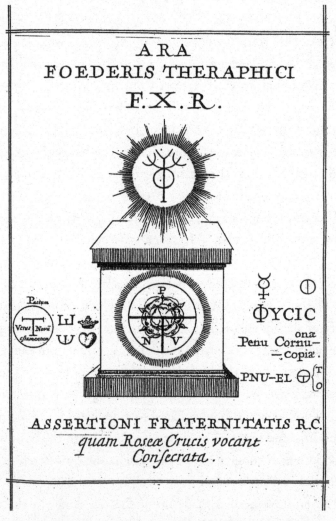

Frankenberg's version of *Ara Feoderis Therphici F. X. R.*

form ᚤᛏᚻᛏᚤᛁ, GÆGHN MIS—*occure mihi,* which means "go to me" or "run to meet me" and is the call or mission of Christ, who is the "caller" of mankind. In *Antiquitates Scanziana* he mentions John 21:19 as the source for this mission.[30] This is the call from above downward. Man, or "the called," answers with the same runes read in a different way, from below upward: ᛁᚤᛏᚻᛏᚤ, SIM ÄGHN K(ynd), *simus possessionis filij, quasi unus,* "We are the possessions of the Son, as one." As is frequent in the works of Bureus, one rune, in this case Kyn, has to signify a whole word: *Kynd.*

The four-stave group of the ravager is made up of the four staves that are left on the rune-cross after the seven staves of the herd and the four staves of the shepherd have taken shape. The excluded runes are ᛏᚱᚾᚦ, TRUL; that is, *troll,* the evil spirits, demons, the spiritual wolves that try to scatter and gobble up the flock. These correspond to the forces of chaos and the thurses in ancient Norse mythology. In the beginning these entice, using law and time (ᚦ & ᛏ); later they press the dupes down into the abyss with the three-pronged pitchfork (ᚼ). If the four staves of the ravager are read in another way one gets LURT, ᚾᚱᛏ, *defraudatorum symbolum,* "the sign of the duped ones," which can be interpreted as filth or muck (LORT).[31]

The third cluster describes the horizontal line of the rune cross that is called "nine staves wide" and its vertical line that is called "seven staves high." In the middle of the rune cross on the crossroads, between the horizontal and vertical lines, stands the Haghal rune. On the right arm

TRUL   LURT

(Images by T. Ketola)

of the nine-staves wide stand the runes ᛏᛅᚱᛁ, which form NORD. This does not, in the first instance, signify the point of the compass north but rather its secret meaning: *"N(ådens) Ord och N(ödens) Ord,"* "the word [Sw. *ord*] of grace and distress." If the runes of the right arm are read in the opposite direction one gets the word *TRON,* which is *fides,* "truth, faithfulness." The Tidher rune signifies, as we saw in the section on the fifteen runes, both *t* and *d*. On the left arm stand ᛏᛈᚾᚱ, which give the word *ÄFUL,* which is to be interpreted by reading the first rune by its complete name. We thus get the word *A(r) FUL,* which means "perpetual fullness," or in its adulrunic reading it stands for *ärofull,* "glorious," "honorable." The two arms can be read as *ära,* "honor," and *trohet,* "faithfulness." The right arm stands for God's word and the left for the spirit of holiness, and "without these two nothing can be called or come."[32] To be called and to come allude to "the Caller," Christ, who cries out from above down to mankind, who is to respond and come to God. From the runes ᚱᛁᛈ on the left arm one can interpret LOF, "praise," but Bureus thinks that the proper adulrunic interpretation should be ᛗᚾᛈ, LYF, which according to him is the old Swedish word for "love," along the lines of the English word, or the German *Liebe.* If we take the runes from both arms, except for the innermost ones (Nådh and Ar)—that is, the whole nine-stave horizontal line without the middlemost runes (*n, h, a*)—the rune cross gives us the word *TROFUL,* "faithful." The nine-stave horizontal line describes various qualities and characteristics that are required for initiatory transcendence as the vertical "seven-stave summit" illustrates.

The seven-stave summit, the vertical rune row of the rune cross, is one of the most important parts of Bureus's adulrunic system. Its runes illustrate a seven-grade initiatory process that can go upward (*ascensus*) or downward (*descensus*). Bureus explains that God's son (Christ/Odin) both descended and was born as a man in this way and reascended to heaven along the same path. The work of man, or of the adulrunic adept, is to advance upward from the lowest rune, Byrghal, to the highest God rune, Thors. The mediator for this process is Christ or Odin, who is

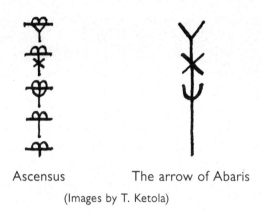

Ascensus   The arrow of Abaris

(Images by T. Ketola)

represented by the Haghal rune.[33] In *Cabbalistica* this seven-grade path of initiation recurs in several versions. It is, for example, connected to the alchemical process and its seven steps to the elixir.[34] In *Antiquitates Scanziana* the seven runes describe Christ's various stages as savior, from conception to resurrection and his reascension to God.[35] While the nine-stave breadth illustrates "the Collector's," Christ's (Byrger's, Odin's), outstretched arms, the seven-stave summit shows the upright length of his body. Thors is the head and Byrghal the feet. The body in between demonstrates the five runes that also symbolize a ladder, "the five-runged ladder," between the divine and humanity. The runes are the rungs of the ladder.

These five rungs of the ladder help Byrghal to climb to the Thors rune. Bureus illustrates this climbing in *Adulruna rediviva* with symbols where Byrghal is combined with the five runes on the path to Thors. This path is the ascending one, or *ascensus*, which is the goal of the runic adept.

Bureus weaves the five rungs of the runic ladder together so that they form a recurring symbol in his work. This symbol is "the arrow," and Bureus connects this symbol to the Hyperborean Abaris, who appears in Greek mythology. This arrow is also a stave or a magical twig carved with runes and bears mystical secrets and magical powers.[36] Through his illustration of the ascension Bureus demonstrates that the goal is a unification of Byrghal and Thors, man and God. This is not a question of a complete absorption by God, without man retaining his

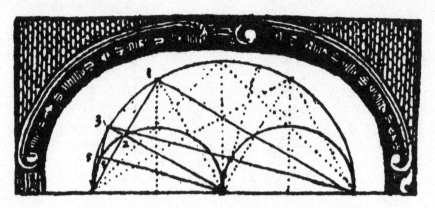

The unification of Thors and Byrghal

distinctive features, as Byrghal illustrates, but rather it is an ascent to a higher level. The symbol of the unification of Thors and Byrghal occurs in various forms in the works of Bureus, but in *Adulruna rediviva* he shows a special version that "indicates the immeasurable power that those who become unified with God receive."[37]

The descent, *descensus*, begins in the Thors stave and is completed in Byrghal only to begin as an ascension in order to be united once more with Thors. Byrghal is interpreted as comprising two gateways; these can illustrate how God descends into matter by exiting one gateway into the world and then returns through the other on the way back to the divine plane. For man Byrghal's two gateways can symbolize birth and death, the womb that conducts us into the world and the grave that conducts us out of the world. The descent begins through the Thors rune, "the door from which all good gifts come."[38] The runes describe, according to Bureus, various levels of the descent: The Kön rune stands for the father's highest kingdom, Haghal accomplished the father's will. Man, or Manna, is the heavenly bread, and Idher stands for repentance that is the result of guilt. The rune Sun represents temptation, and Byrghal is the dungeon in which man sits shackled in irons and in fear of impending death. Bureus explains that the one who sits in this dungeon wishes for a savior, and this is only doubted by someone who does not understand that life is the foremost reward.[39] The seven rune steps correspond with the Lord's Prayer in Matthew 6:9–13.

Thors   Our Father, hallowed be thy name
Kön   Thy kingdom come
Haghal   Thy will be done in heaven as well as on earth
Man(na)   Give us our daily bread
Idher   Forgive us our debts as we forgive those who owe us debts
Sun   And lead us not into temptation
Byrghal   But deliver us from evil.

In *Cabbalistica* the meaning is then developed into the initiatory seven-staved ascent. This corresponds to the alchemical process for producing the tincture or elixir of life.

Calcinatio	ᛟ	Byrghal
Sublimatio	ᛁ	Sol
Solutio	ᛁ	Idher
Putrefactio	ᛦ	Man
Destillio	✳	Haghal
Coagulatio	ᛦ	Kön
Tinctura	ᚺ	Thors[40]

On the same page in *Cabbalistica* the alchemical process is enumerated: (1) *sublimatio*, (2) *descensio*, (3) *destillatio*, (4) *calcinatio*, (5) *solutio*, (6) *coagulatio*, (8) *cæratio*, (7) *fixio*. Why 8 comes before 7 is not quite clear. Because we are dealing with a handwritten manuscript it could simply be a mistake. But adulrunic and Hermetic meanings for this inversion cannot be ruled out.

The seven-stave vertical line is also a Hermetic path of enlightenment. The adept is raised from the darkness of ignorance *tenebræ* (ᛟ) through *splendor* (ᛁ), *lumen* (ᛁ), *lux* (ᛦ), *luminare* (✳), and *modus entis* (ᛦ)

to *principum absolutæ primum* (⚊). The seven runes are situated upon a double-graded scale where the three lowest ones (Byrghal, Sun, and Idher) belong to evil (*mala*) and the four highest ones (Man, Haghal, Kön, and Thors) to the good (*bona*).[41] The seven-stave vertical line also describes man and his constitution.

6–1: *Unum*

5–2: *Mens*

4–3 *Ratio*

3–4 *Opinio*

2–5: *Natura*

1–6: *Corpus*

Byrghal[42]

The fourth flock (cluster) concerns the calculation of time derived from the numerical mysticism of the rune cross. The numbers Bureus assigns to the runes are presented in his *Runa ABC-bok*. The right arm of the rune cross consists of the runes *t, r, o, n,* which have the numerical values 300, 9, 7, and 50, which add up to 366. Hildebrand's runes were supposed to add up to 362, even though following Bureus he says that the sum is 366. The number 366 is, according to Bureus, supposed to correspond to a solar year, while the rune Haghal in the middle of the rune cross has the numerical value of 30 and corresponds to a cycle of the moon.

The left arm of the rune cross consists of the runes *a, f, u, l,* which have the numerical values 90, 1, 3, and 700, which add up to 794. That, according to Bureus, corresponds to the number of years between conjunctions of Saturn and Jupiter ("Jovis"). Bureus explains that "with ✳ Adulruna effects the bride's presence, embrace, and double delight pointing to the year 1648 away from the previous embrace."[43]

The previous embrace was therefore the birth of Jesus, so here we are dealing with a calculation of an apocalyptic event. By the expression "the bride's presence" Bureus means that the Haghal rune should be included in the calculation and that "the embrace and double delight" means that the sum should be multiplied by 2. The conjunction of Saturn and Jupiter, or the "embrace," 794, is added to the number of the Haghal rune, 30, and that is multiplied by 2. This gives 1648, a year that stands out prominently in the adulrunic texts. To understand the meaning of this date we have to see what occurred on the previous arm: A solar year is there extended by one year (366), so we can derive the actual solar year by subtracting one year (366 – 1 = 365). We have to deal with the left arm in the same way. By subtracting one year we can arrive at the actual meaning, which is 1647. This year has great meaning in the work of Bureus in contrast to the year 1648, which does not have any especially pronounced meaning, despite the fact that the Treaty of Westphalia, ending the Thirty Years War, was concluded in that year. Bureus identifies himself with the lion spoken about in the book of Revelation 5:5, as well as the cherub who appears as a lion at God's throne in the book of Ezekiel. In this same way Bureus identifies himself with the lion from the North, *Der Mitternacht Löwe*, which is talked about in the prophecy of Paracelsus. Bureus saw himself as the prophet of the new age who would reawaken the adulrunes and the ancient wisdom.

> Then the last herald, the lion, began to act, the eschatological process is dramatized more and more. The signs and events begin to accumulate. The third empire, Solomon's kingdom, has its inception in 1641, but a greater thing happened in 1647, the year of the second coming of the Holy Spirit and the veritable judgment (Mishpat), when nevertheless only the righteous shall be judged. In this year the sixth seal of the book of Revelation shall be broken and the sixth bowl poured into the Euphrates.[44]

The year for the return of Christ is 1666, when the first judgment comes preceding the thousand-year reign. We understand from Bureus's speculations surrounding the number 666, the number of the wild beast, that the year 1666 has a special meaning.[45] Everything that is supposed to come to pass in 1666 will have already come about in 1647 due to the fact that the year 1666 is to be reduced by nineteen years. Bureus gives many mystical and intricate explanations for this.[46] Bureus explains that in 1647 there would appear a sign on the moon, and the number 19 has been connected to the moon. In the Nordic rune calendars that Bureus studied a row was found with so-called golden numbers with the help of which the exact date of Easter can be calculated. These calendars were constructed according to the prin-

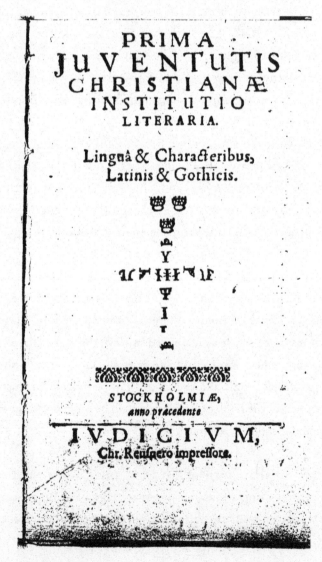

ciple found in Christian calendars that it took nineteen years for the lunar cycles to be repeated on the exact same day. On the runic calendar Latin numerals were replaced by runes.[47] Bureus writes concerning the number 19 and these rune staves:

> Because the golden number of the Moon is Nineteen years, there is first Twelve common years in the calculation, then Seven additional years, which most every farmer in Uppland knows how to make out as the Rimstaves have them.[48]

The number 19 recurs in the work of Georg Stiernhielm, a disciple of Bureus. He compares Greek myths about Apollo's return every nineteenth year with the golden numbers that are found on the rune calendars.[49]

After 1647/1666 a time of supreme happiness comes about that consists of six years in which every day is like a thousand years. In the seventh year, 1673, the final judgment occurs.[50] Thereafter the eternal kingdom of God begins.

The vertical line of the rune cross contains the runes *b, s, i, m, h, k, th,* which have the numerical values: 500, 100, 70, 900, 30, 10, and 5, the sum of which is 1915.

In connection with the computations of the seven-stave summit, a picture of a monument is shown with a cryptic legend: "therewith he set up an adulruna monument for his wife." On the monument was written *adulrunakuml,* ADVLrVnakkVML (= adulruna monument). The capital letters signify Latin Roman numerals, which give the year 1615, DVLVVML = 500 + 5 + 50 + 5 + 5 + 100 + 50. In the same way we substituted the number 1 from each side of the nine-staves across, we will, according to Bureus, subtract 1 from the beginning and 1 from the end of the seven staves of the vertical. This gives us the year 1613, "commonly written as IVDICIUM" (= 1 + 5 + 500 + 1 + 100 + 1 + 1,000), the day of judgment 1613.[51] It was in this year that Bureus received his enlightenment concerning the secrets of the adulrunes. In the late autumn of that year he was on a journey with King Gustavus Adolphus for the purpose of organizing the new printing of the Bible. When they were in Tuna in Dalarna on the fifth of December at twenty-two minutes after six o'clock Bureus was overcome by a *momentum excitationis,* a moment of rapture. He heard a voice that said in song: "RIVos IaM CLaVDe pVer sat prata bIberVnt," "Boy stop up the rivulets, for the meadows have drunk enough."[52] In these words are concealed the Roman numerals for 1673, when the world, according to Bureus, was supposed to end.

The events of 1613 would affect Bureus forever, and he would change earlier conceptions after this and instead take on the role of one initiated into the mysteries, a prophet in the midst of the confused world around him. The manuscript *Cabbalistica* in the diocesan library in Linköping is introduced with the words:

> *This book is mostly (fantasies)*
> *Collected before I*
> *Received knowledge in 1613*
> *of the hidden*
> *Truth*
> *No author can reveal it.*[53]

According to his way of thinking Bureus (Byrghal) was united with the divine (Thors) in 1613 by means of a mystical runic path of initiation that the seven-staved vertical line of the rune cross illustrates.

The fifth flock shows the three kingdoms and their rulers. It is constructed out of the runes *t, o, f* (i.e., the divine triad TOF) and *k, n, e* together with *h.*

The sixth flock shows the staves in the quintet of the offspring (i.e., the last of the three groups in the row of adulrunes), which here are called the crucified's quintet of wounds. The rune Sun is nailed through both feet, Tidher through the right hand, Lagher through the left, Byrghal has both feet fettered, and the rune Man is found at the

The three kingdoms and their rulers   The quintet of the wounds

(Images by T. Ketola)

heart like a spear thrust into it with a stream of blood coming from the heart.

The seventh and last flock in the third section of *Adulruna rediviva* shows "the threat of the guide of the law." Here the rune cross has become a bow and arrow with an arrow pointed toward its target, which is humanity/Byrghal, called the single-stave target. The highest rune, Thors, is called the single-stave string; the nine-stave crossbeam is called the nine-stave bow; and the five-runged ladder has become the arrow of Abaris—that is, the five-stave arrow that occurs in many ways in the works of Bureus. It is worth noting that the point of the arrow is formed by the rune Sun, which corresponds to the sun and especially to its rays. Abaris catches one of Apollos' arrows; that is, one of the rays of the sun. Therefore the arrow of Abaris is a ray of sunlight or an arrow of Apollo. Apollo himself is the sun and can be connected with the Thors rune, which Bureus usually equates with the sun on the horizon.

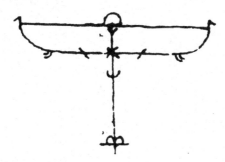

The bow and arrow

THE KING CLAD IN RUNES

The fourth section or chapter in the *Adulruna* work shows a king who has the runes on his clothing and crown. He is the shepherd in his royal office. The king is clad in a shining white tunic with a belt around his waist and crowned with a golden crown. In the pictures he is most often shown carrying a scepter and orb. On the crown is the first quintet of the progenitor, on the belt the quintet of generation, and on the hem of the tunic the quintet of the offspring.[54] In *Antiquitates Scanziana* we see the shepherd or king without his scepter or orb, and instead he is standing with outstretched arms. He is clothed in the three runic quintets, but here the crown is a piece of headgear that looks like the Thors rune.[55]

THE INNERMOST VAULT AND TREASURY OF THE ADULRUNA

Bureus devotes the fifth section to what he calls "the innermost vault and treasury of the Adulruna." At the center of Bureus's mysticism is found this symbol from which the fifteen runes of the rune row have their origin. He calls this symbol the treasury of Adulruna, where "the creator's holiest name is revealed." It has the form of a solar cross with three rings within one another. The two outer rings are geometrically perfect circles, while the innermost ring has the shape of a heart. The heart consists of a semicircle on the lower part and on the upper part that of a divided circle, the two halves of which lie over the lower semicircle, which give the form of a B lying on its side. From the inside of the second circle there is an equal-armed cross that produces the rune Haghal, which is a central rune. The Adulruna symbol is therefore constructed on the basis of an equal-armed cross, a cross and three rings that correspond to the three levels of existence. The solar cross is an ancient symbol that has been found in the North since heathen times. Bureus was also inspired by John Dee's Monas Hieroglyphica, which, similarly, is a universal symbol that contains other symbols within itself. The signs of all the planets can be seen in Dee's Monas Hieroglyphica.[56]

All fifteen runes can be traced in the Adulruna symbol, and Bureus has an elaborate system for how that is to be done. The first group of five runes, the quintet of the progenitor, is extracted for the most part from the outermost parts and outermost rings of the Adulruna. The quintet of the progenitor corresponds to God the Father, the creator. These runes are, after they are extracted from the Adulruna, the five largest in size as compared with the next ten runes. The next group, the quintet of generation, corresponds to the mediator. These runes are derived from within the outer circle and from the middlemost circle and are smaller than the former group. The last group, the quintet of the offspring, is derived from within the middlemost circle and from the heart form. These last five runes are

Adulruna

the smallest of all. Among these runes are found the rune of matter and duality, Byrghal, and these last five correspond to the plane of matter and the physical body.

HOMO TRIPLEX AND THE THREE QUINTETS

Before we investigate the structure of the Adulruna we should take a closer look at Bureus's ideas about triplicity. The world, as well as the human being, is made up of three main levels. These ideas commonly occur within Hermeticism and Neoplatonism. There is a divine level and a material level. Between these is found a mediating level that has been called the astral level or the world soul. This triplicity is a recurring theme in the work of Bureus. Besides the creator and that which is created, there is also the process of creation itself. To this level belongs "the mediator," which corresponds not only to the son, Jesus, but also to Odin and Byrger Tidesson. The universum consists of three books written by God. The first book is God's word, which can be interpreted as the Bible, and also as the mystical word John describes (1:1): "In the beginning was the Word, and the Word was with God, and the Word was God." The second book is the macrocosmos, nature and the world around man. The third book is the microcosmos, man and his inner world.[57] The world was created in three main sections: sky, earth, and sea. More precisely, Bureus is strict about not confusing heaven and earth with the ordinary sky or material earth. The first and lowest of the parts of the world was the ocean. In the beginning it is found as a primeval abyss. From the ocean, which corresponds to the principle of physicality, the sensible external world originates. The second, middlemost world was the earth, but a nonphysical earth of a higher type that corresponds to paradise and the garden of delight. The third level is heaven, which is the divine world and which should not be mixed up with the ordinary sky.[58] Bureus thought that in the same way man was a *Homo triplex,* with a threefold nature. He derived support for this from Hebrews 4:12, that man also consisted of two higher parts besides the physical body. He indicated that the initials of man's threefoldness formed the Paracelsian word SAL.

S—*Siel* (soul), a replica of God's body. *Homo spiritualis.*

A—*Anda* (spirit), the sum of all human powers, a medium of which reason is a part. *Homo rationialis.*

L—*Lekamen* (body), matter, human flesh, and blood. *Homo carnalis.*[59]

The letter *T* in the alchemical principle SALT can also be found in the work of Bureus. The body and corpse of Christ is crucified on a T as Bureus notes in one of his Adulruna commentaries. This would correspond to the occult idea that the cross upon which Christ was hung corresponds to the *Tau,* the final letter in the Hebrew alphabet. It marks the end and the point in time when man can return to his divine origin. Because Bureus equates Christ and Odin, this symbolism is interesting from the ancient Nordic perspective since Odin hangs himself on the world tree, Yggdrasil, which has been associated with the *t* rune.

Among occultists there is disagreement as to whether the spirit or the soul was the highest substance of man. In his revelation of 1613, Bureus has the idea that the soul was ranked above the spirit, but after his experiences in Tuna he thought the better of it and reverted to his earlier view that he revised: "At that time I knew not that Spiritus is the highest *in homine.*"[60]

Bureus explains that the body is earthly, heavy, and downward striving while the spirit is divine and "mightily high-soaring." Body and soul are unified by the medial substance that is the soul. The soul is the soul of the body and is also the body of the spirit.[61] The soul is feminine, while the spirit and matter are by contrast masculine, and they are like suitors courting the soul. Bureus writes:

> The spirit, who first sought her hand in marriage, very much wants to elevate her, make her his bride and thus make her his lawful wife and queen; but the body, like a seducer, flatters her and wants to lure her away from her bridegroom, down into a dark cave in the earth, to make her into a whore.[62]

In the Nymäre verses Bureus writes:

> *Our soul has the temperament of a bride,*
> *and the spirit is of the nature of the husband.*[63]

The soul is a bride whose favor the body and spirit fight over. The bride allows herself to be lured down into matter by the body, which is called a common or unredeemed man.

> *Now it was not long,*
> *Before a Commoner,*
> *Came into the company,*
> *He enticed her away with flattery,*
> *Into a Cave with him,*
> *Way down under the Earth.*
> *The dark and ugly,*
> *And there he did dishonor her.*[64]

It is only by sacrificing the body on the cross or on the world tree like Christ or Odin that the human soul is united with the spirit.

Triplicities occur in the Adulruna symbol of Bureus with its three circles from which the three runic quintets can be derived. The three circles correspond to spirit, soul, and the body. The outermost level corresponds to God and the spirit, while the middle one is thought to stand for the mediator and the soul. The innermost heart-shaped ring corresponds to the body that is crucified.

THE ADULRUNA

In the different versions of *Adulruna rediviva* and in *Antiquitates Scanziana,* Bureus describes the development of the runes from the archetypal principles out of which his adulrunic solar cross is constructed. He also describes the construction and principles of the Adulruna symbol. In *Antiquitates Scanziana* he shows how the solar cross is built upon a circle that represents the *theologia negativa,* the knowledge of the divine that cannot be described in word or concept. This is the undifferentiated primeval principle of unity. On the other hand, the cross represents the positive and affirmative knowledge of the divine, the *theologica affirmativa.* Bureus connects this affirmative knowledge of the divine with Paracelsus and his teachings. Bureus identified himself with Paracelsus, and Bureus's initials, ITAB, which stood for Iohannes Tomae Agrivillensis Bureus were also indicated as meaning Iohannes Theophrastus Aracelsus Bureus in signatures. The initials ITAB could have other symbolic meanings as well.[65] The equal-armed cross corresponded to the sun and its influence as well as to the presence of the divine. Bureus also explained the structure of the cross. The horizontal line stands for the horizon of eternity. In agreement with Platonic tradition it can represent how the creator divided the world into two parts and separated heaven and earth, spirit and matter. Above and below are, however, reunited by the vertical line. The descent by God's son (Jesus, Odin, the mediator) unifies the two worlds. This thereby makes possible the ascent of man.

From the symbol with a circle divided by a horizontal line Bureus derives the first name of the creator, which is GUD (God), which consists of the runes Kön, Ur, and Thors. The runes Kön and Ur gave rise to the runes Frey and Odhen, and Bureus finds in the word GUD the original Gothic trinity TOF: Thor, Odin, and Frigga. When the solar cross is completed, and the vertical line is added, the name of the Gothic tetragrammaton can be found. The vertical line corresponds to the descent of the son and his appearance as an *I* could be associated with "Iesus." The four-staved Gothic tetragrammaton is thus GUID. In *Antiquitates Scanziana* he compares the name of the tetragrammaton in different languages. In Latin it is DEUS, in Arabic ALLA, in Hebrew IHVH, and so on.[66] In any illustration of the tetragrammaton, however, the Hebrew IHVH has the foremost place among tetragrammatons in different languages. The Thors rune represents God the Father, the Ur rune corresponds to the son, Odin, and Christ, and the vertical line (which is similar to the rune I) stands for the descent of the son into human form. The Kön rune represents the Holy Spirit.

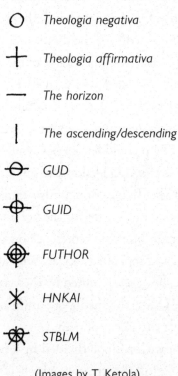

O   *Theologia negativa*

✝   *Theologia affirmativa*

—   *The horizon*

| *The ascending/descending*

⊖   *GUD*

⊕   *GUID*

⊕   *FUTHOR*

✳   *HNKAI*

✳   *STBLM*

(Images by T. Ketola)

Seeing that Bureus first produced GUD and then GUID, the Gothic tetragrammaton could be interpreted as God + the son.

In the next level of the Adulruna symbol there is found a circle within the first one. From this symbol the creator's other name can be discovered. From the equal-armed cross with two circles Bureus's entire first group of runes, the quintet of the progenitor—*f, u, th, o, r*—can be derived. These runes form the word *FUDOR*, which Bureus interprets as father. This is the creator's, or progenitor's, other name, as well as the first quintet of the three. The runes that give rise to GUID FADER are of the same size.

In the next group the runes become a degree smaller. Now a cross has been formed on the inside of the other rings. This cross, together with its vertical line, forms a Haghal rune. Bureus associates this rune with Christ and the Holy Spirit, which are the mediators that will unite man (Byrghal) and God (Thors).[67] This is also the quintet of the mediator, the quintet of generation, which is symbolized by the three scepters that express the official power of the three crowns. The runes in this quintet are *h, n, k, a, i*. Bureus has the runes *n, a,* and *k* represent NotAriKyn (*notarikon*), the cabbalistic teaching where initial letters form a word, as in ITAB.

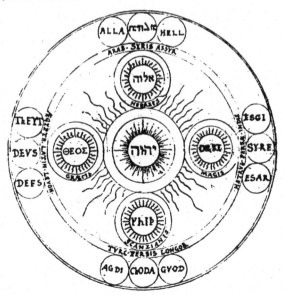

The last group, the quintet of the offspring, consists of the runes *s, t, b, l, m,* and these form the symbol of the crucified heart that has three nails in it. This represents Christ on the cross. By placing Byrghal on its side on top of a man rune a heart-shaped symbol is made. It appears as a heart crucified on a T, which can correspond to the Tau cross. The rune Tidher corresponds to the nail in the right hand; the Lagher corresponds to the nail in the left. The Sol rune in its simple so-called hanging form penetrates from above, between the two halves of Byrghal. The Sol rune corresponds to the nail through the feet. This runic quintet represents matter, flesh, and blood and consists of smaller runes than the ones in the foregoing groups.

The three basic symbols in the Adulruna are the solar cross with two rings, the three nails, and the crucified heart with three nails. These three basic symbols each represent a runic quintet. Additionally these are preceded by the simple solar cross with a ring that stands for the Gothic tetragrammaton, GUID.

GUID   The solar cross, tetragrammaton.

FUTHOR   The solar cross with two rings (sun and moon). "Id Sol et Luna Adulrunæ,"[68] quintet of the progenitor, "Father." The divine world. Thor.

HNKAI*   The three nails, quintet of generation, the mediator, the son. The astral world. Odin.

STBLM   The crucified heart pierced through by three nails, the quintet of the offspring. Matter. Frigga/Frey.

THE THREE CROWNS

The sixth section in *Adulruna rediviva* concerns the three crowns, "the eldest coat of arms of the Swedish realm." The number 3 is a holy and

---

*The usual order of these runes, which he has, among other places, in his *Runa ABC-bok,* is *k, h, n, i, a.*

magical number in the work of Bureus and recurs in many contexts in his philosophy. In the chapter about the three crowns Bureus explains that the Swedes were originally ruled by the ancient one who was called the Ancestor. Over time the mass of people grew and the ancestral father's task became too difficult, so he installed a high priest and a judge who took over some of his duties. He himself was called the king and was the most prominent of the three. The Swedish realm was also divided into three countries, and on the advice of Byrger Tidesson the king, or *drighten,* gave each country a crown, and the three crowns were to become the heraldic device of Sweden as a whole.

The so-called folklands is a collective way of designating Tiundaland, Attundaland, and Fjärundraland in Uppland. These were juridical districts. They were united in and by the enactment of the Law of Uppland (1296) into one common jurisdiction. The origin and development of the folklands before 1296 is veiled in darkness, but their existence is known from the the eleventh century onward. The names of the three folklands indicate that they originally comprised ten (Tiundaland), eight (Attundaland), and four (Fjärundraland) so-called *hundaren* (hundreds); that is, jurisdictional districts or district courts. Around 1300 the interior parts of Gästrikland were still counted as part of Tiundaland. The word "folk"in the term *folkland* appears to have originally meant "warrior band." Before the inception of the Upplandic Law the folklands were independent domains of "law men" who had a religious function. Byrger Tidesson was, according to Bureus, a law man in Tiundaland.

The younger Västgötland Law asserted that the Swedes possessed the right to elect the king of the realm. According to the Upplandic Law this right was incumbent upon the three folklands. The Södermanna Law established that the election should take place at the legal assembly of Mora. Magnus Eriksson's national law established that the law men from all the jurisdictions of the realm should elect the king at the legal assembly of Mora. On the meadow of Mora in the parish of Lagga, about six miles from Uppsala, on the border between Attundaland and Tiundaland, the election of the king was conducted during the legal assembly of Mora, when the people chose their king. During the Middle Ages an oath stone was situated on the meadow of Mora. It was called the Mora stone. The exact original location of this oath stone is now unknown. It was probably displaced back in the Middle Ages. But it was supposedly to be found in the vicinity of a house that was built in 1770, where it is preserved today in eight pieces of stone. Some of them are whole and others fragmentary. The three crowns were depicted on the Mora stone. A classic drawing by Scheffrus shows the Mora stones, where one of the stone fragments bears the symbol of the three crowns.[69]

The three crowns also symbolize the three functions: the king, the judge, and the high priest.[70] For Bureus the three crowns are in no way merely associated with mundane concerns. They are in the highest-degree symbols for metaphysical and esoteric reality. In several illustrations the three crowns surmount the rune cross. From the chapter titled "The Three Realms and Their Rulers" in *Adulruna rediviva* we can draw the conclusion that the three realms that the three crowns symbolize are derived from the Gothic trinity TOF, so that the three crowns are those that crown Thor, Odin, and Frigga. Sweden's national emblem is therefore also derived from the Gothic trinity.

THE ADULRUNA AND ITS SCIENCES

In *Cabbalistica,* Bureus lists seven sciences according to the hierarchical ordering of the seven vertical staves of the rune cross.

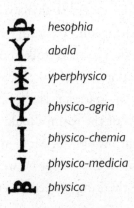

hesophia

abala

yperphysico

physico-agria

physico-chemia

physico-medicia

physica

THE SUCCESSORS OF BUREUS

The esoteric researches of Bureus were known to those outside Sweden, and he received several visits from guests from faraway countries who desired to be instructed in "the truth about the adulrunes."[71] The Dano-German author Conrad von Hövelen for a time owned one of the seven manuscripts of *Adulruna* by Bureus. Conrad von Hövelen was inspired by the contents, and when he traveled to Sweden in 1659 to write ballets and plays, he also wrote "Die Auf-läbende Adelrune oder Schwedens Alten und Neuen Herligkeit," presented in 1664 but now lost.[72] The famous Rosicrucian Joachim Morsius visited Bureus. Jacob Böhme's prominent pupil, Abraham von Franckenberg, expressed his admiration for Bureus in several letters that have been preserved.[73] Even if he also met with opposition to his domestic plan, Bureus had a small band of followers.

Bureus's most advanced apprentice was the poet and civil servant Georg Stiernhielm (1598–1672). Stiernhielm became the royal antiquary after Bureus and was strongly influenced by his teacher. On certain topics he would tone down Bureus's mystical speculations, in other contexts he went even further than Bureus. Stiernhielm was fascinated by Neoplatonism early on and opposed the scholastics and the tedious "quarreling" of Aristotle, which he abhorred. "Eagles don't catch flies," was his commentary on the Aristotelians. Instead he read the *Enneads* of Plotinus and mystics such as Ficino, Robert Fludd, and Giordano Bruno. He was the first in Sweden to accept in all respects the ideas of Bruno concerning an infinite animated universe with countless stellar worlds. Like Bureus, Stiernhielm thought that the true philosophy was found among the ancient wise men such as Plato, Moses, Zoroaster, and Hermes Trismegistus. In his uncompleted philosophical life's work, *Monile Minervae* (Minerva's Necklace), Stiernhielm describes how elements in nature are woven together. The main theme is the doctrine of nature's three principles: the dark, the soul, and the light. According to Stiernhielm the biblical account of creation describes how these three principles work together to produce our world. Out of the night, the empty nothingness, emerged the first principle, *prima materia,* primeval matter, which was a misty mass of water, the abode of the dark and cold. Primeval matter was formed and received its structure from the principle of the soul (*mens*). The soul is an emanation of God's essence that deposited the ideas, or seeds, of things in matter. These are first made ready or actualized by the light (*lux*) that functions as the instrument of the soul and drives away the night so that nature rises out of the depths like Venus from the waves.[74]

Stiernhielm was also a linguist, and his linguistic writings are marked by the influence of Neoplatonism and of his teacher, Bureus. In the chapter about the treasury of Adulruna, Bureus shows how the runes and words correspond to spiritual reality. Therefore the original Gothic language is not only supposed to represent reality but also directly reflect it. During the Renaissance it began to be called into question as to whether Hebrew was the original divine language. Bureus toyed with the idea that the original Gothic language was the oldest, but he nevertheless ascribed a special position to Hebrew as the original divine language above any other. Stiernhielm would go all the way and declare Gothic to be the original language that corresponded exactly to the things it describes.[75] The idea comes from Plato's dialog *Cratylus,* in which words are seen as not merely arbitrary signs but rather as something that reflected their own content and corresponded to actual things. Even the individual letters and their sounds corresponded to certain principles: *R* signifies movement, *L* ease, and so on.[76] Stiernhielm shows how the letters represent gradations of spirit or matter. The vowels correspond to the spiritual plane; the highest of them is the letter *A,* which corresponds to God himself, the source of all things. After *A* come the other vowels in the hierarchical order: *Ä, E, Ö, I, Y, Å, O, U.* The letter *A* corresponds to the light and clarity, while *U* corresponds to the dark and night. The consonants represent matter, but the vowels *I* and *U* are close to being materialized, and by losing light the sounds are transformed into *J* [*Y*] and *V.* If *V* condenses and materializes further it becomes an *F* and ultimately a *P.* Of the consonants the *H* is closest to the spiritual. It is almost immaterial. To the lowest consonants belong the *N* and finally the *M* that corresponds to the earth and more, darkness and silence. Here we see a similarity to the description by Bureus of the fifteen runes where M is the last rune, "the one that shuts the mouth." Perhaps it was this Platonically influenced linguistic teaching caused Bureus to place the rune M last. In the usual sixteen-rune row it is the fourteenth rune. That Stiernhielm was to a high degree influenced by Bureus is clearly indicated by the title of his first more exhaustive linguistic work, *Adelruna sive Sibylla Sveo-Gothica*.[77] In the manuscript *Specimen philologicum in priman literam A,* Stiernhielm devotes himself to the concept of *adelruna antiqua*.[78] In *Mysterium Etymologicum* he starts out from the fifteen adelruna row of Bureus.[79]

After Stiernhielm, Olof Verelius (1618–1682) would become the royal antiquary. Unlike Bureus, Verelius did not consider the runes to be keys to some positive esoteric knowledge, but rather he thought that they had been used as means for the practice of black magic. He did consider, in agreement with Bureus, that the runes had several layers, or levels, that were only accessible to the initiated runemaster. Following the directions of the Icelander Olof Rugman (1636–1679) he made an inventory of the magical uses of the runes. There were *málrúnar*—that is, written signs—but there were also magical runes. These latter runes were the magical forms of runes, and they could be divided into twenty grades, or alphabets, with progressively more mysterious powers. In the first grade each rune had a name according to what it was supposed to represent. The rune Man signifies "man" or "human being." In other grades certain characteristics or properties were added such as in this example, *madher er moldar auki,* which means "man is the increase of dust." Grade for grade the signification of the runes was expanded, and already with the seventh grade one required the wisdom of a poet to understand the meanings, for here the really dark runes began, such as the harmful runes, flax runes, weaving temple runes, and so forth. Those who were initiated into the highest degrees knew how to use them to "call up the dead and conjure spirits."[80]

Olof Rudbeck was influenced by Bureus, and in chapter 28 of the first volume of *Atlantica* he refers to the research of Bureus.[81] In the same chapter is found a picture of a caduceus staff in the image of which Rudbeck shows how all the runes can be seen. This staff with its two serpents, which belonged to Mercurius, or the *merkesmann,* as Rudbeck calls him, illustrates the three governmental authorities ascribed to the three crowns. Rudbeck shows how the three runes that symbolize the authority of the three crowns are found in the caduceus. These runes also represent Har, Jafnhar, and Thridi, the mystical chieftains whom King Gylfi meets in Snorri's *Edda.* Jafnhar is represented by the *i* rune, Har by the *h* rune, and Thridi by the *t* rune.[82] Rudbeck's way of finding all the runes in the Hermetic symbol and gathering correspondences with Gothic and national motifs is reminiscent of procedures used by Bureus.

A farmer by the name of Jon Olofsson quoted Bureus as he traveled around in the Upplandic countryside spreading a daring form of religious propaganda. He was gripped by apocalyptic speculations and considered himself to be a "prodigy" and world savior who spoke daily with an angel.[83]

Although Bureus had a small group of admirers, it does not seem that his adulrunic esotericism received any wider distribution. His most prominent pupil, Stiernhielm, distanced himself from Bureus's cabbalistic mysticism and is more tinged with Neoplatonic ideas. Neither does it appear that Bureus's theories were committed to any sort of practice, even if they invited such application. Perhaps his *Adulruna* was too subjective and obscure to win over any successors.

13

ESOTERIC GOTHICISM
AFTER BUREUS

A re Bureus, and possibly Stiernhielm, ultimately examples of an esoteric Gothicism? Did esoteric ideas live on in later Gothicism? A meaningful answer to this would require a thorough survey not only of Gothicism but also perhaps even more so of the development of esotericism from the early 1600s onward. The history of esotericism during the time of Gothicism passes through the Rosicrucian awakening that influenced Bureus but that then exhibited a continuing presence that assimilated itself to other forms in the development of Freemasonry and an order-based culture. It appears that Gothicism continued to be influenced by the esoteric subculture, but it also went through the same transformations as esotericism in general. Whether or not Bureus was influenced by the inner Rosicrucian awakening, a society that came later, the Manhem League, was marked by a secularized Freemasonically inspired enthusiasm for the idea of orders. Whether the Manhem League should be principally classified as an esoteric society depends on whether by "esoteric" one means such things as initiatic orderlike culture and secrecy. A spiritual or religious dimension was unambiguously found within the Manhem League, which did include initiations, an orderlike culture, and secrecy. It is nevertheless uncertain whether it can be called an esoteric society and whether it can be compared to the esoteric Gothicism that distinguished Bureus. At the end of this chapter I will avail myself of Antoine Faivre's method to analyze the esoteric traits of the Gothicism of Bureus.

JOHAN GÖRANSSON'S *IS ATLINGA*

One of the few who bravely stood up for the Gothic fantasies of the period when Sweden was a world power once these ideas had become hopelessly unfashionable during the 1700s was the runologist Johan Göransson. In a book with the title *Is atlinga; De är: De forna göters, här uti Svea rike, bokstafver ok salighets lära, tvåtusend tvåhundrad år före Christum, utspridde i all land; Ingenfunden af Johan Göransson* (1747), Göransson developed his theories about the origin of the runes, languages, and religions. Like Bureus he claimed to have rediscovered the original truth about the runes. He describes the holy numbers that were very meaningful to the Sveo-Goths and to which different runes in the sixteen-rune row corresponded.[1] Following Bureus he explains that the rune row's initial runes *f, u, th, o, r* indicate Father, which proves that the secrets of Christianity are concealed in the runes. He considered that every rune had a great symbolic significance, and he thought that every rune was also a sermon. Using the Icelandic rune poem from the 1400s as his point of departure, he describes the meaning of every rune in a column that also shows its number in the rune row and which letter it signifies.[2] Further on in the book he discusses Odin's wife, Sibyllan (who is not found in the works of Bureus), who prophesies Christ through the rune row that corresponds to different years and epochs in history. The first rune (ᚠ) corresponds to the Golden Age of peace, bliss, prosperity, and happiness. Göransson offers his runic sermon:

> Adam, created in God's image in a condition of bliss, owned the riches of the earth, even the Highest Peace that can be given. In the *Edda* this age is sometimes called Frei's and sometimes Thor's golden age; even by the Greek and Latin historians.[3]

Rune for rune Göransson takes the reader through history, especially with biblical references. By multiplying the number of the rune in the rune row by 200 he produced the historical years the rune describes. The Nöd rune, which is the eighteenth rune, stands for sixteen hundred years after creation, the year when the great distress, the Deluge, occurred. Göransson is one of the least noticed of the series of runologists who ascribed symbolic meanings to the runes. Unlike Bureus, he is not especially marked by an esoteric strain but, if anything, represents a mystical Gothic Christianity with a strain of numerology and ideas about prophecies.

THE INITIATORY GOTHICISM OF THE MANHEM LEAGUE

Later Gothicism has its inception during the early 1800s. It had been preceded by a period of what the predecessors of later Gothicism experienced as one of disinterest in anything Nordic. The earlier Gothicism and Rudbeckianism had disappeared or been ridiculed in learned circles, and only a few people such as Björner and Johan Göransson had carried on the cause of the earlier form of Gothicism during the 1700s. As a reaction against this the Gothic League was founded in 1811, with the poet Erik Gustaf Geijer being one of its leading figures. The league's aims were literary as well as cultural and patriotic in general. They wanted to revive the "spirit of freedom" and "manly courage." The common heroic history of the North, the old Nordic myths, and Icelandic sagas were emphasized.

Another similar patriotic league was the Manhem League. The members were partially the same as the ones in the Gothic League. Both groups stressed the importance of physical, spiritual, and moral strength. Only a strong and hardy people could save the fatherland. Influenced by Germany's growing gymnastics clubs with Friedrich Ludwig Jahn at their helm, the league considered that the health of the people and "a sound soul in a sound body" were important elements together with instruction and education of the people. Above all, the

Manhem League had as its ambition the development and improvement of the new generations. Physical exercises and patriotic songs would develop the upcoming generation into new Vikings. The Manhem League developed a nine-degree path of initiation that would teach Gothic virtues to the young adepts.

The name *Manhem* comes from Old Icelandic *mannheimar,* "the world of man" or "mankind's abode(s)." The mannheimar are mentioned by Snorri Sturluson in the *Heimskringla* as a name of Svithjod, the land of the Swedes, and which contrasts with Gudhem, Gothem, or Godhem ("abode of the gods"). Manhem is the name of the world of mankind. Midgård is a common designation for the world of mankind, but it is really the name of the fortress in which mankind lives. In the same way, Asgård is the fortress where the Æsir live, while the real name of their world is Gothem.[4] In the work of Eyvindr Skáldaspillir, Manhem is said to be the dwelling place of Odin and the goddess Skadi. Snorri's interpretation made it so that the prominent figure of Gothicism, Olof Rudbeck, used it as a synonym for Sweden in the Swedish translation of *Atlantica: Atland eller Manheim.* The word *manhem* has frequently been used in Gothicism (e.g., Erik Gustaf Geijer's poem "Manhem").

The symbol of the Manhem League was the Madher rune (Ψ), which stood for "man" or "*manhem.*" Above the rune stood the letter *M,* and on their greater seal above that there was a symbol of the trinity surrounded by a radiant ring. Around the border appeared the motto of the league, *Thette eR vaR nidleitni,* "this is our aim," inscribed in runes. The educational character of the Manhem League was connected with the fact that the league was founded by teachers at the Afzeliuska School in Stockholm.

The search for the "innocence of being" was the goal of initiation into Manhem. This is represented by seeking after Balder, who, after he had been killed by his brother Hödur through Loki's treachery, disappeared into the realm of the dead, Hel. The path of initiation consists of nine degrees that can be compared to the nine days that Odin's son Hermod traveled when he went to meet Balder in the realm of the dead. The number 9 also occurs in connection with Odin's initiation during nine nights on Yggdrasil. For the brothers in the Manhem League initiation denoted a form of education the aim of which was to improve themselves on both an outer and inner level. In the final degrees the brother in the order would go the whole way out into the ordinary world and work within society with the teachings of his initiation as part and parcel of who he was. The adepts were mainly young men, and the league had no age restrictions, although an informal proclamation indicated that they did not admit anyone under twelve. The initiation would unite the youths with the adult brothers of the order through a shared initiatory experience.

THE PATH OF THE NINE DEGREES OF INITIATION IN THE MANHEM LEAGUE

One of the leaders of the Manhem League was the author Carl Jonas Love Almqvist. He developed the nine initiatory degrees. In both the Gothic League and the Manhem League there was originally a strong strain of neo-paganism and criticism of Christianity. But over time they became increasingly Christian, something that, among other things, found expression in the later degrees of the Manhem League. The descriptions of the degrees of the Manhem League come from Almqvist's collected works, which are published in a digital version by the Svenska vitterhetssamfundet (Swedish Knowledge Society). Citations of Almqvist's work are drawn from there. I also availed myself of Greta Hedin's *Manhemsförbundet: Ett bidrag till göticismens och yngre romantikens historia* from 1928.

1. The Dark Grove. The first degree is a preparation for entrance into the course of initiation within Manhem. First the adept must enter into a dark phase in which he realizes that impurity and ignorance marked the world and his earlier life. The first degree is a melancholy degree corresponding to darkness and death. The adept has to answer some riddles and learn to read the runes. For this degree the adept is supposed to read the myths that belong to the nightside of the ancient Nordic world, which contain myths about giants, trolls, and dark elves. The Asa god who belongs to this degree is the god of blindness, Höder, the brother and murderer of Balder. His blindness corresponds to the external enlightenment that characterizes the uninitiated and that can be exploited by an evil will, such as Loki possesses. The adepts in this degree are called "Höder's children." They wear the Madher rune on a dark band. It represents mankind in its dark predicament. Almqvist describes this degree:

If Manhem were a place, a ceremonial veil would hang in black cascades over the whitewashed walls in the first of the nine halls. Because the world is said to be white, but here it should be revealed that the black waves of darkness, in invisible swells, but with quite deep sighs, extends over the whole and lie upon it like a ceremonial veil. A tomb, in the work itself, is the world in this position. As the usual world lives, concluding with death, Manhem's drama conversely begins by dying, so that the life to come may be without end.

To leave the first degree and enter into the next degree the adept has to declare himself ready to live for love and truth, and he must be convinced that the vices and follies of his present life are things that ought to be abandoned once and for all in exchange for something much better.

2. Balder's Grove. The second degree is intimately connected to the first one and at the same time they are complements of one another. The adept has turned away from the darkness of the previous degree and searches inward. In the search for self-improvement the adept asks himself how to improve himself on this level, and the answer is by acquiring a strong body. Games and gymnastics belong to this degree. The purity and innocence of the body is to be developed in this degree, while the innocence of the soul is to be developed in the later degrees. To keep themselves aware of the fact that the body is not everything, the adepts cried out: "Woe . . . Woe . . . Balder still lies in Hel!" during their gymnastic exercises. The adepts of the second degree are called "Balder's children," and they wear a Tvimadur (a double form of the Madher rune) hanging on a white band. The adept receives a sword upon initiation into the second degree. Readings from the light side of the *Edda*—the mythology concerning the gods—belong to this degree.

The first two degrees are called the child degrees and function as preparation for the higher degrees.

3. Hlidskjalf. The third degree is named for Odin's fortress and corresponds to "the high chief ruler Odin's magnificently dazzling Valhalla." Now the adept has passed through the two preparatory child degrees and enters into the actual Manhem League with the third degree. The Hlidskjalf degree is the first of the three degrees that correspond to the Asiric life and the three main Gothic gods, Odin, Thor, and Frigga (or Frey), described by Adam of Bremen. The third degree is characterized by nature poetry, and fitting readings are the holy Nordic poems such as the "Voluspa" and royal sagas such as the *Volsunga Saga* and *Heimskringla*. According to Almqvist, the spirit of the degree should be marked by

> the carefree, independent gaiety that man inhales with a deep breath when he feels himself to be living a sound, glorious, natural life. The delight in the power of physical life: the feeling of the enormity of the Asa chieftains who increase our own confidence, seeing as they belong to us and our own land: the earth's own gleaming delight as every thing appears as if living through myth.

Members of the third degree are called "Odin's warriors," and they wear a symbol of Gungnir, Odin's spear, on their breasts hanging on a sky-blue band, a color that should remind the adept of Valhalla and the heaven of his forefathers. They now receive the shield. The adepts should set about developing their physical strength but should not forget the search for Balder, which is the task of initiation. Although

Hlidskjalf corresponds to Odin's golden halls and the golden age, the initiates may not remain without asking the question about whether they can find Balder here. As an answer they get:

> Lo, Odin himself went to look for Balder but did not find him. But now the traveling companions remain behind! And your joyous repose among the ancients; and your play here, until the age merges, to further beginnings to depart toward your goal.

From the third degree onward the degrees correspond to epochs in Swedish history. The third degree corresponds to the oldest Asiric period, which is called the Yngling Age.

4. Thrudvogner. The name of Thor's fortress designates the fourth degree. This degree represents the Gothic warrior life and heathen chivalry, or knightly virtue. It is a darker and more warlike degree than the third degree. The nature poetry of the previous degree is replaced by military force, and the beautiful strains of Valhalla are replaced by the roar of the sea and storms. The physical strength and warlike capacity of the Asa god Thor places its stamp upon the adepts of this degree, and they are called "Thor's warriors." Heathen chivalry distinguishes itself from Christian chivalry—into which the adept is initiated in the higher degrees—in that the Christian knight fights for principles outside himself, such as his lady or God. Heathen warriors fight only for themselves.

> The heathen warrior embraces unbridled independence bordering on savagery, as the individual, fully aware of his strength, rushing over land and sea, considers everything to be his own, as it is subjugated by his strength, and recognizes no rights among others or obligations for himself other than those to which he himself is willing to consent.

The symbol of this degree is the hammer of Thor, Mjölnir, on a steel-gray cord. The adepts now receive the coat of mail. Adepts ask whether Balder is to be found here and receive a negative answer but hear of a mystical island where he can perhaps be found. The adept then thinks: "We have to go this island!"

5. Fensal. The fifth degree is named after the abode of Frigga. This degree represents the return of the heathen warrior or Viking to the land of his forefathers. Love of the fatherland marks this degree as the last of the Asa degrees. The degrees of this level belong to the physical makeup of man and his nature period. After this, spiritual development begins. Almqvist explains that the land of the forefathers is for man's nature period what heaven is for his spirit.

> Therefore this degree is the last one in this period. The idea of the Fatherland is the blossom of Heathendom. Its spirit is the calm inner desire in which people realize that they belong to a specific land upon the earth, and for the welfare of which they will gladly offer every effort with a childlike enthusiasm. Still only in an earthly fashion (never aiming toward heaven, except in their innermost beings, as yet in an unconscious way), the Fatherland is everything to the warrior: the peaceful womb out of which he emerged, and to which he lovingly returns after gleaming adventures all over the world; he wishes to return, to be sunken down one day, to be united with his ancestral soil. The coloring of the league, dazzling in the third degree and gloomy in the fourth, here transitions into a silent, airy mild brilliance—like the daylight in which a landscape appears on a beautiful summer evening. This degree is the evening of the natural life.

In a certain way Frigga represents Mother Earth, but after this degree it is time for the adept to try to get away from the nature period, to go upward into the higher regions. The adepts of the fifth degree are called "Frigga's warriors" and wear an encircled golden ax on a green band. Frey also belongs to this degree. Adam of Bremen reported that a Fricco was worshipped alongside Thor and Odin. This was later interpreted as meaning Frigga, but during the 1800s it was understood that it referred to Frey. Frigga certainly fits better in the context of the fourth degree. It is also interesting to note that Bureus's Gothic trinity consisted of Odin, Thor, and Frigga. Geijer's *Odalbonden* and Thomas Thorild's *Göthamanna sånger* were appropriate readings for the fifth degree. Initiation into the fifth degree takes place in a nighttime setting beside a runestone. The adepts have to look down into Frigga's shrine, and there they see a picture depicting the island they heard spoken about in the fourth degree, Thrudvogner. They ask to see more, but the shrine is closed again and the torchbearers in the ceremony say with a sigh: "Nothing more is to be seen herein." The adepts, who earlier had received a sword, shield, and coat of mail, complete their armament in the fifth degree with the reception of a helmet. In a stately manner they now stand as the king's men, defenders of the fatherland.

6. Degree of Hope. Despite the bright-sounding name of the sixth degree, Almqvist explains that if the fifth degree represented the twilight, then the sixth corresponds to the degree of the night. This is the degree of the abyss and Ragnarök. The ancients collapse, and the adepts go from the physical degrees into the spiritual ones. The sixth degree is connected to the previous degrees in that both are preparatory degrees. The other degrees constitute the outer preparation, and the sixth degree is the inner one. The other degrees prepare the adept to enter the real side of the league (the Asa life of the third, fourth, and fifth), while the sixth degree prepares the adept to enter the league's ideal side (the seventh, eighth, and ninth). The hope that the adept experienced in the other degrees was horizontal and directed out over the earth, while the hope in the sixth degree is vertical and strives toward heaven.

The initiation ceremony for the sixth degree symbolizes Ragnarök. The words of the Norns are read for the adepts who are dressed in their full armor, but they have their eyes blindfolded. They learn that the forces of the abyss are loose. The Asa gods fall in the battle against these, and the Æsir as well as the forces of chaos die in this struggle. One after the other of the different pieces of ceremonial armor are taken from the adept. Lastly the sword is taken away from him. The adept has taken an oath in which he swears to remove all weakness of the will, all narrow-mindedness of thought, and all meanness in his actions. The adepts are offered a ritual drink of wine, and the blindfold is taken from their eyes. All the members already initiated into the league are dressed in white, and above the president a large star that represents the degree of hope is seen.

Once the old gods fell, Balder's meaning was rediscovered. Balder lived among the gods as the spirit does in nature. Balder's dealings with nature ultimately result in his plunging into Hel as the world's innocence is lost. Now innocence is returning like the island the adepts sought, or like the morning star that announces the coming day. The adepts once more receive their swords in exchange for their promise to use their physical force free of egotistical aims. They wear as a sign a silver star on a white band with black edging. The star represents the star of hope in the night, the northern star in the vault of heaven. With the sixth degree the adept makes the transition from Swedishness into universality. The adept is to have his feet on the earth of the fatherland but is to raise himself over selective love. The adept is called "the knight of the morning star" in this degree.

7. The Garden of the Bird of Paradise. The seventh degree represents the lower element of Christian "chivalry" that corresponds to courtly love for the lady. The adept possesses the same force and strength as the warrior in the lower degrees but does not fight for himself alone but for something outside of himself. This degree involves the life of Romanticism and the beginning of the higher spirit. In this degree the members receive a special order name. The symbol of the degree is a golden heart hanging on a light red band with white borders, and the adept is called a "knight of the golden heart." The shield belongs to the seventh degree. The reading for this degree is the Old Testament. Swedish history from Birger to the Kalmar Union is the epoch corresponding to this degree.

8. The Temple. The degree actually bears no name, because it is consecrated to Christianity itself. The degree should be distinguished by a life that is Uranian and the higher completion of the spirit. The Romanticism of the previous degrees is to become Uranian or heavenly in this one. Here the adept should be marked by unselfishness and unity with God. The adept is called a "knight of the cross" and wears a golden cross on a purple band. A helmet and cuirass belong to the eighth degree. The period between the Kalmar Union and Gustav Vasa is the historical epoch of the degree, and its reading is the New Testament.

The seventh and eighth degrees form the Christian cavalry.

9. The Heart. The ninth degree signifies a kind of exit from the league out into society at large. The degree represents "the view over the whole, life's contradictions reconciled, a coincidence of the degrees under one heading, beyond the league." In a long commentary, Almqvist explains that the adept has to realize that he is basically a yeoman and that all social classes or estates are built upon this farmer class. The king represents the ideal and the farmer represents the real, but they are basically unified in the same principle: "in the work itself (i.e., when the forms are penetrated down to their basic levels) everything in Sweden belongs to the yeoman class." Unity arises in "the Social Union, Kingdom." The four estates, or classes, represent the different degrees in the Manhem League. The farmers form the basis. After this comes the nobility. Above the nobility stands the citizenry, and the highest, the ninth degree, is represented by the priests. In the ninth degree the adept lays his chivalric name and armor aside, but at solemn occasions he wears a cloak and a wreath of oak leaves. They are called Noblemen in the Manhem League. When the graduates of the highest degree associate with one another they are all clad in black as a sign of their equality and call one another Freeborn Swedish Men. The epoch that corresponds to this degree is from Gustav Vasa up to the present day.

The initiatory path of the Manhem League, as Almqvist describes it, fulfills an educational function for young men who are to be formed so that they may become good fellow citizens in society. The adepts begin by having their feet planted in the Swedish or Gothic soil, which corresponds to the five lowest degrees, but raise themselves to the universal and Christian level that is represented by the four uppermost degrees.

Through the Manhem League and other manifestations of Nordic mysticism we can see how the influence of Bureus and the currents of runic Gothicism have reached through the nineteenth century and to the present day. As noted above, I will now analyze Bureus's cabbalistic system according to Antoine Faivre's criteria to see if it meets the definition of esotericism.

ADULRUNIC MYSTICISM AND FAIVRE'S CRITERIA

Are the adulrunic mysticism and Gothic Cabbala esotericism of Bureus outside the criteria Antoine Faivre established and of which I gave an account in chapter 10? Faivre's six criteria are (1) correspondences, (2) living nature, (3) imagination and mediations, (4) experience of transmutation, together with (5) traditional concordance and (6) transmission. The last two named here are not primary, but only relative, and do not need to be present in all forms of esotericism.

On the first point, correspondences make up a central part of the adulrunic argumentation. The runes do not merely represent different principles but instead correspond to them directly on a spiritual plane. Bureus demonstrates this in the universal symbol of the Adulruna into which the runes all fit. The seven runes of the seven-stave summit—that is to say, the vertical line of the rune cross—correspond to the levels of the human soul, alchemical stages, and biblical events. It seems that Bureus was able to discover a great deal in this one line of seven degrees. In the same way the number 3 can be found in different parts of existence. Viewed in a way other than as a division into seven levels, the human being consists of three parts (= SAL = the Swedish *siel, ande, lekamen;* "soul," "spirit," "body"), just as creation is constructed from earth, water, and air. God is triune, which the ancient Sveo-Goths knew as their trinity, TOF. In the same spirit Bureus explains that the Svea-realm consists of the three minorities represented by the three crowns. Reality is revealed in three forms—scripture, the macrocosm, and the microcosm—and these express the same universal truth.

Regarding the second criterion, Faivre writes that the idea of a living nature proceeds from the view that the cosmos is a complex, manifold, and hierarchical unity where nature assumes an important place along with God and humanity. Alongside of God's direct revelations or the studies of humanity itself, the macrocosm and nature are the most important sources of knowledge for Bureus. Faivre explains that esotericists observe that nature is permeated by a light or a fire and is rich with potential revelations and therefore may be read like a book. Bureus often returns to how divine signs are naturally to be discovered in nature, directly recorded in natural objects. Nature is filled with signs and secret information. The relatively positive view of Byrghal reveals that Bureus does not wish to turn his back on nature but instead have it be reunited with the divine. The adept is not to retire from nature but rather unite nature and God.

On the subject of imagination and meditation, the runes, number, and language function as the mediating principles between the divine world and the terrestrial one. On this point Bureus is entirely an esotericist and not a mystic, according to Faivre's third criterion in which he explains that esotericism differentiates itself from mysticism by its emphasis on the intermediary levels between the terrestrial and the divine. Bureus consistently returns to the idea of the intermediary worlds and their meaning. Christ, Odin, Byrger Tidesson, and not least of all, himself, are mediators between planes. The division of human beings and worlds into three levels implies some intermediate plane, and Bureus ascribes great importance to this idea. In the Gothic trinity TOF, Odin was the mediator, and for the threefold construction of man, SAL, the soul functioned as the mediator. Bureus earlier thought that the spirit was the middle level, but he himself reports that he revised his conception after 1613. Consequently the formula SAL (soul, spirit, body) was thereafter reformulated to ASL (spirit, soul, body), but the order of the letters in the formula appear not to have played an especially important role for Bureus, as SAL continued to refer to a Paracelsian principle.

The fourth criterion is experience of transmutation. On this point too, Bureus is a typical esotericist seen from the perspective of Faivre's criteria. The Adulruna and the Gothic Cabbala do not merely constitute a passive view of the structure of the cosmos, but rather Bureus intends to show a path from one plane to the next by means of his system. The word *transmutation* is derived from alchemy, and Bureus makes direct references to the alchemical process in his *Cabbalistica* and draws parallels between it and his runo-cabbalistic stages of initiation. Adulruna is a path of transmutation in which Byrghal is to rise up and be unified with Thors.

From the standpoint of Faivre's four primary criteria, Bureus is a typical esotericist. Of the two secondary criteria, the first one accords partially with the viewpoint of Bureus, while the latter one is difficult to assess in a clear-cut way.

On Faivre's issue of concordance, in the spirit of the Hermeticists Bureus is an adherent of the *philosophia perennis*, or perennial philosophy, an original tradition that transmits the hidden truth. The ancient Sveo-Goths too had known of the trinity and the true doctrine of which their trinity, TOF, gave evidence. The true doctrine was distorted by sorcerers who represented themselves as being the three Nordic gods. The sorcerers got the Northmen to cease praying to the trinity and instead to begin praying to idols made of wood. Bureus illustrates this by showing the tetragrammaton in different languages, which can be seen as a sign that he was implying that the true doctrine can be found in different religions. Certainly Christianity and the wisdom of the Hebrews have a primary place, as well as the Sveo-Gothic primeval wisdom, which he thought he could reawaken with the Adulruna.

On the last criterion of transmission, it is more difficult to judge how Bureus thought that his teachings would be transmitted, since no structured order or any initiatory school was formed around his Adulruna. Not even Stiernhielm, who otherwise was Bureus's foremost disciple, took up the Gothic Cabbala.

Bureus unified esotericism and Gothicism. In the works of Bureus the theme of Gothicism merges with the esotericism of the age such as alchemy, Cabbala, Hermeticism, astrology, and magic. What is particular to Bureus is that he utilizes the Gothic theme to describe an individual path of initiation that leads to an alchemical and cabbalistic fusion with God. Ordinary Gothicism, of both the older and the younger types, is restricted to using the theme of the mystical Goths to emphasize the kingdom or nation in a mythologized depiction of history. The Adulruna and the esoteric Gothicism of Bureus utilize the Gothic theme for initiatory purposes. The Goths were thought to be the mystical carriers of the forgotten truth that mankind stood on the verge of rediscovering.

For Bureus language and words are mediators between man and the divine. The runes are the original signs that mediate between the creator and the created. Through a comparison with the Cabbala, Bureus was convinced that the runes also had different dimensions, in part as written characters but also as esoteric and magical symbols. He developed a Gothic Cabbala. He called the secret dimension of the runes adulrunes or adelrunes. He constructed a symbol he called the Adulruna that contained all fifteen adulrunes. Thus Bureus had a universal symbol that he called Adulruna, while at the same time he spoke of fifteen runic characters that were also called adulrunes and that went into the larger symbol. The universal Adulruna was supposed to function as both a symbol for humanity and for the universe, for the microcosm and for the macrocosm. The universal Adulruna is a map of the universe and the development of man through different levels of existence. Out of the Adulruna the runes emanate and group themselves in different constellations as the three rune crosses on the

An example from Bureus's *Magiska fyrkanter*

falling stone, or in a greater rune cross that contains all fifteen runes. This rune cross contains the esoteric seven degrees of man's initiatory path as illustrated by the seven runes. These runes are endowed with numerous meanings in the writings of Bureus in which they are compared to the life of Jesus, alchemical processes, and different levels of the soul.

Bureus lived during a time when speculations such as his were widespread. In the conflict between Protestants and Catholics, the teachings of Paracelsus were picked up by the Protestants and Reformed groups. For a period during the time of the reign of Gustavus Adolphus, Paracelsism would enjoy a great influence in Sweden. The prophecy of the lion made by Paracelsus would be used in propaganda for the Swedish king during the Thirty Years War. Bureus participated in the spread of this propaganda, but the whole time he suspected that it was rather he himself who was the lion who had been prophesied. Bureus was influenced early on by the Rosicrucian pamphlets that were being distributed in Europe. Among the Rosicrucians the prophecies of Paracelsus were cited, and everyone awaited the lion who would come from the North and save the righteous.

Bureus was a multifaceted man who had the command of several languages. When he was older he studied Arabic and attempted to develop a runic writing style based on the Arabic mode of writing. Bureus vacillated between being a fairly sober scholar and having curious whims, as when one morning in 1609 it occurred to him that he should create an *alphabetum vegetable,* a plantlike mode of writing that was not supposed to be written in a line but rather blossom out in all possible directions. Johannes Bureus made invaluable efforts for the Swedish language and runology, but he himself thought that the Adulruna and the Gothic Cabbala were his most meaningful contributions to the future world.

NOTES

INTRODUCTION TO PART 2

1. Enoksen, *Runor: Historia, tydning, tolkning,* 185.
2. Bureus, *Antiquitates Scanziana,* F.a., p. 61.
3. Andersson, *Runor, magi, ideologi: En idéhistorisk studie,* 100.
4. Flowers, *Johannes Bureus and Adalruna.*

CHAPTER 10.
GOTHICISM AND WESTERN ESOTERICISM

1. Bogdan, "Västerlänsk esotericism som nytt akademiskt ämne," 75.
2. Bogdan, *From Darkness to Light: Western Esoteric Rituals of Initiation,* 9ff., 22.
3. Bogdan, "Västerlänsk esotericism," 76.
4. Faivre, *Access to Western Esotericism,* 61.
5. Faivre, *Access to Western Esotericism,* 35.
6. Olav Hammer, *Claiming Knowledge,* 37.
7. Hanegraaf, *New Age Religion and Western Culture,* 384f.
8. Hanegraaf, *New Age Religion and Western Culture,* 385.
9. Tiryakian, *On the Margin of the Visible,* 499.
10. Ahlbäck, "Spiritism, ockultism, teosofi och antroposofi," 166f.
11. Faivre, *Access to Western Esotericism,* 5.
12. Faivre, *Access to Western Esotericism,* 13–19.
13. Faivre, *Access to Western Esotericism,* 13.
14. Hanegraaf, *New Age Religion and Western Culture,* 385ff.

15. Bogdan, "Västerlänsk esotericism," 79.

16. Bogdan, "Västerlänsk esotericism," 80.

17. Cornell, *Den hemliga källan: Om initiationsmönster i konst, litteratur och politik,* 21ff.

18. Eliade, *Rites and Symbols of Initiation,* xii, 30.

19. Bureus, *Adulruna rediviva,* Rål. 9 8°, p. 67.

20. Hedin, *Menhemsförbundet,* 140ff.

CHAPTER II.
THE PROPHETS OF GOTHICISM

1. Malm, *Minervas äpple,* 12.

2. Eriksson, "Göticism," 35.

3. Eriksson, "Göticism," 36.

4. Eriksson, "Göticism," 35.

5. Andreas Nordin, foreword to Jordanes's *Getica: Om goternas ursprung och bedrifter,* 21.

6. Nordström, *De yverbornes ö,* 100.

7. Mierow, *The Gothic History of Jordanes,* 4:25.

8. Tacitus, *Germania.*

9. Stenroth, *Myten om goterna,* 46f.

10. Stenroth, *Myten om goterna,* 120.

11. Eriksson, *Rudbeck 1630–1702: Liv, lärdom, dröm i baroxkens Sverige,* 263.

12. Malm, *Minervas äpple,* 13.

13. Newly published in paperback as Olaus Magnus, *Historia om de nordiska folken* (Gidlunds, 2001).

14. Malm, *Minervas äpple,* 13.

15. Andersson, *Runor, magi, ideology,* 94.

16. Enoksen, *Runor,* 173.

17. Olaus Magnus, *Historia om de nordiska folken,* 64.

18. Eriksson, *Rudbeck,* 263.

19. Svärdström, *Johannes Bureus arbeten om svenska runinskrifter,* 7.

20. Lindroth, *J. Th. Bureus, Den svenska grammatikens fader,* 1:1ff.

21. Enoksen, *Runor,* 178.

22. Andersson, *Runor, magi, ideologi,* 96.

23. Enoksen, *Runor,* 182.

24. Frängsmyr, *Svensk idéhistoria,* part 1, 84.

25. Andersson, *Runor, magi, ideologi,* 99.

26. Frängsmyr, *Svensk idéhistoria,* 84.

27. Åkerman, "The Use of Kabbala and Dee's Monas in Johannes Bureus' Rosicrucian Papers."

28. Enoksen, *Runor,* 20.

29. Enoksen, *Runor,* 184.

30. Enoksen, *Runor,* 185.

31. Lindroth, *Svensk lärdomshistoria. Stormaktstiden,* 161.

32. Ross and Lönnroth, "Den fornnordiska musan: Report från ett internationellt forskningsprojekt," 35.

33. Malm, *Minervas äpple,* 15.

34. Björner, *Prodromus tractatuum de geographia Scandinaviæ,* 29–48.

35. Lindroth, *Svensk lärdomshistoria,* 652.

36. Lindroth, *Svensk lärdomshistoria,* 654.

37. Lindroth, *Svensk lärdomshistoria,* 653.

38. Lindroth, *Svensk lärdomshistoria,* 653.

39. Johan Göransson, *Is atlinga,* 79.

40. Enoksen, *Runor,* 201.

41. Lindroth, *Svensk lärdomshistoria,* 655.

42. Atterbom, "Skaldar-Mal," 9–10.

43. *Iduna,* vol. 10 (1824): 20–62.

44. Enoksen, *Runor,* 205.

45. Enoksen, *Runor,* 206.

46. Lilegren, *Run-Lära,* 15.

47. Ross and Lönnroth, "Den fornnordiska musan," 44.

48. Ross and Lönnroth, "Den fornnordiska musan," 29.

49. Ross and Lönnroth, "Den fornnordiska musan," 23.

50. Ross and Lönnroth, "Den fornnordiska musan," 38.

51. Stenroth, *Myten om goterna,* 10.

52. Stenroth, *Myten om goterna,* 70.

53. Stenroth, *Myten om goterna,* 47.

54. Stenroth, *Myten om goterna,* 48.

55. Malm, *Minervas äpple,* 29ff.

56. Stenroth, *Myten om goterna,* 148ff.

57. Fyhr, *De mörka labyrinterna: Gotiken i litteratur, film, musik och rollspel,* 36ff.

58. H. P. Lovecraft, *Selected Letters,* vol. 1, 1911–1924.

59. Raudvere, "Mellan romantik och politik: Midgårds-projektet och den samtida utmaningen," 18.

60. Gardell, "Gudernas återkomst," 285ff.

61. Stenroth, *Myten om goterna,* 147.

62. Lönnroth, "Fenrisulven från Vallekilde," 160ff.

63. Watkins, *American Heritage Dictionary of Indo-European Roots.*

64. Andreas Nordin, introduction to Jordanes's *Getica,* 21.

65. Stenroth, *Myten om goterna,* 53.

66. Hildebrand, *Minne af riksantikvarien Johannes Bureus,* 4.

67. Nordström, *De yverbornes ö,* 12.

68. Nordström, *De yverbornes ö,* 13.

69. Lindroth, *Paracelsismen i Sverige till 1600-talets mitt,* 24.

70. Nordström, *De yverbornes ö,* 37.

71. Nordström, *De yverbornes ö,* 14.

72. Lindroth, *Paracelsismen,* 255.

73. Lindroth, *Paracelsismen,* 29.

74. Lindroth, *Paracelsismen,* 16.

75. Lindroth, *Paracelsismen,* 24, 62.

76. Lindroth, "Johannes Bureus: Mystikern och profeten," 230.

CHAPTER 12.
THE ADULRUNES

1. Bureus, *Cabbalistica,* Codices Lincopeneses N 24, p. 61.

2. Ståhle, *Vers och språk i vasatidens och stormaktstidens svenska diktning* (1975), 218.

3. Bureus, *Adulruna,* Rål. 9 8°, p. 44.

4. Lindroth, *Paracelsismen,* 107.

5. Bureus, *Cabbalistica,* 61.

6. Bureus, *Cabbalistica,* 73.

7. Flowers, *Johannes Bureus and Adalruna,* 16.

8. Ståhle, *Vers och språk i vasatidens och stormaktstidens svenska diktning,* 258.

9. Lindroth, *Paracelsismen,* 103.

10. Lindroth, *Paracelsismen,* 191.

11. Enoksen, *Runor,* 208.

12. Enoksen, *Runor,* 208.

13. Pennick, *Secrets of the Runes,* 35.

14. Pennick, *Secrets of the Runes*, 36ff.

15. Lindroth, *Paracelsismen*, 193.

16. Hildebrand, *Minne af riksantikvarien Johannes Bureus*, 42.

17. Åkerman, "The Use of Kabbala and Dee's Monas in Johannes Bureus' Rosicrucian Papers," 57.

18. Hildebrand, *Minne af riksantikvarien Johannes Bureus*, 312.

19. Bureus, *Adulruna*, Rål. 9 8°, p. 53.

20. Bureus, *Adulruna*, Rål. 9 8°, p. 55.

21. Flowers, *Johannes Bureus and Adalruna*, 15.

22. Susanna Åkerman, "Rosenkorset i Norden," 87.

23. Bureus, *Adulruna*, Rål. 9 8°, p. 55.

24. Quoted from Hildebrand, *Minne af riksantikvarien Johannes Bureus*, 322.

25. Bureus, *Adulruna*, Rål. 9 8°, p. 59.

26. Bureus, *Adulruna*, Rål. 9 8°, p. 61.

27. Lindroth, *Paracelsismen*, 138.

28. Bureus, *Adulruna*, Rål. 9 8°, p. 63.

29. Bureus, *Adulruna*, Rål. 9 8°, p. 61.

30. Bureus, *Antiquitates Scanziana*, Codices Holmienses F. a. 3, p. 175.

31. Bureus, *Adulruna*, Rål. 9 8°, p. 61ff.

32. Bureus, *Adulruna*, Rål. 9 8°, p. 66.

33. Lindroth, *Paracelsismen*, 138.

34. Bureus, *Cabbalistica*, 73.

35. Bureus, *Antiquitates Scanziana*, 158.

36. Nordström, *De yverbornes ö*, 120.

37. Bureus, *Adulruna*, Rål. 9 8°, p. 68.

38. Bureus, *Adulruna*, Rål. 9 8°, p. 67.

39. Bureus, *Adulruna*, Rål. 9 8°, p. 67.

40. Bureus, *Cabbalistica*, 73, 93.

41. Bureus, *Cabbalistica*, 47.

42. Bureus, *Cabbalistica*, 53.

43. Bureus, *Adulruna*, Rål. 9 8°, p. 69.

44. Lindroth, *Paracelsismen*, 234.

45. Sandblad, "Eken vid Güstrow och de sju inseglen," 73.

46. Sandblad, "Eken vid Güstrow och de sju inseglen," 83.

47. Enoksen, *Runor*, 159.

48. Quoted in Sandblad, "Eken vid Güstrow och de sju inseglen," 83.

49. Nordström, *De yverbornes ö,* 128.

50. Sandblad, "Eken vid Güstrow och de sju inseglen," 84.

51. Bureus, *Adulruna,* Rål. 9 8°, p. 70.

52. Lindroth, *Paracelsismen,* 140.

53. Bureus, *Cabbalistica.*

54. Bureus, *Adulruna rediviva,* F.a. 22.

55. Bureus, *Antiquitates Scanziana,* 115.

56. Åkerman,"The Use of Kabbala and Dee's Monas in Johannes Bureus' Rosicrucian Papers."

57. Lindroth, *Paracelsismen,* 191ff.

58. Lindroth, *Paracelsismen,* 198ff.

59. Bureus, *Antiquitates Scanziana,* p. 44.

60. Lindroth, *Paracelsismen,* 197.

61. Lindroth, *Paracelsismen,* 194.

62. Quoted in Lindroth, *Paracelsismen,* 195.

63. Bureus, *Nymäre Wijsor.*

64. Bureus, *Nymäre Wijsor.*

65. Åkerman, *Rose Cross over the Baltic,* 64.

66. Bureus, *Antiquitates Scanziana,* 190.

67. Lindroth, *Paracelsismen,* 138.

68. Bureus, *Aniquitates Scanziana,* 196.

69. Schück, "Kulturminnesvård genom tre sekler," 27.

70. Flowers, *Johannes Bureus and Adalruna,* 24.

71. Enoksen, *Runor,* 184.

72. Lindroth, *Paracelsismen,* 502.

73. Bureus, Codices Lincopeneses Br. 2.

74. Lindroth, *Svensk lärdomshistoria,* 164f.

75. Lindroth, *Svensk lärdomshistoria,* 268.

76. Ståhle, *Vers och språk i vasatidens och stormaktstidens svenska diktning,* 253.

77. Stiernhielm, Fd 13.

78. Stiernhielm, Fd 13.

79. Stiernhielm, Fd 3.

80. Andersson, *Runor,* 101f.

81. Rudbeck, [d.ä.], *Atland eller Manheim . . .* , 832.

82. Rudbeck, *Atland eller Manheim,* 856.

83. Lindroth, "Johannes Bureus: Mystikern och profeten," 229.

CHAPTER 13.
ESOTERIC GOTHICISM AFTER BUREUS

1. Göransson, *Is atlinga,* introduction.
2. Göransson, *Is atlinga,* 2.
3. Göransson, *Is atlinga,* 106.
4. Enoksen, *Fornnordisk mytologi enligt Eddans lärdomstexter,* p. 88ff.

BIBLIOGRAPHY

WORKS OF JOHANNES BUREUS

Primary Sources by Bureus and His Followers

Codices Holmienses

Bureus, Johannes. *Adulruna redivia*, F.a. 21.

———. *Adulruna redivia*, 22.

———. *Adulruna redivia*, Rål. 9 8°

———. *Adulruna redivia*, Rål. 6 12°

———. *Antiquitates Scanziana*, F.a. 3.

———. *Burerunor*, F.a. 11.

———. *Runarafst*, F.a. 14.

Stiernhielm, Georg. *Adelruna sive Sibylla Sveo-Gothica*, Fd 13.

———. *Mysterium etymologicum*, Fd 3.

———. *Specimen philologicum in primam literam A,* Fd 13.

Codices Upsalienis

Bureus, Johannes. *Adulruna redivia*, R 551.

———. *Adulruna redivia*, R 552.

———. *Sigilli mysteria*, Y 31.

Codices Lincopeneses

Bureus, Johannes. *Cabbalistica*, N 24.

———. *Diverse bureska fragment*, H 47.

———. Om språkens upkomst, Spr. 1.

Franckenberg, Abraham von. brev till Burues, Br. 2.

Published Sources

Bureus, Johannes. *Ara foederis theraphici F.X.R. assertion fraternitas R. C. quam roseae crucis vocant, consecrate.* 1616.

———. *Den svenska ABC boken, på thet enfalligeste så stält, at de vanlige bokstavarne lämpa sigh efter runerne, och bådhe semias medh wår vanlighe pronunciation.* Uppsala, 1624.

———. *Fama e Scanzia redux. Buccina iubilei ultimi, Eoae hyperboreae praenuncia: montium Europae cacuminal suo clangore feriens, inter colles & convalles araba resonans.* Stockholm, 1616.

———. *Hebraeorum philosophia antiqvissma.*

———. *Monumenta sveo-gothica hactenus exsculptura, U. o. tr. å.* Uppsala, 1624.

———. *Nordlandalejonsens Rytande, Som aff Koppar Altarsens Mätning, Vppenbarar Skriftennes Tijda Räkening.* Uppsala, 1644.

———. *Nymäre Wijsor.* Uppsala, 1637.

———. *Runa ABC-boken.* Stockholm. 1611.

———. *Runa ABC-boken.* Uppsala. 1624.

———. *Runa revx Dän danske k. Waldmars prophetia, om rvnas hem-flycht, funnen I Danmark, uti en norsk bok, skalda benemd, vtaf den höglärde ... D. Olao Worm ... och af honom där sammestädes latit af prenet vtgå år 1636. Vnder däd namnet Literatvra: danica.* Stockholm, 1643.

———. *Smaragdina tabula chronologiae cherubinicae hactenus sigillatae, pro assertion veritatis evangelicae ex ungvibus bestiae, in confirmationem fidelium Augustanae confessionis et solatium gementium et in fidelium emendationem.*

———. *Svenska ABC-boken medh runor.* Stockholm 1612.

OTHER REFERENCES

Åkerman, Susanna. *Rose Cross over the Baltic: The Spread of Rosicrucianism in Northern Europe.* Leiden, the Netherlands: Brill, 1998.

——."Rosenkorset i Norden." In *Rosenkorsets rop: Fyra seklers levande tradition.* Haarlem, Netherlands: Rozekruis Pers, 2002.

——. "The Use of Kabbalah and Dee's Monas in Johannes Bureus' Rosicrucian Papers." In the proceedings of the IAHR conference in Durban, South Africa, August 2000, edited by Antoine Faivre and Wouter Hanegraaff.

Agrell, Sigurd. *Lapptrummor och runmagi.* Lund, 1934.

——. *Runornas talmystik och dess antika förebild.* Lund, 1927.

——. *Rökstenens chiffergåtor och andra runologiska problem.* Lund, 1930.

——. *Senantik mysteriereligion och nordisk runmagi.* Stockholm, 1931.

——. *Zur Frage nach dem Ursprung der Runennamen.* Lund, 1928.

Ahlbäck, Tore. "Spiritism, ockultism, teosofi och antroposofi: Några historiska linjer." In *Att se det dolda,* edited by Owe Wickström. Stockholm: Förlag Natur & Kultur, 1998.

Andersson, Björn. *Runor, magi, ideologi: En idéhistorisk studie.* Umeå, 1995.

Aswynn, Freya. *Leaves of Yggdrasil.* St. Paul, Minn.: Llewellyn Publications, 1994.

Atterbom, Per Daniel Amadeus. "Skaldar-Mal." In *Phosphoros* (January–February 1811).

Bernston, Martin, and Henrik Bogdan, eds. "Västerlänsk esotericism som nytt akademiskt ämne." *Religionsvetenskap i Göteborg* 25 år, 2002.

Bkarke, Bodvar. *Runa.* Sollentuna, 1988.

Björner, Erik Julius. *Prodromus tractatuum de geographia Scandinaviæ veteri, et historiis gothicis: exhibens succinctum judicium de scythiæ, svethiæ et gothiæ etymo, ut et runarum in cippis helsingicis ac medelpadicis inventarum ætate, usu atque explicatione.* Stockholm, 1726.

Bogdan, Henrik. *From Darkness to Light: Western Esoteric Rituals of Initiation.* Göteborg: University of Göteborg, 2003.

——. "Västerlänsk esotericism som nytt akademiskt ämne." *Religionsvetenskap i Göteborg,* 75.

Cornell, Peter. *Den hemliga källan: Om initiationsmönster i konst, litteratur och politik.* Sweden: Gidlunds, 1988.

Dumezil, George. *Gods of the Ancient Northmen.* Edited and translated by E. Haugen. Berkeley: University of California Press, 1973.

Eliade, Mircea. *Rites and Symbols of Initiation.* Woodstock, Conn.: Spring Publications, 1995.

Ellis Davidsson, H. R. *Gods and Myths of Northern Europe.* Harmondsworth, UK: Penguin, 1964.

———. *The Road to Hel.* Cambridge: Cambridge University Press, 1943.

Enoksen, Lars Magnar. *Fornnordisk mytologi enligt Eddans lärdomstexter.* Lund, Sweden: Historiska Media, 2000.

———. *Runor: Historia, tydning, tolkning.* Lund: Historiska Media, 1998.

Eriksson, Gunnar. *Rudbeck 1630–1702: Liv, lärdom, dröm i baroxkens Sverige.* Stockholm: Bokförlaget Atlantis, 2002.

Eriksson, Nils. "Göticism." In *17 uppsatser i svensk idé- och lärdomshistoria,* 1991.

Faivre, Antoine. *Access to Western Esotericism.* Albany: State University of New York, 1994.

Flowers, Stephen. *Johannes Bureus and Adalruna.* Smithville, Tex.: Runa Raven Press, 1998.

Frängsmyr, Tore. *Svensk idéhistoria.* Part 1. Stockholm: Förlag Natur & Kultur, 2000.

Friesen, Otto von. *Runora i Sverige.* Uppsala, 1928.

Fyhr, Mattias. *De mörka labyrinterna: Gotiken i litteratur, film, musik och rollspel* Lund: Ellerströms, 2003.

Gardell, Mattias. "Gudernas återkomst: Asatro, rasmystik och etnisk identitet i Förenta Staterna." In *Svensk religionshistorisk årskrift,* 1998.

Göransson, Johan. *Is atlinga; Det är: De forna göters, här uti Svea rike, bokstäfver ok salighets lära, tvåhundrad år före Christum, utspridde i all land; Igenfunden af Johan Göransson.* Stockholm, 1747.

Grimsson, Atrid. *Runmagi och shamanism.* Stockholm, 1990.

Hammer, Olav. *Claiming Knowledge: Strategies of Epistemology from Theosophy to the New Age.* Leiden, the Netherlands: Brill, 2000.

Hanegraaf, Wouter J. *New Age Religion and Western Culture: Esotericism in the Mirror of Secular Thought.* Albany: State University of New York Press, 1998.

Hedeager, Lotta. *Skuggor ur en annan verklighet: Fornnordiska myter.* Finland, 1997.

Hedin, Greta. *Menhemsförbundet: Ett bidrag till göticismens och den yngre romantikens historia.* Göteborg: Elanders boktryckeri, 1928.

Hildebrand, Hans. *Minne af riksantikvarien Johannes Bureus.*1910.

Hultkrantz, Åke. *Vem är vem i nordisk mytologi.* Denmark: Prisma, 1991.

Iduna. Vol. 10. Stockholm, 1824.

Johannesson, Kurt. *The Renaissance of the Goths in Sixteenth-Century Sweden: Johannes and Olaus Magnus as Politicians and Historians.* Translated by James Larson. Berkeley: University of California Press, 1991.

Jordanes. *Getica: Om goternas ursprung och bedrifter.* Translated by Andreas Nordin. Stockholm: Atlantis, 1997.

Kummer, S. A. *Rune Magic.* Translated and edited by Edred Thorsson. Smithville, Tex.: Runa Raven Press, 1993.

Lilegren, Johan. *Run-Lära.* Stockholm, 1832.

Lindroth, Hjalmar. *J. Th. Bureus, Den svenska grammatikens fader.* Lund: Berlingska boktryckeriet, 1911.

Lindroth, Sten. "Johannes Bureus: Mystikern och profeten." *Ord och bild* 56 (1947).

——. *Paracelsismen i Sverige till 1600-talets mitt.* Uppsala: Almqvist & Wiksell, 1943.

——. *Svensk lärdomshistoria. Stormaktstiden.* Stockholm: Norstedt, 1975.

List, Guido von. *The Secrets of the Runes.* Translated and introduction by Stephen Flowers. Rochester, Vt., Inner Traditions, 1988.

Lönnroth, Lars. "Fenrisulven från Vallekilde." In *Skaldemjödet i Berget.* Stockholm: Atlantis, 1996.

Lovecraft, H. P. *Selected Letters,* vol. 1, *1911–1924.* Edited by August Derleth and Donald Wandrei. Sauk City, Wis.: Arkham House, 1965.

Magnus, Olaus. *Historia om de nordiska folken.* New edition. Sweden: Gidlunds and Michaelisgillet, 2001.

Malm, Mats. Minervas äpple: Om diktsyn, tolkninig och bildspråk inom nordisk göticism. Ph.D. diss., University of Göteborg, 1996.

Mierow, Charles C. *The Gothic History of Jordanes in English.* 1915. Reprint. Cambridge: Speculum Historiale, 1960.

Nordin, Andreas. Foreword to Jordanes's *Getica: Om goternas ursprung och bedrifter.* Stockholm: Atlantis, 1997.

Nordström, Johan. *De yverbornes ö.* Stockholm: Bonniers, 1934.

Palm, Thede. *Trädkult: Studier i germansk religionshistoria.* Lund: Gleerup, 1948.

Pennick, Nigel. *The Inner Mysteries of the Goths.* Chievely Berks: Capall Bann Pub., 1995.

———. *Practical Magic in the Northern Tradition.* New York: HarperCollins, 1989.

———. *Runic Astrology.* Chievely Berks: Capall Bann Pub., 1995.

———. *Secrets of the Runes.* London: Thorson's, 1998.

Raudvere, Catharina. "Mellan romantik och politik: Midgårds-projektet och den samtida utmaningen." In *Myter om det nordiska: Mellan romantik och politik,* edited by Catharina Raudvere, Anders Anrén, Kristina Jennbert. Lund: Nordic Academic Press, 2001.

Ross, Margret Clunies, and Lars Lönnroth. "Den fornnordiska musan: Report från ett internationellt forskningsprojekt." In *Myter om det nordiska: Mellan romantik och politik,* edited by Catharina Raudvere, Anders Anrén, and Kristina Jennbert. Lund: Nordic Academic Press, 2001.

Rudbeck, Olof. d.ä., *Atland eller Manheim . . .* (T.I.) Upsalae: Henricus Curio, 1679.

Sandblad, Håkan. "Eken vid Güstrow och de sju inseglen: Till tolkningen av Johannes Bureus religiösa mystik." In *Lychnos,* 1959.

Schück, Adolf. "Kulturminnesvård genom tre sekler." In *Svensk kulturminnesvård: ett 300-årsminne.* Centralkommittén för Gustav-Adolfs-fonden för de svenska kulturminnesmärkenas vård, 1930.

Ståhle, Carl Ivar. *Vers och språk i vasatidens och stormaktstidens svenska diktning.* Stockholm: Norstedt, 1975.

Stenroth, Ingmar. *Myten om goterna.* Stockholm: Atlantis, 2002.

Strömbeck, Dag. *Sejd.* Lund, 1955.

Sturlason, Snorri. *Snorres Edda.* Translation and introduction by Björn Collinder. Stockholm: Forum, 1970.

Svärdström, Elisabeth. *Johannes Bureus arbeten om svenska runinskrifter.* Stockholm: Wahlström & Widstrand, 1936.

Tacitus. *Germania.* Translation and commentary by J. B. Rivas. Oxford: Oxford University Press, 1999.

Thorsson, Edred. *Futhark: A Handbook of Rune Magic.* York Beach, Maine: Weiser, 1984.

———. *Northern Magic: Mysteries of the Norse, German & English.* St. Paul, Minn.: Llewellyn, 1993.

———. *Runelore: A Handbook of Esoteric Runology.* York Beach, Maine: Weiser, 1987.

———. *Rune Might: The Secret Practices of the German Rune Magicians.* Rochester, Vt.: Inner Traditions, 2018.

Tiryakian, Edward E., ed. *On the Margin of the Visible: Sociology, the Esoteric and the Occult.* Hoboken, N.J.: Wiley, 1974.

INDEX

Page numbers in *italics* indicate illustrations.

BOOKS OF RELATED INTEREST

Nordic Runes
Understanding, Casting, and Interpreting the Ancient Viking Oracle
by Paul Rhys Mountfort

The Return of Odin
The Modern Renaissance of Pagan Imagination
by Richard Rudgley

Rune Might
The Secret Practices of the German Rune Magicians
by Edred Thorsson

The Secret of the Runes
Translated by Guido von List
Edited by Stephen E. Flowers

The Fraternitas Saturni
History, Doctrine, and Rituals of the Magical Order of the
Brotherhood of Saturn
by Stephen E. Flowers, Ph.D.

Icelandic Magic
Practical Secrets of the Northern Grimoires
by Stephen E. Flowers, Ph.D.

The Norse Shaman
Ancient Spiritual Practices of the Northern Tradition
by Evelyn C. Rysdyk

Runic Lore and Legend
Wyrdstaves of Old Northumbria
by Nigel Pennick

INNER TRADITIONS • BEAR & COMPANY
P.O. Box 388 • Rochester, VT 05767
1-800-246-8648 • www.InnerTraditions.com

Or contact your local bookseller